THE
TRUMAN
PERIOD
AS A
RESEARCH FIELD

EDITED BY

Richard S. Kirkendall

UNIVERSITY OF MISSOURI PRESS

COLUMBIA • MISSOURI

PUBLICATION OF THIS BOOK HAS BEEN AIDED BY

THE TRUMAN LIBRARY INSTITUTE FOR

NATIONAL AND INTERNATIONAL AFFAIRS

Contents

Opportunities for Research

✤

RICHARD S. KIRKENDALL

T HIS VOLUME rests upon a set of assumptions about the Truman period as a research field. The authors are not united in their evaluations of President Truman and his Administration. Perhaps the dominant view of him among students of the Presidency is reflected in the Schlesinger poll that rated him a "near great" President, chiefly because of his major decisions on foreign policy.[1] If this is the dominant view, then some of the contributors here represent the development of a "revisionist" interpretation characterized by doubts about the necessity and value of the containment policy and by a belief that Truman could have accomplished much more than he did in domestic affairs. The writers are united only by their assumptions that presidential libraries provide rich opportunities for research,[2] that research in the Truman Library is in a very early stage, and that the work that lies ahead could be assisted

---

[1]Arthur M. Schlesinger, *Paths to the Present* (Boston, Houghton Mifflin Company, 1964), 105–6.

[2]For my attempts to appraise those libraries, see Kirkendall, "Presidential Libraries—One Researcher's Point of View," *The American Archivist*, 25 (October, 1962), 441–48, and Kirkendall, "A Second Look at Presidential Libraries," *ibid.*, 29 (July, 1966), 371–86.

I

significantly by an inventory of what has been done and what needs to be done.

The volume is a product of a conference of historians, political scientists, and archivists held in the Truman Library in mid-April, 1966.[3] The meeting, sponsored by the Truman Library Institute for National and International Affairs, brought together scholars who had conducted important work on recent United States history, especially those who had emphasized the Truman period and had studied in the Truman Library. While this was the Institute's fourth conference, it differed from the earlier three. More time was devoted to it; for the first time, formal papers were presented and discussed.[4] In the hope of providing stimulus and direction for research and writing on the Truman Administration, the conference sought ways to serve the needs of scholars contemplating work in this area, research directors, the staff of the Truman Library, and the Institute's Committee on Grants-in-Aid. Thus, the group took stock of research and publication on the Administration and surveyed the work that has been done, the research in progress, and the problems that need to be explored.

As both the papers and the discussion were, in the main,

---

[3] The participants, in addition to the contributors to this volume, were Herman Kahn, Assistant Archivist of the United States for Presidential Libraries; Robert H. Ferrell, Indiana University; Alonzo L. Hamby, Ohio University; Alan D. Harper, Queens College of the City University of New York; Samuel P. Hays, University of Pittsburgh; Francis H. Heller, the University of Kansas; J. Joseph Huthmacher, Rutgers University; Richard P. Longaker, University of California, Los Angeles; Allen J. Matusow, Rice University; Alfred B. Rollins, Jr., Harpur College of the State University of New York; Gaddis Smith, Yale University; Donald C. Swain, University of California, Davis; and Athan G. Theoharis, Wayne State University. Others participating were Philip C. Brooks, Director of the Truman Library, and several members of the Library staff.

In a summary session concluding the conference, the following members of the Board of Directors of the Truman Library Institute took part in the discussion: Thomas C. Blaisdell, Jr., of the University of California, Berkeley; Cyrus Eaton, of Cleveland, Ohio; Arthur Schlesinger, Jr., of the Institute for Advanced Study; and Earl Warren, Chief Justice of the United States.

The contributors are grateful to the Board and Dr. Brooks for the opportunity that they provided and to them and other participants in the conference for their assistance in the preparation of this volume. The editor also wishes to thank Dr. Brooks and his staff for their help with editorial tasks.

[4] Reports on the earlier conferences are available in the Truman Library.

devoted to the substance of the Truman years, the volume can assist those who are seeking to enlarge their understanding of the life and times of Harry S Truman rather than those who are searching for topics to explore. Nevertheless, the papers and the discussion served the dominant aim of the conference; many conclusions emerged regarding the work that needs to be done. Numerous aspects of the Administration's background and situation as well as of its thought and behavior await the attention of serious scholars willing to explore the sources in the Truman Library and other research centers. This introductory essay will survey the recommendations that were made.

As to the background of the Administration, we need to know much more about the lives before 1945 of people who played major roles in the Truman period. Only a very small number of significant biographies are available now. In addition to substantial studies of the President, useful explorations could be made of the careers of Cabinet officers, of members of the White House staff, and of other Washington personalities, including military leaders, congressmen, and representatives of major interest groups. What experiences, personalities, and points of view did these men and women bring into the events of the period? What relations had they established with one another?

The domestic history of World War II is another major part of the background of the Truman period that needs much more attention than it has received. Worthy topics are the basic economic policies—stabilization, mobilization, demobilization, and reconversion; the relations between government and business, both large and small; the allocation of contracts; and the wartime agencies—their structures of power, the activities of businessmen on their staffs, their relations with the military, industry, and finance, and the assumptions of their top officials. The economic thought of economists and government officials, postwar planning by official and private groups, and Roosevelt's efforts to educate the public on postwar problems should be explored. We also need studies of the politics of the period. How, for example, did the conservative coalition develop and operate?

Turning away from the background out of which the Administration emerged and looking at the situation in which it functioned, one finds some of the largest opportunities for research—and some of the most difficult, including public opinion. Was the public dominated by a conservative mood that doomed to defeat the Administration's innovating tendencies in domestic affairs? Why did such a small number of voters go to the polls in 1948? What did the public think of the limited accomplishments of the Eighty-first Congress? When did the public become fearful of subversive influences? How much support did McCarthy have? Was the public dominated by concerns about status? What were its attitudes toward government spending, unbalanced budgets, economic growth, and economic stability?

The public should be divided into the formal and informal groups of which it was composed, and these groups need to be explored. Changes in the attitudes of liberals, such as increasing attention to civil rights and civil liberties and declining concern about poverty and Big Business, should be studied, as should the thought of professional economists on policy questions. To what degree, for example, was Keynesianism accepted by economists and other groups? Did these groups place other values above a balanced budget? (Both rhetoric and behavior need to be examined.) Pressure groups, such as the NAM, the Chamber of Commerce, the CIO, and the Farmers Union, their structure, ideology, behavior, and leaders, including Lewis, Green, Murray, and Patton, deserve closer attention than they have received. The distribution of power and influence needs to be analyzed. Was Big Business the dominant group? How much influence did scientists wield? What relations did these groups have with the federal government? What were the relations among businessmen, military men, and scientists? Were government agencies, like those in the field of social welfare, playing political roles, such as the promotion of proposals for reform, that once had been played by private groups? Did groups like the American Medical Association manipulate public opinion, and did they manipulate it more successfully than the President?

Many questions concerning congressional politics remain unanswered. Did the conservative orientation of Congress explain the Administration's failures in domestic affairs? To deal with this basic problem, Congress must be analyzed with great care. The leaders, their interrelationships, and the membership of the major committees need to be explored; the structure of Congress needs to be defined. Did Congress contain conservative and liberal coalitions? Congressional and presidential parties? If it did, what were their ideologies? How did these blocs function? What were their strategies and tactics? Did key figures like Sam Rayburn blunt proposed liberal legislation in order to avoid a dangerous feud within the party? How much power did these blocs have? Did their composition and strength vary with time and issues? Was Congress more complex than these concepts suggest? Was it characterized by many blocs rather than by two major ones? Did congressmen identify with Congress as an institution as well as with their parties and their constituents? How strongly did congressmen identify with each? Did Congress accurately reflect public opinion on the major questions of the period?

The parties and the elections must also be studied. Was there a centrist faction in the Democratic party? If so, when was it formed? Who were its members? Was party unity its dominant aim? How much did it accomplish? Who were the Dixiecrats? Why did they bolt? Had other party leaders expected this? How significant did the bolt seem to them? How did they prevent other Southerners from breaking with the party? How did the bolt affect the outcome of the election? How were the Dixiecrats treated when they returned to the Democratic party?

Many other aspects of politics in 1948—Republican strategy, Dewey's campaign methods, the dominance of domestic considerations—deserve study and explanation, and the politics of the period should be explored in the states and local communities as well as on the national level. Did local Democratic leaders urge the Administration to "go slow" on domestic questions because the Democratic coalition had ceased to be a "have-not" coalition and had become interested chiefly in maintaining the gains that had been made? Were local political machines being undermined by the social welfare programs of the national government?

Although the conference discussed the background and situation of the Administration, its thought and behavior received heaviest emphasis. As with every administration, certain fundamental questions about decision making and the Administration's place in the flow of history need to be explored systematically. How did those obliged to make decisions define the situations that faced them? . . . the direction that forces were moving? . . . the goals they wished to reach? . . . the alternative courses of action that were open? . . . the limits upon action? Such questions need to be asked in relation to the Administration's significant decisions. Similarly, its parts need to be divided into those that represented change and those that represented continuity. Each important aspect needs to be looked at from this historical point of view so as to determine the Administration's historical significance.

At present, most students assume that the Truman Administration was significant, first of all, for the innovations it made in American foreign policy and for the consequent impact this policy had on developments outside the United States. Work in this area is in a very early stage. High on the list of needs are studies of the influential men, their backgrounds, their recruitment, and their basic ideas and values. How influential were military men? Was there a change from Roosevelt to Truman in the conceptions of the past that influenced behavior and policy? Was thinking in the late stages of the Roosevelt Administration dominated by memories of the way the American people had behaved in 1919–1920, while thinking in the Truman Administration was heavily influenced by awareness of the tendency of European affairs to get out of control? How were the national interest and the national purpose defined? Did definitions change during the period? How much did the period contribute to the vast enlargement of the definitions that has taken place in this century? What happened to the anti-imperialism or anticolonialism that had influenced the Roosevelt period? What were the beliefs of top officials as to how social reality could be manipulated and influenced? Did they see the United States as a stabilizing or as a revolutionary force in the world? Did they have accurate views of the country's power in the world and its impact upon other nations? How did they interpret to themselves and to the public what the United States was doing? We need, in short, studies of the intellectual side of the history of American foreign policy.

The very early years of the Administration's foreign policy deserve careful attention. Important themes here include the rise in the influence of the State Department and the pattern of its relations with the President. Scholars should take a close look at the changes in American attitudes toward Great Britain from 1944 to 1947 and the consequent changes in policies; they should study the relations between the United States and the United Nations in the early years of the latter's operations. What were the attitudes of American officials toward the U. N. at the end of the war? What role did the organization play in international politics during 1946? Did the Russians' use of the veto cause American officials to lose confidence in the effectiveness of the organization? What were official attitudes toward the organization early in 1947? And what of official conceptions of Russian ambitions and capacity? What changes took place in those conceptions from 1945 to 1947? How did they compare with realities? Did Kennan's cable from Moscow in February, 1946, influence the State Department's planning during that year? What was the military capacity of the West during those years? Were officials thinking of the relations between available weapons and the goals of their foreign policy? How useful did available weapons seem to the policy makers?

In this area, the impact of the atomic bomb on the thinking in this period is a controversial subject worthy of fresh study. How did the bomb influence the thought and behavior of the Administration? Did American policy makers view atomic weapons as devices that could be used to bring about change in the international situation? Did they seek to exploit the advantage that possession of the bomb provided? Did it enable the country to act effectively on the international stage? Did possession of it cause Administration leaders, including the President, to change their ideas about the importance of the Army? What limits did officials put upon the use of the bomb? Did a view that it should not be used retard development of a nuclear arsenal?

Other aspects of military policy, such as the development of the theories of massive retaliation and limited war, need to be explored. Of great importance are the military budgets. What economic, military, and political theories shaped them? What roles in their development were played by the President, the Defense Department, other departments, the armed services, their industrial and scientific allies, and their organizations of retired officers? A closely related and significant area is the story of the relations of the federal government, industry, and science. How did it develop during the Truman years? And what of a very new feature of American life, the United States as an occupying power? What was the impact of this experience upon the countries that were occupied? What was the impact upon the U. S.?

Much remains to be done on the major developments from 1947 to 1949: the Truman Doctrine, the Marshall Plan, the Berlin Airlift, the North Atlantic Treaty Organization, and Point Four. The assumptions and factors upon which the decisions were based need to be explored much more deeply than they have been. Did factors in the domestic situation, such as Republican control of Congress and determination to cut back on government expenditures and reduce the nation's role in international affairs or the belief in the desirability of relying upon the U. N., place limits upon the possible courses of action open to the Administration? Did the Truman Doctrine help to prepare the people and the Congress for acceptance of the Marshall Plan? To what degree did the Administration regard this plan as the final answer to the situation in Europe? Why did the Administration wish to promote greater cooperation among European countries? What assistance did the aid program provide for American industries and firms? What attempts did they make to influence purchases and European developments? What was the impact of the plan and of Point Four? What American experiences were drawn upon in these programs? Who were the people involved in them? How were they administered? What attitudes toward revolution influenced Point Four? What decisions did the Administration make from March to June, 1948, concerning its relations with the Brussels Treaty Powers? What was Vandenberg's intention in his resolution of June, 1948? Was it the brain child of the State Department? What decisions were made by the State Department while NATO was in the planning and negotiating stage? Other matters demanding exploration are Acheson's roles—his dealings with the Senate Foreign Relations Committee and with the Europeans—and the political and psychological significance of NATO—the factors that made it possible, the refutation that it provided of the Communists' claim that capitalist nations could not cooperate, and the means that it supplied for the management of problems outside of Europe.

American policy in Europe after 1949 should be studied. How much change took place in that policy in 1950? How good were the chances for successful negotiation between East and West in 1951–1952? Why did no negotiations take place?

Students of American policy in the Far East could also make contributions. They could, for example, probe the belief that Europe was of greater importance than Asia, the conceptions that officials had of Asia, the influence that Asian experts had upon Far Eastern policy, and the assumptions involved in the effort to redefine that policy after the fall of China to the Communists. In need of study and definition are various aspects of the Korean War, such as the Administration's handling of the situation in the U. N. following MacArthur's defeat, the failure to keep pressure on China after that country had become interested in an armistice and the impact of the war upon U. S. relations with Asia, the Administration's thinking about Russian and Chinese ambitions, and military thought and policy.

The list of research possibilities in the field of foreign policy has not been exhausted. U. S. relations with Latin America and with Israel, the overseas information program, and foreign policy and party and congressional politics after 1949 deserve attention. What, for example, was Senator McCarthy's impact upon foreign policy? How did the President respond to McCarthy's attack? Did Truman provide an adequate defense of his Secretary of State? And, to raise a very large and difficult question that could command the attention of many scholars, What were the reactions of other countries to the role that the United States was playing in the world? In addition, much could be done with the impact of that role upon domestic affairs. Did it hamper efforts to develop a domestic program and force the Administration to make compromises in that area in order to build and maintain support for its foreign policies?

Although the Administration's accomplishments in foreign affairs surpassed its achievements at home, domestic affairs also provide research opportunities. The impact of the G. I. Bill, for example, is a major subject that has not been explored, and the social and economic thought of the Administration needs to be analyzed. To what extent was it restrained by a belief in the importance of a balanced budget? Did the officials themselves place a high value on this, or did they merely assume that most Americans did? What theories guided the Administration's thinking about inflation? . . . about Big Business? How did the Administration explain the survival of poverty in American life? Did officials pay much attention to this factor? Were they concerned about particular impoverished groups, such as migratory workers? Did the officials come up with new programs in this area, or did they rely merely on programs that had been developed earlier? Did those programs help the poor? Did conservatives in the Administration, like John Snyder, frustrate efforts to develop a liberal program?

Much could be done with the Administration's relations with business, labor, and science. Important departments and agencies, such as the Reconstruction Finance Corporation, the War Assets Administration, the Antitrust Division of the Justice

Department, and the regulatory agencies, and important policies, including antitrust, conservation, reclamation, and tariff, provide research opportunities. What relations did the Department of Commerce have with business groups? What attempts did it make to advance their interests? Who were the men in charge of the Federal Reserve System? What relations did they have with various interest groups and the federal government? What relations did the Department of Interior have with mining, oil, and lumber interests? How did the federal government's greatly expanded role in science and technology contribute to economic growth and to the growth of particular firms? Policies need to be looked at from the point of view of their impact upon regional development, and unsuccessful as well as successful efforts in this area, like the failure to establish additional river valley authorities, should be examined. The economic policies of the Korean War should be added to this list. How did they affect particular firms? How were they influenced by business and military leaders? How did the tax increases affect the distribution of income? Why was organized labor unhappy with the stabilization program?

Civil rights and civil liberties moved to new positions of prominence in the Truman period. Truman's thinking on civil rights needs to be clarified, as does the background to his important message on civil rights in February, 1948. The Administration's relations with civil rights pressure groups and leaders should be explored. Did the officials think these people spoke for Negro America or for only the middle-class segment of it? The attitudes and roles of the Justice Department in both civil rights and civil liberties should be probed deeply. We need studies of the establishment of the Administration's loyalty-security program, its handling of security matters before the public became aroused about them, the pressures on the Administration in this area, the Administration's handling of the public relations side of it, the Administration's responses to McCarthy's charges, and its enforcement of the Internal Security Act of 1950.

The White House staff provides another large and significant subject for research. Who were the men involved? How were they recruited? How did they define their roles? . . . the President's roles? . . . the problems he faced? . . . the values that should guide his handling of them? How well did they do their work? What were their relations with the President, with one another, with other government officials, with Congress, and with interest groups? How were responsibilities distributed among the staff? How were power and influence distributed?

Finally, Truman's methods and abilities as a leader loomed large in the essays and in the discussion of them. Several fundamental aspects received attention: What preparations had he made for his role as leader? What values, attitudes, and personality characteristics shaped his understanding of the Presidency? How did they influence the way he used the office and affected the development of it? What was his attitude toward power? How had it developed? Was he more sensitive to power considerations at some points in his career than at others? Did he seek personal power? Did he have confidence in his use of it? Did he have realistic assumptions about the way people behave? When did he learn that people would not always anticipate what was needed and do what they were ordered? What were his ideas about the ways in which social change takes place? How did he define his situation and the possibilities that were open to him in it? Did he seek to unite or to divide the body politic?

To gain a more complete understanding of Truman as a leader, much work must be done on his relations with his staff and other aides. When, if ever, did he learn to use staff? How did he select staff members? Did he choose men who were capable of helping him to realize his goals, have confidence in them, listen to them, and defend them against attack? Did he organize staff work effectively? . . . make adequate demands upon his staff for work and briefing? . . . rely too heavily upon his assistants? . . . rely upon the right people at the right time? . . . tap enough sources? . . . rely upon one adviser much more than others? To what degree did he rely upon others to prepare his speeches? How did he decide what should be in them? How did he assign responsibilities for them?

Truman's varied relations with Congress provide another area for investigation. How were they influenced by his own experiences in the Senate? What members of the Administration had major responsibilities in this area? Did he rely heavily upon personal contacts? With whom did he deal? Did he adhere to the agreements he made with them? Did he supply an agenda and drafts of bills? Did he devote enough of his own time to efforts to build support in Congress for his proposals? Did his approach to Congress, especially in calling the special session in 1948, exaggerate the partisan dimension of that body, neglect its institutional character, and consequently alienate its members, including Democrats? What were the attitudes of congressmen toward him and his Administration? When did he begin his preparations for the election of 1948? How did he treat Congress in the preparatory period? What were his strategy and tactics, expectations and priorities in his dealings with the Eighty-first Congress? Why did he fail to obtain approval of such proposals as health insurance and federal aid to education? Did he neglect opportunities to take important steps that did not require endorsement by Congress?

Interpretations of Truman as a leader of public opinion tend to stress his shortcomings and warrant very careful analysis. How did he define the President's relations with the people? Did he attempt to educate as well as respond to public opinion? Did he do all that he could to educate the public on international affairs, the policies he developed to deal with them, and his domestic proposals? Did he take advantage of all of the opportunities that the press conference provided? Did he make enough speeches? Did he make the right kinds of speeches? Which speeches were effective, and which were not? Did his speeches stimulate fears on which his opponents capitalized? Did he fail to develop the stature needed to put down the challenges that came to him from such men as Senator McCarthy and General MacArthur? Were personal qualities basic to his failures in public relations?

These, then, are the suggestions for research that emerge from the essays that follow and from the discussion they stimulated. There are limits, of course, on our ability at present to follow these suggestions. Many of the sources, especially for foreign and military policies, are not open to scholars. Nevertheless, much can be done now, and much more will be possible in the near future. The quantity of available materials in the Truman Library is large and growing, and restrictions upon access to sources there and elsewhere will soon begin to drop away.[5]

---

[5]See Appendix A.

Foreign and Military
Policies

❖

DAVID S. McLELLAN

JOHN W. REUSS

Iᶠ FOREIGN AND MILITARY POLICIES during the Truman Administration had to be summarized in a word, that word would be *seminal*. Ask yourself how many of the decisions made in 1945–1953 control policy today. Current criticism of United States policy looks back to the Truman years either with such admiration as to suggest that it was a golden age or with regret for having marked the beginning of the Cold War. Neither attitude is correct. The era was, rather, a seedtime for mid-century foreign and military policy.

Some understanding of the immediate background of the Truman years is necessary to understand the problems that faced Truman and his aides. The dilemma here, as in any similar enterprise, is where to begin. Cold-war pathologists treat the years 1945–1947 as the period in which the Grand Alliance collapsed. We have had studies of the Potsdam Conference, of encounters with the Soviets at the Council of Foreign Ministers meetings, and of the Russians' increasing unwillingness to apply the Yalta Declaration to Eastern Europe. Considerable debate rages over the precise origins of the

Cold War; some historians trace its roots to some distant point in the past.[1] Such analyses are desirable for understanding the past, but unfortunately they miss the important point. Too often the burden of such works is to infer from the historical record some kind of inevitability about the East-West crisis that became a way of life after 1947. Other studies, which suggest that the outcome of such a struggle could, would, or should have been different, fail largely to comprehend the context in which events and decisions were taken. Studies of the Cold War that trace its origins to 1840, 1871, or 1914–1917 lead to a number of theories, or rather moods, about the nature of international relations and Soviet–American relations. They rest finally on some conviction that the Cold War was either inevitable or the result of bad policy.

Two major themes emerge, however, from America's World War II experience. First, the war was managed in traditional terms. Winning the battles was left to the generals; in Washington, the peace was planned in the State Department.[2] The two efforts were uncoordinated. The assumption controlling all this activity was that the Grand Alliance would continue after the cessation of hostilities. The mechanism through which this cooperation was to be sustained was the United Nations. Unity among the Big Three in the United Nations, it was believed, would lead to the peaceful and equitable solution of European problems.

Secondly, American participation in the Second World War meant almost certain victory for the Allied Powers. The application of the principle of unconditional surrender was the international analogue of total mobilization of American resources. Priorities of every kind were determined by military

---

[1]For example, W. W. Rostow, in *The United States in the World Arena*, cites the decades after 1840 as the historical period at which Russia and America entered on a collision course. John Lukacs, in *A History of the Cold War*, traces the Cold War to the origins of the American Republic. The Rostow volume constitutes one of the most ambitious attempts to explore the Cold War. It is full of suggestive hypotheses and contains an excellent bibliography.

[2]This American propensity to treat war and peace as discrete and essentially unrelated phenomena was the source of many of Truman's severest problems. His Administration had to take up the peacemaking at an excruciating juncture, with no realistic political foundations for the peace in being.

need. The economy was rigidly regulated. Consumer desires were sacrificed, but everyone knew that after the war a swift reconversion of the domestic economy would allow the American people to regain what had been lost, to return to what has popularly become identified as the "American way of life." The war had been fought to enable the United States to determine for itself what course it should take. The war over, the United Nations launched, what else needed to be done? That this was not also the prevalent feeling among the political and diplomatic leaders in Washington raises questions of some importance.

Still, despite the remote origins of the Cold War, despite the failure of Americans during the Second World War to coordinate their diplomacy with their military policy, despite the hopes of the American people during the war for a beautiful world thereafter, it was in the immediate postwar era that the Cold War came into full bloom. It is therefore to the years beginning in 1945—that is, the Truman years—that the historian must go to re-examine the assumptions of American diplomatic and military planners.

Some effort must be made to differentiate those responses and behaviors that were distinctly the product of the Truman Administration's role from those that were extraneous to it. Recognition of this need does not imply that positions taken by the Truman Administration did not have a feedback effect on the environment and vice versa, but it means that history must judge that Administration's performance in terms of the appropriateness of its perceptions and of the wisdom with which it translated those perceptions into action.

It will be in the light of the Truman Administration's idea of American security and destiny in the world after 1945 that historians and social scientists will examine its foreign and military policies. When we speak of the Cold War we mean more than the Soviet–American duel; we mean the adaptation of the United States to the revolutionary ethos that awaited the world on the morrow of victory over the Axis Powers.

Turning, then, to the method of examining the Truman years: What approach should the historians and social scientists take? One way to arrive at generalizations is by induction —through the study of large numbers of isolated facts that eventually combine into propositions, hypotheses, theories, laws. Evidence will almost invariably relate to actions of participants who behaved in given ways. Upon a minute and exhaustive study of the record the researcher builds a superstructure of interpretation and theoretical analysis. The most successful examples thus far of this approach to the study of the Truman Administration are the works of Herbert Feis,[3] of Tang Tsou,[4] and of Stephen G. Xydis[5] and in the field of politics, strategy, and government the studies by Samuel Huntington,[6] Bradford Westerfield,[7] and of Warner Schilling and Paul Hammond.[8]

Another approach might employ the deductive method, in which the researcher begins with certain theoretical and orienting ideas he then tests against evidence in the public record, in the memoirs, and in whatever archival materials are available. This latter approach is the more widely employed, but it is not always used as scrupulously as scholarship requires.

Another way to understand the Cold War is through theorizing, and here one has such students as William A. Williams, Joseph P. Morray, and D. F. Fleming, notably, although there are others. These three observers contend that the capitalistic West has been unrelievedly hostile toward the Soviet Union and thus caused the Cold War.[9] According to W. A. Williams:

The majority [of Truman's policy makers] rapidly embarked upon a program to force the Soviet Union to accept America's traditional conception of itself and the world. The decision represented the final stage in the transformation of the policy of the open door from a utopian idea into an ideology, from an intellectual outlook for chang-

---

[3]Herbert Feis, *The China Tangle; Between War and Peace: The Potsdam Conference;* and *Japan Subdued.*

[4]Tang Tsou, *America's Failure in China: 1941–1950.*

[5]Stephen G. Xydis, *Greece and the Great Powers: 1944–1947.*

[6]Samuel P. Huntington, *The Common Defense: Strategic Programs in National Politics.*

[7]Bradford Westerfield, *Foreign Policy and Party Politics.*

[8]Warner Schilling and others, *Strategy, Politics, and Defense Budgets.*

[9]W. A. Williams, *The Tragedy of American Diplomacy;* D. F. Fleming, *The Cold War and Its Origins, 1917–1960.*

ing the world into one concerned with preserving it in the traditional mold.

Particularly after the atom bomb was created and used, the attitude of the United States left the Soviets with but one real option: either acquiescence in Amerian proposals or be confronted with American power and hostility. It was the decision of the United States to employ its new and awesome power in keeping with traditional Open Door Policy which crystallized the Cold War.[10]

For a time after 1945 this view was of more than academic interest. It is a point of view, with roots in American populism, that has been given a Marxian veneer. Under the leadership of Henry A. Wallace it constituted a source of no small importance. The Wallace defection from the Administration's foreign policy found its rationale in the argument that America was attempting to impose some form of economic imperialism on the world.[11]

According to this interpretation, the United States employed the A-bomb in the closing moments of the war in order to beat Russia to the punch in ending the war in the Far East and to institute a form of atomic blackmail to impose an American design upon the world.[12] Another device that is often cited as being used by the United States against the Soviet Union is its economic power and, specifically, its power to give or withhold a loan to facilitate Russian recovery. It is generally held by those who attribute the Cold War to American imperialism that Harriman and others "shared the State

[10]Williams, *Tragedy of American Diplomacy*, 205–6.

[11]Wallace's philosophy is probably more complex and confused than at first appears. In his Madison Square Garden speech of September 12, 1946, Wallace called upon the United States to recognize that "we have no more business in the *political* affairs of Eastern Europe than Russia has in the political affairs of Latin America, Western Europe, and the United States." Calling for cooperation with Russia, he argued that "we want to be met half-way." Wallace seemed to be saying that, if only we could respect each others' political spheres, a community based upon economic interests would be possible.

[12]W. A. Williams buttresses his argument for the case that America's need for an open door caused the Cold War, by claiming that "the United States had from 1944 to at least 1962 a vast preponderance of actual as well as potential power vis-à-vis the Soviet Union" (*Tragedy of American Diplomacy*, 208) and that "the United States used or deployed its preponderance of power wholly within the assumptions and traditions of the strategy of the *Open Door Policy*. The United States never formulated and offered the Soviet Union a settlement based on other less grandiose terms." (*Ibid.*, 208.)

Department's view that the lever provided by Russian weakness and devastation could and should be used to insure a predominant role for America in all decisions about the postwar world."[13]

This school generally contends that Soviet foreign policy was essentially defensive in character and that, because of the destruction visited upon Russia, the Kremlin was exhausted by the war and too preoccupied with domestic recovery to have the will to pursue an expansionist foreign policy. According to this interpretation, Russia would have been content to have consolidated its power in Eastern Europe.

In the eyes of the America-the-Imperialist school, United States opposition to Soviet moves in Eastern Europe is usually attributable to America's rapacious need for markets. This interpretation holds that Roosevelt bequeathed his successors "little if anything beyond the traditional outlook of open-door expansion. They proceeded rapidly and with a minimum of debate to translate that conception of America and the world into a series of actions and policies which closed the door to any result but the cold war."[14] This school takes for granted that overwhelming economic preponderance produced an expansion in American foreign policy.

A similar mechanistic interpretation attaches to America's possession of the atomic bomb; America had a monopoly, *ergo* America employed that monopoly in a wholly conscious, consistent, and ruthless fashion to attain its objectives.[15] Holders of this view make little if any effort to examine the assumption that, because America possessed power, it intended—or understood how—to employ it in a ruthless fashion. This assumption leads Alperovitz to conclude that positions attained by the United States in the Far East by victory over Japan and by Soviet promises to respect the *status quo* in Manchuria held good for all time.

A second school of thought holds that the United States was

---

[13]Williams, *Tragedy of American Diplomacy*, 221.

[14]Williams, *Tragedy of American Diplomacy*, 229.

[15]This is the gist of Gar Alperovitz, *Atomic Diplomacy: Hiroshima and Potsdam.*

soft and naive in its dealings with the Soviet Union and that Communist power thereby expanded unchecked. This is the school that erroneously contends that at Yalta Roosevelt turned Poland over to Stalin; that China passed under Communist rule because of American policies at Yalta; that the United States lost the Korean War because American political leaders, inept or worse, frustrated the sensible purposes of brave generals; that socialism is entrenched in most of Western Europe; and that socialism is the prelude to communism.[16] The conspiracy theory constitutes an extreme variant of this interpretation. In effect, liberals, with their mistaken assumptions about human nature and about internationalism and communism, permitted and even abetted and encouraged Communist victories. Even containment appears flawed in the minds of those who espouse this viewpoint. Their chief complaints against the Truman Administration's policy have been that it was not active or aggressive enough, that its actions were rooted in the immoral assumption that the free world must try to get along with the Communist world, and that it mistakenly believed that Communist power, if contained, would show internal contradictions that would blunt its dynamic force.

A third interpretation of the Truman Administration's foreign and strategic policies derives from the theory of realism usually associated with Hans J. Morgenthau and George F. Kennan, which we shall call Academic Realism. Academic Realism captured the field in the late forties after collapse of America's dream of an orderly postwar world and after publication of Morgenthau's *Politics Among Nations.*

Beginning with the assumption that in the past American foreign policy had been committed to a moralistic and legalistic view of the international order and had, therefore, been hopelessly naive and irresponsible, Academic Realism called for a power approach to international politics. The interesting thing about this school is that it has never been happy with the "realism" exemplified by the Truman Administration.

Academic Realism consists of precepts from eighteenth- and

[16]John L. Snell, "The Cold War: Four Contemporary Appraisals," *American Historical Review,* 68:1 (October, 1962), 69.

nineteenth-century international relations. Academic Realism made popular a notion of a universe of international politics distinct from domestic—a universe in which statesmen who were free from irrational pressures of mass democracy and self-serving interests and bureaucracies would use reason in the adjustment of their nations' interests. They saw a world in which competing interests could be accommodated. Unfortunately, the view of international relations held by Morgenthau and Kennan appeared just as the United States was making a dramatic break with the past. The conditions for sustaining foreign policy after World War II required the mobilization and allocation of vast resources. This in turn broke down any artificial compartmentalization of international and domestic affairs and involved the masses most intimately. The necessity for these changes has been neither welcomed nor understood by Morgenthau and Kennan.

The new statecraft is programmatic; it requires alliances, bases, economic aid, propaganda, and a host of strategies. Efforts to fulfill these needs have tended to usurp the control over foreign relations usually reserved to traditional diplomatic practices. The growth of programmatic foreign policy has ruptured the traditional distinction between domestic and international relations and has involved in our diplomacy all kinds of nontraditional experts. The new statecraft emerges from a highly political process; it involves the participation of a much wider range of the populace in foreign policy. The mobilization of vast domestic resources for use abroad means that bargaining for them must be done at home; it is democratic, and it is messy. No one responsible for the conduct of foreign relations can be wholly satisfied with the new state of affairs; certainly Dean Acheson resented the massive intrusion of the public as much as anyone, but the question is, are you willing to live with the changed situation and make the best of it? Because the exponents of Academic Realism have never reconciled themselves to the new ethos, their interpretations of the Truman Administration have expressed a certain animus.

Academic Realism usually draws a sharp distinction between

the so-called "golden age" of American initiative and the period that began with the Truman Doctrine and included the Marshall Plan, Point Four, and, with reservations, the North Atlantic Treaty. They argue that after 1949 rigidity and militarization of American foreign policy set in, rendering American diplomacy insensitive to changes in the international environment. Globalism and all the sins thereof are traced back to this period (1950–1952).

The somber tones in which the academic realists color the last years of the Truman Administration is the more surprising because of their own dark and sanguinary theories about international relations:

Thus Morgenthau and others have argued that men and states, being fundamentally aggressive, must be deterred by the aggressiveness of others, or by some other balancing device. It could be that the introduction of this deterrence may have been the prime provocation of aggressiveness. . . . Clearly an expectation of aggression or greed can promote responses which will ensure aggression and greed; and remedies based on the assumptions of Man's aggressive nature such as the balance of power, can establish conditions in which the balance of power would seem to be required, even though there were no original aggressiveness.[17]

Given the evil nature of man, man's *animus dominandi*, and given the nature of the State (as if it were but a projection of man writ large, with the human personality transposed to an abstraction called the State), Russia and America were bound to oppose one another. All that remains is for the statesman to ensure that he conducts policy with prudent regard for the national interest defined as the maximization of power.

It would appear that these interpretations tend to be a priori theories that are unproven and more expressive of mood than of logic. In recent years a considerable theoretical literature has developed that questions these reigning theories of international politics. More recent theory throws doubt on the realists' assumption that aggressiveness either in states or in the men who govern states underlies the Cold War. Psychologists

---

[17]John W. Burton, *International Relations, A General Theory,* 33.

generally agree that aggressiveness is an emergent or dependent state of mind. "One cannot cite man's inherent aggressiveness as a fact that makes war (or rivalry) inevitable."[18] The nature of aggressiveness suggests that the Cold War has a more complex explanation and that its seat is not necessarily in the presumed aggressive instincts of men and states.

Another fault of traditional realist theory has been its view of the relation between states. According to Academic Realism, conflict between states is inevitable because their relations are based on nothing better than chance.

Wars occur, firstly, because there is no control or order in relations between States, and secondly, because there is nothing to prevent them. States are not by nature aggressive; but their relationships are ones in which power and conflict are inherent. On this thesis wars are likely to occur between identical States . . . whatever type of internal organization might be postulated. The argument is not necessarily that States are aggressive, but that in the absence of world order or world government, they will come into conflict.[19]

Academic realists have taken for granted that power and conflict are inherent in relations between states, without much inquiry as to the causes of this condition. That one state or set of states wishes to change the *status quo* and another set to preserve it, is about the extent of their inquiry into causation. Nor does their theory require that nations be responsible for the conditions that are producing a demand for change.[20] Yet, one must ask if concern to accommodate and guide change has not been one of the marks of postwar international relations. More recent theory argues that the study of international

---

[18]Fillmore H. Sanford, *Psychology: A Scientific Study of Man,* 212.

[19]Burton, *International Relations,* 44. As a corollary to this, nation-states are not supposed to form permanent attachments, but if the balancing process is to function, each must be ready to switch partners. This postulate of realist doctrine seems to be confounded by the special relationship that Britain has adopted toward the United States. Has Britain a national interest distinct from that of the United States?

[20]In line with this, the West did not consider the degree to which Western nations were directly or indirectly responsible for Italian, German, or Japanese aggressions. In the nuclear age, this characteristic expression of national interest realism, the attempt to repress apparent aggressiveness, as an alternative to the removal at an early stage of the underlying causes of the so-called aggression, would be foolhardy in the extreme.

relations ought to be on the causes of change, the demand for change; that it is in the stresses and strains of adapting to unexpected and unrelenting change that one finds the sources of the Cold War. "It is when the relationship is a dynamic one in which states are required to make adjustments to changes which are taking place in each of them and between them, that conflict is likely to develop."[21]

Everyone seems to agree that the changes in the landscape left by World War II and the political changes that followed were bound to be disconcerting. Suddenly two nations, both animated by utopias and unaccustomed to dealing with each other, found themselves face to face. Active in this enfacement also was the ideological force of communism—especially potent in a spiritually defeated Western Europe. Another factor was the imprecision of each other's goals. The war had narrowed the strategic distance between Washington and Moscow without defining any clear spheres of influence. The United States was bound to be shocked by the change because it had indulged an exaggerated faith in Soviet-American friendship and in the United Nations.

The eclipse of Germany, Japan, Britain, France, and Nationalist China represented a revolution in power relations. All the familiar dikes to encroachment through overweening power by one or another of the Great Powers had been swept away. For a time Washington tried to keep alive the hope that Great Britain would continue to perform its traditional function of maintaining order and security within the vast and turbulent perimeter stretching from Gibraltar to Hong Kong. This hope proved to be an illusion.

America's sudden confrontation with Russian power in Central Europe was doubtless matched by Russian suspicions of American intentions, especially of an America possessed of atomic bombs and unparalleled wealth. Then followed the near collapse of Greece, the fall of Czechoslovakia, the Berlin blockade, the collapse of Nationalist China, and the war in Korea—all within five years. History has seldom known such pace of crises.

---

[21]Burton, *International Relations*, 72.

Not enough account has been taken of the effect of the environment on the policies of the two superpowers. Each has maneuvered within a rapidly changing frame of forces. More political change occurred in the twenty-five years between 1940 and 1965 than in all recorded history. It is true that each of the Great Powers had security interests that prompted each to consolidate power within its sphere of influence, but we believe that more attention must be paid to change as a factor for generating tension.

We exist in a new age and in a new ethos of international politics in which, out of fear of nuclear holocaust or out of the lamentable experience of two wars, statesmen and people alike have determined to measure their actions; study of our foreign policies calls for more systematic approaches. *Risk calculation* and *crisis management* are new terms. They betoken a self-conscious awareness that gains can no longer be made by crude resort to war (although war is an omnipresent factor) but that the advancement of one's interest requires a concern for the other fellow and some calculation of his responses. Analogies with poker and other games of strategy may sound callous and idiotic in discussing across-the-table conferences of diplomats, in the light of the human beings and civilizations whose lives are at stake, but much of the same tactical skill is needed there. In point of fact, if change and competition are endemic to the nation-state system as presently organized, then an approach that calls on statesmen to measure their decisions in the light of their effects on one's opponents' expectations and sense of security represents an advance over the previous condition in that human intelligence is now applied to the resolution of international conflict.

Such a process assumes a high rationality in goals and in choice of means. Success seems to call for scoring gains that do not threaten or damage the vital interests of one's opponent. Logically, such a concern or process lends itself to rationality or logic. If the statesman is striving with all logic at his command to achieve a gain for his side without prompting an irredeemable irrationality or destruction from the opponent, then the scholar has incentive to study decisions in

similar terms. Such an approach, which is commonly designated
as the decision-making approach, need not reduce the analysis
to taxonomy nor preclude recognition of the uniqueness that
invests every human act. The story is told that at a meeting
of the Yale Corporation to discuss the Political Science Department's budget Robert Taft and Dean Acheson fell to discussing whether politics was a science or an art. They agreed
that it was an art. There is no need to go against the combined
judgment of two such seasoned operators and to deny that
politics in its best sense and practice is an art. It is also, in
its highest form, the application of human reason to human
problems, and it is therefore susceptible to analysis. The plain
fact is that most statesmen, while striving to increase their
nation's security and interest, are also striving to avert catastrophe. Men may fail through ignorance or lack of self-control
or because, caught up as playthings of their gods, they find
that events are too compelling for their puny powers. But
unless they are scoundrels like Hitler, or men unversed in
politics, their desire to improve their country's position while
avoiding an irreparable catastrophe obliges them to behave
logically.

From a generalized understanding of the range of variables
that constitute the statesman's or decision maker's environment
(range of choices) it ought to be possible to isolate and re-
construct those factors that he recognized and to which he
assigned importance in any particular decision. Naturally, for
the decision maker, the criteria of decision and the decision
itself are a blend. Precisely because the Truman Administration manifested a marked propensity toward prophylactic actions designed to avoid "no option" situations and precisely
because it sought to avoid losing control of situations, as in
Korea, it deserves the kind of analysis the decision-making
approach provides.

Too often the study of international relations and foreign
policy is a study of the archives and of the documents, without adequate attention to the political and emotional context
in which twentieth-century statesmen are obliged to act. A
decision-making approach would raise all the variables to the

level of analysis—including some of which the decision maker ought to, but may not have been, aware. Were the questions asked by men within the Administration the right ones? How did they arrive at them? What was the quality of the advice they were receiving? Did this advice take into account a sufficient range of variables? Were the variables properly appraised?

It is especially essential that American scholars pay greater attention to the influence of the demands of other countries upon United States foreign policy. For example, American scholars have been prone to criticize the military emphasis upon NATO and to overlook the demands of the Europeans for American troops in Europe.[22]

Just as American policy must be studied as a function of the policies of other countries, so more attention must be given to the support that developments in international relations brought to American policy.

The statesman is constantly confronted by a dilemma. He wishes to influence the external environment in a particular way, but by the very act of acting he alters (often for the worse) the perspectives of those whom he is trying to influence. In order to act he must have the support of his own people and of allies and friends, but their terms for cooperation are often profoundly at odds politically and psychologically with the conditions he is trying to induce in the international environment. The act of statecraft is like the attempts to hit a target on the wing or to put a BB in a particular hole without dislodging all the others. This need for precision and delicacy demonstrates why the decision-making approach has a great deal of merit despite criticisms raised against it. It

---

[22]This failing prompted the British scholar D. C. Watt to complain that, methodologically, American historiography in dealing with foreign policy does not get much beyond an examination of domestic forces: "This leads inevitably to their main interest being directed to the causes of a particular foreign policy, rather than the consequences of its adoption and the chain of actions and interactions in the development of world politics it may promote. Inevitably, too, this leads to their approaching the history of America in foreign policy in terms of the interplay of domestic politics, pressures, and personalities." "American Diplomatic History," in *The Review of Politics* (October, 1965), 556.

alerts the observer to the dynamics of statecraft and to its pitfalls. Every decision must be examined on two levels of analysis, first, on the theoretical level of the ends the statesman wants to accomplish, and then on the practical level of the means to package and sell the decision to the public. It is quite surprising how often old hands, such as George Kennan, Walt Rostow, Henry Kissinger, and others, miss this crucial consideration in their analyses. They talk of foreign policy without understanding the difficulty of being effective abroad while at the same time securing popular approval at home. This task of statecraft confronted the Truman Administration in an excruciating form.

The application of a decision-making approach to foreign and strategic policy under the Truman Administration serves to focus upon the much-neglected topic of leadership. The study of leadership is an important subject in its own right, but it serves also to throw light upon the philosophic roots or mainsprings of a nation's actions. "Historians differ radically in their estimates of the impact leaders have on great events. Some see deep and inexorable forces as the key determinants; others argue that particular men in places of power create and direct the energies of their time. The truth undoubtedly lies somewhere between these positions."[23]

The distinctive contributions of the men who made American foreign policy under the Truman Administration has been all but ignored. A few important memoirs and biographies are available, but for the most part scholarly discrimination has been swamped by waves of unfounded generalizations. Rather than assigning the conduct of American policy to this or that doctrinal position, one might learn a great deal, especially about its distinctive features, by studying the perceptions of its leadership and the manner in which these men responded to the problems pouring in upon them. The *Weltanschauung* of the Truman Administration must be studied in terms of a distinctively American philosophic and political tradition, a tradition, we would suggest, that is not fatalistically wedded

---

[23] James D. Barber, *Political Leadership in American Government*, 4.

to the grim necessities of power politics nor devoid of optimism nor grounded in a tragic view of life.

Regarded in generational terms, most of the men who were President Truman's associates in the conduct of foreign policy were either born and educated in the era before World War I or came of age in the twenties and thirties. The failure of the League, the rise of the dictators, and the lesson of Munich were important intellectual experiences. It may well be that it was precisely because men like Truman, Marshall, and Acheson were not Academic Realists that enabled them to see the relevance of economic assistance and domestic reconstruction to the containment of communism and that inspired them to back the Truman Doctrine, the Marshall Plan, and Point Four.

Those were uniquely American programs, woven out of moral idealism and hard-headed American experience with economic development and well-being. The decision makers were prepared to respond to world conditions in new and innovative ways; they were not prepared to wait fatalistically until all options were closed but one—war. They were prepared to mobilize and employ national resources in unique and revolutionary ways—the Marshall Plan, Point Four, and aid to struggling allies in Asia and the Middle East. They were also prepared to take their chances with public opinion and with wrath in Congress to make good on their ideas and plans. Power and ideals were never divorced in Truman policy. The Truman Administration never gave up its belief that it was the moral obligation of all nations, and especially of the Great Powers, to foster freedom, justice, and order as well as their narrower national interests.

The relationship of ideas to action has been grossly neglected or oversimplified in analysis of the Truman Administration, perhaps in part because it espoused no major ideology of foreign policy beyond containment but concentrated instead on action.

It is difficult if not impossible to explain the distinctiveness and success of what was accomplished under Truman without referring to the American tradition of politics. It is precisely the American political ideal of a common good or public interest, vague and uncertain though it may be, that made American foreign policy relevant to the new international environment. Had United States foreign policy been grounded in a view of politics as essentially evil and expedient, in exercise of which statesmen arrive at diplomatic accommodations on the basis of a contingent balance of power, where would American policy be today? We suggest that it is precisely in the American tradition that political action ought not to be divorced from moral purpose, that it should dignify and enlarge man's life, that we will find the inspiration for the Truman Doctrine, the Marshall Plan, Point Four, and even the North Atlantic Treaty. Its emphasis upon reason and innovation made the Truman Administration's foreign policy relevant to the new international environment.

The post-World War II world was not the stable and well-ordered Europe-centered universe of the eighteenth and nineteenth centuries. It was a world of revolution bordering on anarchy; the power of the Soviet Union was more than that of the Red Army, and this power lay in the strength of its appeal to the hopes of men longing for a principle of order and for escape from the wreckage of capitalism and nationalism. Where would the United States have been had it acted only out of sordid self-interest and pursuit of power?

In turning away from utopianism the architects of the Administration's foreign policy did not seize upon Academic Realism. Realism, in the doctrinaire sense of power politics, does not explain the foreign policy of the Truman Administration any more than the constant invocation of Hamilton explains the statecraft of the Founding Fathers. American foreign policy repudiated utopianism after 1945, but it continued to draw upon a distinctively American political tradition for its responses. It is frequently averred that pragmatism is the touchstone by which American foreign policy can be explained. This may be true, in the sense that the Truman Administration had no grand political strategy other than containment and that policy was essentially innovative and responsive to situations and crises.[24]

---

[24]In line with American experience, the Truman Administration may have

Clearly, the Truman Administration could not have defined the issues, educated the people, and made the decisions it did had it not been animated by some powerful if not always well articulated sense of America's purpose and by some understanding of how to manipulate and influence social reality. It may seem astounding, but no one has studied this most fundamental of all problems. Neustadt has given us a treatise on Presidential rationality and prudence in decision making, but Truman and his cohorts had to believe in something first. They had to possess some sense of values and goals by means of which to orient and order their calculations.

We venture to suggest that we look to that part of the American political tradition that is concerned with the moral equality of all men and to the principle of the common good. While turning away from utopianism the Truman Administration did not turn away from the idea of the common good of mankind. It is true that the congruence between American idealism and the common good found its most complete expression in the Marshall Plan and Point Four, but even in the formulations of its policy toward the Soviet Union and in the development of its military strategy a concern for the common life and the common good of mankind still found expression.[25]

The relationship of values to American foreign policy must be studied through men and their relationship to the American people on the one hand and to foreign governments on the

---

placed too much reliance upon constitutional and institutional arrangements to order its foreign relations. For instance, it may have placed too much faith in the formal institutional structure of NATO, EDC, and foreign aid to order its relations with its allies and may not have made sufficient allowance for the volatility and changeableness of politics that is characteristic of a system of sovereign nation-states. While the Truman Administration was always keenly aware that governments are the ultimate sovereign will of a nation's actions, it may have overestimated the centripetal force of such arrangements as NATO.

[25]The decision never to recognize the Communist regime as the legitimate government of China, taken out of understandable bitterness with the government's role in Korea, seems to have accomplished little practical good and may be viewed as an exception to the general spirit of reason and tolerance with which the Truman Administration conducted its foreign policy.

other hand. We know very little of the President's political philosophy. A reading of the Truman *Memoirs* is not very revealing from this point of view. We note the importance of a pragmatic outlook and, above all, Truman's historic sense of the office of the Presidency.

We know a good deal more about certain of Truman's lieutenants. This is especially true for James V. Forrestal, whose *Diaries*[26] has been published and whose papers are available on a restricted basis at the Princeton University Library. Two noteworthy studies of Forrestal have been published.[27] James M. Byrnes has published two volumes of his memoirs,[28] and an account of his diplomacy is now available in the *American Secretary of State* series edited by Samuel F. Bemis and Robert Ferrell. Studies of George C. Marshall have either been published or are forthcoming.

A great deal less is known of John Snyder, Robert Lovett, Dean Acheson,[29] Averell Harriman, Paul Hoffman, Louis Johnson, and others. Of the military leaders who figured in the Truman years, a great deal is known about General MacArthur but much less about Omar Bradley, who played an extremely important role both in the transition to the Joint Chiefs of Staff concept and also as an adviser and supporter of the President in many crises.

Publication of David Lilienthal's *Journals*[30] as well as of the first volume of the official history of the Atomic Energy Commission has helped fill a major gap in our knowledge of the relationship of atomic matters to grand strategy and diplomacy.

Not nearly enough research has been done on Truman's organization and management of the executive branch. We have some excellent studies of the reorganization of the de-

---

[26] Walter Millis, ed., *The Forrestal Diaries.*

[27] Arnold A. Rogow, *James Forrestal: A Study of Personality, Politics and Policy,* and Robert G. Albion and Robert H. Connery, *Forrestal and the Navy.*

[28] James F. Byrnes, *Speaking Frankly,* and *All in One Lifetime;* George Curry, *James F. Byrnes.*

[29] The first volume of Dean Acheson's memoirs, *Morning and Noon,* gives us significant insights into the philosophy of a major figure.

[30] David E. Lilienthal, *The Atomic Energy Years,* Vol. II, *The Journals of David E. Lilienthal.*

fense sector under the Armed Services Act of 1947,[31] and we now have some excellent studies of the National Security Council,[32] of the Council of Economic Advisers,[33] and of the State Department.[34] But of the general organization of the White House for initiative, execution, management, and control of foreign policy we have next to nothing. Yet, it should be noted here, subsequent administrations built largely on Truman's experience.

We know next to nothing, also, of the relationship of the various departments and individuals within the Truman Administration to each other. The shift in the United States' attitude toward the Soviet Union can almost be charted by the exclusion of Henry Morgenthau, Harold Ickes, and Henry Wallace from the Cabinet. Their departure from the Government appears to have coincided with the rise in influence of the State Department, which President Truman sought to restore to its proper function. A model of what can be accomplished in research in this area without access to the complete record is Paul Hammond's "N.S.C. 68: Prologue to Rearmament."[35]

We suggest that it would make more sense to approach the study of the Cold War and of Truman's foreign policy, not in terms of monistic and deterministic theories of imperialism or power maximization, but in terms of leaders faced with desperate and compelling choices, forced to act under circumstances of greatest uncertainty, and acting while straining to avoid plunging the world into a new maelstrom. We think the Cold War could best be studied as a series of successive adaptations to rapidly changing environmental demands in which hostility was hardly avoidable but in which a constant regard for the necessity of change has helped to avert a calamity.

---

[31]Walter Millis, *Arms and the State,* and Huntington, *The Common Defense.*

[32]Paul Hammond, *Organizing for Defense.*

[33]Edward S. Flash, Jr., *Economic Advice and Presidential Leadership.*

[34]James L. McCamy, *The Conduct of the New Diplomacy,* and Robert Elder, *The Policy Machine.*

[35]Paul Hammond, "N.S.C. 68: Prologue to Rearmament," in W. Schilling and others, *Strategy, Politics, and Defense Budgets,* 267–378.

Truman's foreign policy was also affected by domestic forces. Because of the importance the corporate-capitalist economy assumes in American society, a number of scholars have inferred an important causal relationship between the needs of the economy and an American responsibility for the Cold War. It is certainly possible, starting from a priori premises, to infer a cause-and-effect relationship between the American economy and foreign policy, especially if one is prepared to ignore the relevance of other factors, but it is much harder to demonstrate the connection with any degree of precision or conclusiveness. In spite of the challenge, surprisingly few of the links have been studied in the chain of analysis that connects the values and interests of particular groups and classes in American society through its institutions to the issues of the Truman foreign policy. Westerfield's study, *Party Politics and Foreign Policy*, while eminently worth while, limits itself to the congressional terrain. It does not seek to go outside the Congress to study the forces animating American politics.

Earl Latham's *The Communist Controversy in Washington* is an important exception to the paucity of studies.[36] Latham has succeeded in identifying an important causal connection between a general set of interests and the importance McCarthyism assumed in American life after 1949. Utilizing indices from presidential and congressional elections, Latham demonstrates that an important conservative impulse had been building for a decade prior to the 1948 election. So long as the chances of a Republican victory in 1948 had looked propitious, Republicans in Congress had gone along with bipartisanship. "The failure of the electorate to effect a change of government in 1948 with such opportunity as the political system might permit for the release of anti welfarist ambitions under conditions of responsibility for the outcome . . . produced a political expression that exploded in McCarthyism."[37]

Here we have a specific linkage between a set of interests (conservative), political institutions, and policy consequences (McCarthyism). While Latham has not attempted to assay the

---

[36]Earl Latham, *The Communist Controversy in Washington*.
[37]Latham, *Communist Controversy*, 398.

impact of McCarthyism upon foreign policy, it is possible to hazard the judgment that it was very great. Immediately after the 1948 election and a year before McCarthy's speech at Wheeling, West Virginia, frustrated Republicans were beginning to zero-in on China policy. Bipartisanship on China policy, never very strong, broke down completely thereafter. By the end of 1949 the China bloc in Congress, hardly very numerous before 1949, had succeeded not only in making hostility to the Administration's China policy a party matter but it had also succeeded in identifying Acheson as the Number-One target of Republican hostility. In this instance we know that they successfully defeated the Administration's efforts to disengage America from the fortunes of Chiang Kai-shek's regime on Formosa and blunted Acheson's efforts to effect a new departure in Far Eastern policy. The thrust and effectiveness of the Republican campaign to discredit and alter the Administration's foreign policy became even more severe with the onset of full-blown McCarthyism.

McCarthyism in this view of the party movements of almost a century was the agent of a fundamentalist conservatism that was prepared to yield public policy to reformers for the relatively short periods required to satisfy grievances but which expected to recover predominance when these intervals were over.[38]

It was easy for the conservative forces to frustrate Truman's Fair Deal in the Congress where the Republican–Southern Democratic coalition tightened its grip upon the committees after 1948, but there still remained the question of the Presidency in 1952. In order to improve their chances the conservative forces in the country intensified their attacks upon foreign policy, with what consequences for foreign policy we still do not really know.

Nevertheless, the logic of Latham's study suggests that the Communist issue was the cutting edge for a conservative attack upon the Administration domestically and that its impact upon foreign policy was largely a function of this attack rather than of any real commitment to shifting American foreign policy

---

[38]Latham, *Communist Controversy*, 423.

from its containment basis to something else. The Republicans once back in power, both McCarthyism and liberation were relegated to the woodshed. Nevertheless, it cannot be denied that McCarthyism exacerbated the Cold War strains in American society, reduced the Administration's room for reasonableness and maneuverability, and gave certain interests a greater influence upon policy than they otherwise would have had.

The challenge to scholarship is to distinguish between the conditions imposed upon Truman's foreign policy by the system of international politics (bipolarity) and those imposed by the economic, political, and group interests of American capitalists, Zionists, Republicans, etc. Group and class interests in America are most often presented in terms of the general interest and are screened through a mesh of culturally held values as well as through a system of party, congressional, and executive institutions with their own corporate interests to protect. In order to triumph, group and class interests must successfully identify with and negotiate their way through this complex screen of values and institutions. It is only by taking such things into consideration that one can ask the really significant empirical questions. How else are we to distinguish a "business" attitude from an "American" attitude on foreign policy matters? How else are we to distinguish between the issues on which a businessman in office is deciding as a businessman or as a government official? Or are we to assume that business ideas, fostered by a corporation-dominated society are so pervasive that the distinction does not have to be made? If so, how do we account for the opposition of Robert Taft and the Republican party, presumably spokesmen for the capitalist viewpoint, to both European involvement and military spending? Such anomalies defy simple explanations. Only the most profound respect for the complexity of political life will give us true insight into the dynamics of the Truman Administration's foreign policy.

Let us now turn away from these general considerations and look at the development of the Administration's foreign policy. Upon assuming the Presidency, Truman was initially obliged to take over Roosevelt's role and commitments. Almost all planning had been on the assumption that the Soviet Union would cooperate in establishing a reasonable international order. Except for those elements of the State Department charged with postwar economic planning and with planning for the United Nations, the State Department had been rather thoroughly ignored as a source of plans for foreign relations and as an agent for implementing them.

Wartime diplomacy had been heavily influenced by the military, and the United States' actions at the war's end—abrupt cancellation of lend-lease, demobilization, etc.—all had their roots in the American view of war as a discrete event. Powerful public and congressional forces were wedded to the view that the war had been a mistake and that the sooner the United States returned to its own affairs the better. Consequently, the Truman Administration began its term of office with the American public psychologically disposed to return to isolationism and oversold on the United Nations; no guarantee existed that the much-hoped-for Soviet cooperation would be forthcoming. Only in the realm of international economic affairs had promising wartime progress been made in the form of the Bretton Woods Agreements, but to secure passage of these through Congress was to require a Herculean effort by the new Administration.

It is our contention that Truman's foreign policy during this period can best be understood as a halting process of adaptation to the shock of recognition that Soviet–American relations were not going to develop in the direction Roosevelt had led the American people to anticipate and of adaptation to swiftly moving changes in the international environment. This can be best illustrated by a brief examination of policies that have been the center of continuing controversy.

A great deal of controversy already surrounds the origins of the Cold War. Why is it that one set of scholars takes it for granted that American policy was principally a response to Soviet intransigence and aggrandizement while another set attempts to weave from the declarations and actions of American statesmen a persuasive case for United States responsibility?[39] We have indicated that the downhill course in Soviet–

American relations had already set in during the Second World War; the incompatible designs of the two superpowers were never resolved but simply plastered over. Once the defeat of Nazi Germany loomed upon the horizon the whole postwar fate of Europe clearly lay before the two superpowers. This extraordinary situation was thrown in relief by the weakness of both Britain and France. The unconditional surrender of Japan and the weakness of China produced a similar bipolarity in Asia. Had there existed other great powers and not simply a vacuum, Soviet–American tensions would not have taken such an acute form.

This complexity still does not explain why certain writers can cite reams of evidence that Byrnes went to London in September, 1945, with "an A-bomb on his hip" and other "proof" of a systematically aggressive tone to American words and actions, while others can demonstrate just as systematically that the Administration worked for a reasonable accommodation. To explain the discrepancy in the evidence introduced by the two parties to the controversy requires a less a priori interpretation. The "get tough" line is there, but it may be more profitable to examine it as a function of the Administration's frustration through failure to achieve the peace projected by Roosevelt and its anxiety over the consequences that would ultimately have to be drawn from that failure.

Those who are determined to show that the United States was seeking an honorable accommodation and that the onus for its failure lies mostly with the Soviets must ask themselves if the terms upon which the United States proposed to settle the peace were realistic. It is quite possible that conditions that might seem reasonable to the United States, which had scarcely been touched by the war, would not seem adequate to the Soviet Union, which had suffered so enormously. Is it sufficient to demonstrate that the United States was trying to be reasonable and accommodating if its terms for the postwar

---

39The controversy was recently reopened in an exchange of "Letters" between Arthur Schlesinger, Jr., and Gar Alperovitz, in *The New York Review of Books,* 7 (October 20, 1966), 37–38.

world appeared wholly inadequate to the needs of the other
great victor?

Santayana's definition of a fanatic is someone who redoubles
his efforts when the realization of his goals becomes unclear
or uncertain. Before we can defend the proposition that the
United States was trying to be reasonable and accommodating
we must judge the validity, in terms of both international
politics and Russian needs, of the conditions of the postwar
settlement to which the Administration was committed. We
must ask if a spheres-of-influence, balance-of-power approach,
which we eventually adopted, would not have provided a
sounder basis for accommodation. The Soviets had but thinly
disguised their intention of establishing a *cordon sanitaire* of
states dependent upon the Soviet Union along its western bor-
ders. Negotiations between Stalin and Churchill in the autumn
of 1943 had formalized their spheres-of-influence approach.
But Secretary of State Hull had turned in horror from the
spectacle, and even Roosevelt had registered his disapproval.
The Declaration on Liberated Europe, as well as other agreements reached at Yalta, attempted to reconcile the Soviet
Union's preoccupation with territorial expansion with the
American ideal of a pluralistic universe in which a presumed
harmony of interests would operate to produce order out of a
situation in which every nation was free to determine its own
best interest. In spite of its rejection by the Americans, the
spheres-of-influence approach continued to run like a thread
through the skein of the early postwar Soviet negotiations.
Byrnes reported to his Cabinet colleagues the obvious advances
by Molotov to settle postwar problems *à deux*, with Britain
being admitted as a junior partner on issues that concerned it.
Byrnes hastened to reassure his colleagues that he intended
to repulse all such advances, and on the few occasions when
he tentatively embarked upon big-power diplomacy he was
swiftly brought to heel by Vandenberg.

Had the United States been able to switch to a spheres-of-
influence approach there is no guarantee that Soviet–American
relations would have turned out any better. The United States
could not avoid being interested in the fate of Western Europe,

which it had just liberated at the cost of so many men and so much money. Moreover, a spheres-of-influence approach does not assume the end of conflict but merely its mutual reduction to carefully controlled dimensions. There would have been a continued need for military forces in being and more, not less, call upon American resources than was envisaged by Washington's postwar planning.

Unable to switch its approach, the Truman Administration was in a quandary. Dismay, irritation, and an inclination to riposte came in the wake of deception. Policy alternated fitfully between efforts to preserve the spirit of accommodation upon which the Grand Alliance had hitherto rested and an inclination to penalize the Soviet Union for failing to live up to America's expectations. Philip Mosely writes that to have made cooperation stick "much more should have been done to assure him [Stalin] of assistance in rebuilding the Soviet economy; as it turned out, Stalin and the Soviet people soon felt that their vast sacrifices were forgotten by less war-damaged allies as soon as the fighting was over. That and other policies would have required a much more integrated policy than American policy seemed capable of achieving during World War II."[40]

Policy presupposes some degree of consistency between a government's perceptions and its willingness and ability to act upon them. Despite its perception that Soviet behavior was not consonant with the wartime assumptions of American policy, the Truman Administration clung to the belief in an underlying harmony of interests among nations, as among men, which needed only to be worked at to be realized. It persisted in the belief that a sensible accommodation could be made between the wartime partners, yet it refused to accept cardinal Soviet conditions for continued collaboration. At the same time it was deterred by pressures for demobilization and a return to normalcy from taking the kind of military and political initiatives that alone might have influenced Soviet behavior short of open contests.

It seems to us that the Administration's ambivalence about

---

[40]Philip E. Mosely, *The Kremlin and World Politics,* 156.

international politics, complicated by the difficulty it knew it would face in attempting to reverse trends at home, deserves more consideration if we are to understand why some scholars see America responding only to Soviet initiatives while others trace responsibility for the Cold War back to the words and actions of the Truman Administration.

The shift in American foreign policy between the time of Roosevelt's death and the conferences at Potsdam and London has been the subject of endless controversy. It is generally agreed that some shift occurred and that it is correlated with Truman's coming to the Presidency. Critics tend to confuse correlation with causation. They observe that American foreign policy changed after April, 1945. They note that Roosevelt died and Truman replaced him at that time, and they jump to the conclusion that Truman's assumption of office was the cause of that change. They do not recognize that certain long-postponed issues were bound to come to a head at this time, regardless of whether Roosevelt had lived or not, and that these would have produced changes under any circumstances. They seldom if ever recognize that, precisely because change was so long avoided by Roosevelt, it was all the more painful when it became necessary under Truman.

No observers agree on the reasons for Roosevelt's delaying so long in coming to a settlement of postwar issues. Feis, Snell, and others contend that he procrastinated as long as he could in order to maintain the alliance until certain unifying arrangements were completed. For example, Hammond writes:

Roosevelt in preferring postponement also had a rationale. The Big Three Alliance was working remarkably well, all things considered. To raise issues of post-war policy could jeopardize it. Moreover, the unknowns of the future—the conditions in Germany, the American public temper towards continuing foreign involvements, and the fate of the Big Three Coalition, to mention a few placed a premium on the maintenance of freedom of action for Roosevelt, or at least so it appears in retrospect.[41]

Others argue that he refrained from dealing with these issues

---

[41]Paul Hammond, "Directives for Germany," in Harold Stein, ed., *American Civil-Military Decisions: A Book of Case Studies*, 410.

until America was in a position to dictate terms at the end of the war. They never square this with the rapid demobilization of United States armed forces.

As a solution to the question, we suggest the following hypothesis: As long as Roosevelt and Truman could believe that the Soviet Union was committed to some genuine degree and form of postwar cooperation, Soviet behavior in East Europe and elsewhere could be treated lightly.

When the British and Soviets pressed Hull for his opinion as to what the character of the postwar Polish and Yugoslav regimes ought to be, he evaded Molotov's "invitation to 'bow out' from the entire complex of East Central European problems, but he made it equally clear that the United States government was not really concerned about this area of Europe, at least in comparison with the 'big' issues"[42] (Soviet–American friendship, the United Nations).

We know that active American opposition to *de facto* implementation of a sphere-of-influence approach was also checked by the military point of view, which represented a controlling influence *during the war.*

Echoes of this persistent military position were heard at the crucial White House Conference of April 23, 1945, called by President Truman. . . . At this conference Secretary Stimson argued that "the Balkans and their troubles were beyond the sphere of proper U. S. action"; he urged caution in opposing Soviet flouting of the Yalta agreement on Poland and the Yugoslav seizure of Trieste.[43]

This position did not mean that Roosevelt had been indifferent to the fate of Eastern Europe or that in approving "democratic" reorganization of East Central Europe he was also approving Soviet domination of the area. His behavior seemed to reflect the view that if the big issues—Soviet–American friendship, the United Nations, etc.—worked out, lesser issues would resolve themselves.

Truman came to office just when the Soviet Union was demonstrating a remarkable callousness toward the big issues (especially in its ruthless treatment of Poland and its cavalier

[42]Mosely, *The Kremlin*, 207.
[43]Mosely, *The Kremlin*, 206.

attitude toward the United Nations) and thereby undermining United States confidence in Soviet support for the idealized American version of a postwar world free of strife. The shock dealt to American expectations by these evidences of unrequited friendship was severe, and it quickly led to a hardening of positions. But were these positions so fundamentally different from those Roosevelt would have espoused? The shock of recognition that the Roosevelt-inspired utopia was not realizable, coming just at a time when the fates of Europe and of the Far East hung in the balance and when it was perfectly clear that American influence was a waning asset, was bound to produce convulsive adjustments in United States foreign policy perspectives. These in turn appear to have jolted the masters of the Kremlin, who had become accustomed to having everything very much their own way.

Rather than starting to analyze the origins of the Cold War from the standpoint of economic imperialism or of an instinctive or systemic-induced aggressiveness or by imputing malevolent intention to the Truman Administation it seems to us that analysis might begin by recognizing the suddenness and uncertainty with which the Truman Administration was suddenly forced to disabuse itself of the assumptions that had buoyed up Roosevelt's diplomacy and by gauging the anxiety the Administration experienced in not knowing what additional change might portend.

Let us take the tortured issue of whether the United States consciously set out to employ the atomic bomb as an instrument of diplomatic blackmail. A recent study concludes that the strategy of delaying negotiation of postwar issues was held inoperative by the Truman Administration, pending the successful outcome of the tests in New Mexico, on the assumption that "its force would permit a new American initiative in European and Far Eastern diplomacy."[44] The same study concludes that on the basis of the bomb the "firm approach so long in suspense could be resumed with the backing of unprecedented military power."[45] While Alperovitz stops short of saying that

[44]Alperovitz, *Atomic Diplomacy*, 187.
[45]Alperovitz, *Atomic Diplomacy*, 225.

the Truman Administration employed atomic blackmail, he imputes a consistently offensive thrust to American foreign policy, after the tests in New Mexico, that worsened Soviet–American relations. Alperovitz gives the impression that it was somehow wrong for the Truman Administration to consider the bomb's utility for deterring Soviet ambitions. He also ignores the fact that, whatever diplomatic leverage the A-bomb may have had in principle, it did not succeed in securing any major concessions from the Master of the Kremlin. In fact, Truman and Byrnes settled for a great deal at Potsdam that was distinctly favorable to the Soviet Union.[46]

A criticism from just the opposite point of view has been leveled by Pierre Gallois:

President Truman, following the same naive train of thought as his Secretary of War, decided to play down the first atomic explosion. "On July 24th I casually mentioned to Stalin that we had a new weapon of unusually destructive force. The Russian premier showed no special interest. All he said was that he was glad to hear it and hoped we would make 'good use of it against the Japanese.'" Churchill added, "I was sure that he had no idea of the significance of what he was being told."

Nothing was done, of course, to make Stalin aware of the significance, so the momentous news did not influence negotiations; instead it was played down by those individuals who could have used it as a bargaining tool. They did not understand the power of the atom. Potsdam reinforced Yalta, and the destiny of Europe was shaped by Moscow despite the powerful trump card which the Americans had just acquired.[47]

---

[46]In his review of the Alperovitz volume, Ronald Steel wrote: "By July 16, the date the Potsdam conference opened, Truman had his answer: the bomb would work. The President was elated, and told Stimson that the bomb 'gave him an entirely new feeling of confidence.' Not only could it be used to make the Russians behave in Eastern Europe, but it now made their entrance into the war against Japan quite unnecessary. The bomb would allow the US to win the war without an invasion and without the Russians. It was the answer to Washington's prayers. Yet oddly enough, *the news did not make Truman noticeably stiffer in his attitude toward Stalin,* nor in his demands that the Soviets comply with the Yalta accords as the West understood them. *If Truman tried to intimidate the Russians in Eastern Europe with the bomb, he failed totally.* As Herbert Feis later wrote, the explosion at Trinity 'filtered into the conference rooms at Potsdam only as a distant gleam.'" *New York Review of Books,* 5 (November 25, 1965), 9.

[47]Pierre M. Gallois, "U. S. Foreign Policy: A Study in Military Strength and Diplomatic Weakness," *Orbis,* 9:2 (Summer, 1965), 342–43.

Here is an event about which scholars hold diametrically opposite views and which obviously needs research. We need to determine the extent to which, following the termination of the war against Japan, American planners viewed the possession of atomic weapons as an acceptable device to bring about change in the international environment. The divergence between the Acheson–Lilienthal and the Baruch proposals for the International Control of Atomic Energy are indicative of the ambivalence and uncertainty with which the United States approached this critical problem, and these differences suggest that alleged employment of atomic force as an instrument of diplomatic pressure and imperialism is not at all evident from the record.

This raises still another point about the A-bomb. There is as yet no study of the limits that America imposed upon itself in so far as the use of the A-bomb was concerned. Aside from *The Just War* by Robert Tucker, no study has been made of how the American government viewed its arsenal of nuclear weapons after 1945 or of how their development was retarded by the controlling view that such weapons ought never to be used.[48]

The issue of free elections in Eastern Europe is another example of those ambiguous situations Truman inherited at Roosevelt's death, which became a focus of controversy in the wake of the shock of recognition that the Rooseveltian model of the postwar world was not going to be realized. A brief examination of this issue illustrates the initial American diplomatic response during the eighteen-month interregnum between the Japanese surrender and promulgation of the Truman Doctrine. We are not certain what Roosevelt had in mind when he secured Stalin's acceptance of the Declaration of Liberated Europe. To Roosevelt its precise significance may have been blurred by the aura of the Big Three's accommodation to which it was intended to contribute. The State Department may have

---

[48]Robert W. Tucker, *The Just War: A Study in Contemporary American Doctrine,* finds in the American attitude toward war an important determinant of American actions. He notes that the argument that "at no time since the inception of the Soviet–American rivalry have circumstances offered a promise of success to a policy of preventive war appears strained."

had a more specific purpose in mind. Certainly, anyone familiar with the basic social and political complexion of the East European societies could not seriously have believed that free elections would produce regimes friendly to the Soviet Union. The Yalta Declaration on Liberated Europe postulated logically contradictory goals. Stalin told Truman at Potsdam that "any freely elected government in these countries will be an anti-Soviet government, and we cannot allow that."[49]

Was the United States wise to make free elections such an important—perhaps the most important—test of Soviet good faith? One cautionary note on the American side came from Secretary of War Stimson, who was not at Yalta, but who warned President Truman shortly after he came into office in April, 1945:

> . . . we have to understand that outside the United States, with the exception of Great Britain, there are few countries that understand free elections; that the party in power always runs the elections, as I well know from my experience in Nicaragua [in 1927].[50]

Some say, with the benefit of hindsight, that it was unfortunate that Truman and Byrnes ignored Stimson's cautionary advice and seized upon the moralistic-legalistic formula of free elections as the condition of America's agreeing to the peace treaties for the East European states. Cold War analysts of the right argue that the Administration should have taken the occasion of the violation of the pledge to hold free elections to redress the balance while it still had a military capability on the Continent. But what do we learn from an examination of their behavior in these minatory terms? At this point the Administration did not fully comprehend the nature of the shift in the balance of power that had been brought about by World War II and by the destruction of the Axis Powers. It was still wrestling with the newness of it all and baffled by the sense that events were not moving toward a happy ending. The

---

[49]Quoted in Theodore P. Wright, "The Origins of the Free Elections Dispute in the Cold War," *Western Political Quarterly*, 14:4 (December, 1961), 850–64.

[50]Henry L. Stimson and McGeorge Bundy, *On Active Service in Peace and War*, 610.

United States had steadfastly rejected spheres of influence during the war; was it now to acquiesce in them under circumstances far less rosy and reassuring? What would serve as the basis of relations if the two leading states could not agree on legal principles? Having little, if any, sense of an alternative basis for conducting Soviet–American relations that would not call for unpleasant and costly changes in America's projected return to normalcy, is it any wonder that Truman and Byrnes seized upon the "legalistic-moralistic" formula of free elections? Far from their insistence upon free elections being an evidence of their desire for American domination of the Eastern Europe free elections, this insistence may be viewed as an expression of their desire to complete their mission in Europe and go home.

For Byrnes, the implementation of the Yalta agreements would lead to the solution of all outstanding postwar problems. It seems never to have crossed his mind that something more fundamental was at issue and that the agreements by themselves would guarantee nothing.[51] There is a great need to see "free elections," like many other policies the Administration espoused at this time, in the light of the deception and anxiety that was developing as it became more and more apparent that Roosevelt's assumptions about the Soviet Union had been based upon hopes and patently contradictory aspirations, such as "friendly governments" and "free elections."

While the British did not raise such a hue and cry about the failure of free elections to be held in Eastern Europe, many British Laborites as well as Conservatives were shocked by the brutal treatment meted out to left-wing Socialists in Bulgaria and Rumania, Hungary and Poland. They were shocked by the crude liquidation of movements of a distinguished democratic and socialist background, and they quickly lost any illusions

---

[51]One catches a sense of Truman's mood in a letter to his mother and sister as he prepared to depart for Potsdam. "I am getting ready to go see Stalin and Churchill, and it is a chore. I have to take my Tuxedo, tails . . . I have a brief case all filled up with information on past conferences and suggestions on what I'm to do and say. Wish I didn't have to go, but I do and it can't be stopped now." Truman, *Memoirs*, 331. It may be appropriate to distinguish between the motives of Truman and Byrnes and those of the State Department. They need not have been the same.

about the nature of the Kremlin's apparatus and operators. Nothing quite surpassed the shock of the rape of Czechoslovakia, however. Labor's respect and affection for Beneš and Masaryk had been unlimited. The shock of the 1948 Prague *Putsch* was all the more terrible. It turned British Labor, right and left, livid. Not enough attention has been paid to the influence that events in Eastern Europe had in arousing Socialists and Laborites on the Continent and in Britain to the stark horror of the Communist monolith. It might come as a surprise to Americans to pick up a slight volume entitled *The Curtain Falls in Eastern Europe,* edited by Denis Healey. In the Foreword to the 1951 printing, Aneurin Bevan wrote:

> The Communist Party is the sworn inveterate enemy of the Socialist and Democratic Parties. When it associates with them it does so as a preliminary to destroying them. There is an old German aphorism which says: "To cast an enemy out it is first necessary to embrace him." That is what the Communists mean when they ask for cooperation and alliance with the Socialists.[52]

The Communists' behavior inspired a horror among most Europeans that is sometimes neglected in American studies of the dynamics of the Cold War. We sometimes forget the passionate hatred that Communist betrayals in Eastern Europe inspired among European socialists and working-class people.[53]

The United States' participation in the United Nations presents a similar example of the ambivalence and uncertainty that marked America's response to the world situations between 1945 and 1947. In many respects the increasing firmness with which Byrnes faced each successive Council of Foreign Ministers meeting during the eighteen months from September, 1945, to March, 1947, gives a powerful indication of how the United States shifted to meet the changes brought about by the havoc of war and by the continuing decline in the prospect

---

[52]Denis Healey, ed., *The Curtain Falls,* 6.

[53]In this connection it is pertinent to point out that a great deal of European writing has been largely neglected by American scholars: F. S. Northedge, *British Foreign Policy;* C. M. Woodhouse, *British Foreign Policy Since the Second World War;* Alexander Werth, *France: 1940–1955;* Alfred Grosser, *La IVe Republique et sa Politique Exterieure; The American Review,* 2:4 (March, 1963), which devotes almost the entire issue to American foreign policy from 1945 to 1952.

for a stable postwar world. The high point, of course, came in December, 1946, when at the New York meeting of the Council, Byrnes threatened to negotiate peace treaties for Rumania, Bulgaria, Hungary, Finland, and Italy, independent of the Russians. The Soviets responded to the challenge, and with few minor adjustments the treaties were signed. Many people forget that the conclusion of this session was hailed as the dawn of a new era in East–West relations. Considering what was to occur in March, 1947, it is in this period that the assumptions with which American policy planners approached the problems of peace in Europe need careful examination.

Of more interest perhaps is the relationship of the United States to the United Nations. Aside from Ruth Russell's[54] superb study of the Charter, the literature is pitifully inadequate. What was the American attitude toward the United Nations during this critical eighteen-month period? We know, for example, that the Rooseveltian postwar world order was almost totally dependent upon the success of the United Nations. Plans for its organization began with the Atlantic Charter, and Truman was committed to completing the arrangements for the conference to be held in late April, 1945. The United States' involvement in the United Nations was superbly engineered by the State Department. Local groups were organized to discuss world order, the department sent speakers everywhere to spread the word, and 2,636 journalists were accredited to report the details from San Francisco. What role did the United Nations play in international politics from 1945 to 1947?

Certainly the use of the veto in the Security Council by the Soviets during 1946 caused some American officials to have doubts as to the organization's effectiveness. But, can we be sure that these doubts dominated official attitudes? Two examples can be cited. In August, 1946, two American military air transports were shot down over Yugoslavia. Acting Secretary Acheson fired off a note to the Yugoslavs, demanding prompt and effective rectification. If not complied with, the

---

[54]Ruth B. Russell, *A History of the United Nations Charter: The Role of the United States, 1940–45.*

United States *would turn the matter over to the Security Council.* Again, the Soviets during 1946 put heavy pressure on Turkey, hoping to force the Turks to revise the Montreux Declaration, which governed the use of the Bosporus. Here again the United States responded to the situation by warning that any attack in the Straits *would result in prompt action by the Security Council.*

The confusion and uncertainty that characterized the American approach to the Soviet posture in Europe until 1947 is well illustrated by these two divergent policies. On the one hand, Byrnes's policy of "patience with firmness" finally threatened unilateral action in New York. The Russians responded. In this respect the United States seemed to be beginning to recognize that the Rooseveltian model was somehow grossly inadequate; yet the State Department continued to act as though the United Nations had the power to redress some grievance or threat to the peace.

Much more attention needs to be given to official American attitudes toward the effectiveness of the United Nations. The American response to the Soviet threat outside the United Nations came about belatedly. It would appear that, while the State Department sold the American people on the efficacy of the United Nations during the war, they sold themselves at the same time. This conviction made the final break with the past—the perception that direct United States action in Europe was the only effective alternative—much more difficult.

Superficially, 1945–1946 is a somewhat inchoate period in American foreign policy. Debilitating uncertainty about America's role in the wake of the collapse of wartime expectations was made more acute by the rapid dwindling of American military and political power. As a result, American diplomacy was characterized by efforts at reasonableness and accommodation, alternating with toughness and stridency. Foreign policy was still at the mercy of domestic forces that were pulling America away from involvement. A crude anticommunism was emerging in public quarters as a substitute for a more reasonable basis of action. Wherever possible in the light of World War II experience, such moves were made as seemed necessary to the security and efficiency of the nation's foreign policy: unification of the Armed Services, loans to Britain and France, and renewal of the draft. These were little more than improvisations based upon the lessons of past experience. They did not go far toward resolving the issues being raised by the Cold War. As Westerfield, perhaps better than anyone, points out, the Administration was caught between fear of making matters worse by bluntly telling the American people that the Cold War had begun and a mounting desperation about America's lack of means with which to warn off the Soviet Union and endow the West with an effective foreign policy.

The impetus from the external environment that would overcome the inhibitions upon American foreign policy and lead to its greatest innovative period came from a direction that had been almost ignored in America's postwar planning—the Eastern Mediterranean—and in the context of changing Anglo-American relations.

Anglo-American relations rightly form one of the most vital and fascinating aspects of postwar diplomacy. A number of searching and suggestive studies have been devoted to the so-called "special relationship," but much remains to be done. During much of the war, Roosevelt had exploited British imperialism as a lightning rod with which to maintain harmonious relations with the Soviet Dictator. But Roosevelt was genuinely anti-imperialist, and his esteem for Churchill in no way mitigated his anti-British attitude on colonial matters.

Following the war's end, a subtle shift occurred in United States policy. With the world rocking on its foundations and American power being swiftly retracted, the Truman Administration was acutely conscious of the importance of British power to world stability. As long as Britain held out, the United States could procrastinate and could avoid facing up to the transformed nature of world relations. The Truman Administration exerted long and desperate efforts to have Britain make good on the role staked out for it by Washington. The 3.25-billion-dollar loan and the general support for British policies in the Middle East and in Southeast Asia was a distinct change-over from the Roosevelt pattern, so much so that it sealed America's solidarity with the Attlee–Bevin wing of the new Labour Government. With acute insight the Kremlin concentrated its fire on British policy throughout 1945–1946 rather than upon the United States.

Given the exhaustion and the financial weaknesses of the British position, there were limits to Britain's capacity to play its imperial role, and these were rather quickly reached. Weakness manifested itself most strikingly in the Eastern Mediterranean. Oddly enough, the Eastern Mediterranean had not figured prominently in American plans, yet it was there that the Soviet gauntlet was thrown down most boldly: As early as the winter of 1945 Moscow sent notes to Turkey demanding codetermination with Turkey of the Straits regime as well as the acquisition of Kars and Ardahan; Yugoslavia persisted in its endeavors to seize Trieste, and Yugloslav–American relations reached the breaking point in the summer of 1946 with the shooting down of U. S. aircraft; finally, the United States was drawn into the Eastern Mediterranean theater by the unleashing of the Greek Communist guerrillas. Stephen Xydis has given us the details of this process in his most comprehensive study. The irony of the situation lies in the fact that the impetus to clarify its policy and to define its world role came to the United States from an area in which the United States had not had the least interest until pressure from the Soviets became intolerable, and it came as a direct result of unambiguous moves on the part of the Soviet Union.

When General George Marshall replaced James Byrnes as Secretary of State in January, 1947, the major outstanding Soviet–American problem appeared to be the negotiation of the German peace treaty. Byrnes had demonstrated at the New York meeting of the Council of Foreign Ministers that his policy of "patience with firmness" paid off in dealing with the Russians, and Marshall seemed confident that a continuation of this policy would result in a German treaty when he met with the Soviets in Moscow in February. The implication here is that while both men obviously considered the Russians as potentially threatening and difficult to do business with, they also believed that under the proper pressure the Russians could be reasonable.

In the light of other evidence this assumption needs further examination. In February, 1946, nearly a year before General Marshall assumed office, George Kennan, American chargé d'affaires in Moscow, cabled the Department of State a lengthy analysis of Soviet intentions, the substance of which was later published as the famous "X" article in *Foreign Affairs*. Kennan was unequivocal in his analysis that under no circumstances could a *modus vivendi* be reached with the Soviets. He noted with some detail their expansive and aggressive propensities, and he suggested that the Western Powers must begin to plan how those propensities could be contained. The Department of State reproduced the report and circulated it to Forrestal and other high officials of the Government. What impact, if any, this statement had on the State Department's planning at the time remains to be studied. Subsequent events would suggest that either it was not taken seriously or that the State Department for some reason was unable at that time to implement its suggestions. Nevertheless, some attention must be given to the policy decisions being made by the State Department prior to the events of March, 1947.

One possible explanation for the crisis that commenced in the executive with the British announcement in February, 1947, that they would be forced to leave Greece by March 31 may be that officials in the State Department simply did not believe it could happen. Following this line of reasoning, some case can be made to suggest that the loan of 3.25 billion dollars to Britain in 1946 was to be used to shore up the British and enable them to continue to check Soviet penetration in the Mediterranean and the Middle East. Even if this were not the rationale for the loan among the leaders of the Administration, it certainly became the dominant theme when the enabling legislation reached the Congress. The traditional Anglophobes in the Congress accused the Administration of attempting to "pull British chestnuts out of the fire." As the debate proceeded and the outcome hung in the balance, the arguments shifted rather abruptly. At first supported for economic reasons, the debate over the loan ended on a distinctly political and security note. Finally, the loan was supported because it would allow the British to uphold the security and integrity of their sphere of influence. The Congress seemed to be saying that, regardless of how distasteful British imperialism might be, it was better for us to pay them to watch the Russians than to do it ourselves. How far this position was from that of the policy planners at the State Department needs further attention.

The dramatic events that transpired between the announcement of the Truman Doctrine in March, 1947, and General Marshall's speech at Harvard University in June, 1947, are critical. It was during this period that the final break with the past occurred and the United States declared to the world that Soviet intentions and acts posed a threat to international peace and security and therefore must be "contained." Surprisingly little is known about this critical juncture in American foreign relations. Joseph Jones's *The Fifteen Weeks*[55] is an uncritical account of the period that is useful primarily for the chronology it provides. It details certain of the major decisions that were made, but fails to lend much depth to the various assumptions and factors upon which those decisions were based. Stephen Xydis's *Greece and the Great Powers: 1944–1947*[56] provides, no doubt, the definitive study of the internal nature of the civil war in Greece and the state of the international environment at the time, but a detailed analysis of the American response is beyond the scope of his volume. What is required is an American analogue to the Xydis book.

We know, for example, that planners in the State Department were aware of the impending crisis in Greece. That they did not think it was strictly a British problem is uncertain, but the rather dramatic presentation by the British of their note explaining to the United States that they could no longer afford to finance the Middle East and the Mediterranean sphere of influence presents some intriguing questions for research. Could it be possible, for instance, that the British felt they had to act precipitately in order to force the United States to

---

[55] Joseph M. Jones, *The Fifteen Weeks.*
[56] Stephen Xydis, *Greece and the Great Powers, 1944–1947.*

respond forcefully to the Communist threat in the Balkans, that, otherwise, the United States, judging by its record up to that time, might not act successfully, responsibly, or perhaps at all?

To understand the nature of the American reaction requires much more than a recital of dates and personages. More attention must be devoted to the study of the various factors that shaped the domestic situation and limited the courses of action that the Administration could take. After being briefed at the White House by Truman and Acheson on the Greek situation, Senator Arthur Vandenberg replied that the President had no alternative but to "scare hell out of the country." The implications of Vandenberg's injunction have not been treated, but we suggest that it offers at least a partial answer to the criticism that the Truman Doctrine was too blatantly ideological in its anti-Communist tone.

An examination of the domestic scene in the early months of 1947 reinforces the appropriateness of the Vandenberg remark. The Congress was controlled by the Republicans; Senator Robert Taft had made it unmistakably clear during the 1946 campaign that the Truman budget would be trimmed by several billions and brought into balance. Furthermore, the Republicans generally disapproved of America's recent venture into active internationalism, and then supported the United Nations only because they hoped it would allow the United States to quietly retreat to older, cherished ways. Support for any foreign adventure that had at one time been connected with the British would not be forthcoming voluntarily from most Republicans. On the other hand, the general public had heard so much from Washington about the United Nations that a major unilateral act on the part of the United States would not go uncriticized.

These circumstances, then, help explain the ideological anti-Communist nature of Truman's speech to the Congress of March 12, 1947. By stressing the threat that totalitarian regimes posed to the security of the European states, the Administration declared Russia the enemy and announced the policy of containment, which was by no means restricted to Greece and Turkey. Kennan, the intellectual father of the containment policy, strongly objected to the tone of the message. But what Kennan and the other critics of the message like Walter Lippmann failed to note was that the British withdrawal meant either total commitment or total abdication. No program of any magnitude could be gained without the support of the people. Even then, gaining a commitment from a Congress which was uninterested in, if not hostile to, foreign involvement, was no small task.

The reaction in the Congress was more or less predetermined by the crisic nature of the situation. The Congress could not afford to reject the President's proposal without totally undermining his position, yet its recalcitrance was evidenced by the fact that the bill was not finally passed until May—two months after the announced British withdrawal.

The pronouncement of the Truman Doctrine on March 12, 1947, which was the United States' declaration of participation in the Cold War, marks the beginning of the Truman Administration's sweeping strategic and programmatic initiatives in foreign affairs. The break with the past had been made, and the Soviet Union had been designated as the enemy. Preparation for the break had required eighteen months but, once decided upon, the United States attempted to mobilize its available resources and repair the situation as quickly as possible.

Congress' leisurely treatment of the Greek–Turkish aid bill was indicative not only of its general reluctance to become involved at all but also of its growing weariness of being forced to act by executive fiat. By mid-April it was reasonably clear to the planners in the State Department that, if the cooperation of the Congress were to be enjoyed, some long-range program would have to be developed in which the Congress could play a major role. Thus it was that, while the Congress was debating the Truman Doctrine, the State Department was slowly arriving at the conclusion that European vulnerability to Communist expansion was due in large measure to the nature of its war-destroyed economic system. If Europe were to survive, the argument went, it must be rebuilt. The fruit of this thinking was to emerge as the Marshall Plan. Here again, aside from cursory and occasional remarks in the Jones volume, little is known about the developments within the State Department during the genesis of the Marshall proposal.

General Marshall's speech on June 5 at Harvard College invited European suggestions for recovery; it was immediately seized upon by European leaders. Within months the Organization of European Economic Cooperation (OEEC) was organized and functioning. The Marshall Plan still awaits its definitive analysis, but much more has been written from the European perspective than from the American. Probably the best of these is Freymond's *Western Europe Since the War*.[57] The American contribution is largely unexplored.

The evolution of the Marshall offer into a plan for European reconstruction illustrates a number of significant changes in the American approach to foreign affairs. Seventeen billion dollars was appropriated by the Congress for the four-year period, 1948–1952. This in itself represents an impressive accomplishment. To do this the executive utilized a number of innovative devices. Congressional cooperation and involvement was engaged by the appointment of Christian Herter to the chairmanship of a House Select Subcommittee on European Recovery. Trips abroad were sponsored by the Administration for members of Congress to enable the skeptics to see for themselves the extent of the destruction. To counteract the public and congressional charge that such an ambitious program would bankrupt the United States, the Administration prepared a report under the direction of J. A. Krug, Truman's Secretary of the Interior, which effectively canceled this objection. A similar study was initiated by the President's Council of Economic Advisers, which clearly demonstrated America's capacity to meet the needs of domestic consumers while at the same time attempting to help the Europeans rebuild their shattered countries. Much support was mustered when Averell Harriman reported to the President on the seriousness of the Europeans' plight. When the bill came before the Congress an impressive array of prominent American businessmen and industrialists testified that such a program would not only

---

[57] Jacques Freymond, *Western Europe Since the War*.

enable Europe to become once again self-sufficient but it would also give the American economy a boost.

What little scholarly attention has been focused on the Truman Doctrine–Marshall Plan period has generally emphasized the Marshall Plan. There can be no doubt that for any number of reasons it was the more popular of the two. The Truman Doctrine involved military aid and promised little in return except security, a factor the American has difficulty in measuring in political terms. The Marshall Plan, the forerunner of foreign aid, was strictly economic in nature, and most Americans were convinced that such a program would be beneficial for all concerned. Seen in traditional American terms, it was more attractive because it was a "sound investment." The proposition that requires some attention is this: Could the Marshall proposal have succeeded without the announcement and acceptance of the Truman Doctrine four months earlier? We suggest that, without the drastic change in American foreign policy attitudes concerning the United States' role in world affairs that was precipitated by the pronouncement of the Truman Doctrine, it is highly improbable that the Marshall Plan would have been acceptable to a majority of Congress and of the American people.

The degree to which the Truman Administration regarded the Marshall Plan as the final answer to the situation in Europe is, of course, another question that requires further study. The crucial event that tested the adequacy of the purely economic program was the sudden fall of Czechoslovakia to the Communists in February, 1948. Most Europeans seemed well aware that their security involved more than economic recovery. The threat posed by the Russians—both internally by various Communist parties and externally by the military potential of the Soviet Union—was more than military; it was psychological. Economic recovery depended upon making the peoples of Western Europe believe that the Czech coup could not be repeated in Italy or in France.

The European response to the situation was the negotiation of the Brussels Treaty, which was signed in March, 1948, by the governments of Britain, France, Belgium, the Netherlands, and Luxembourg. Pledging the members to a fifty-year period of economic, social, and cultural collaboration, the principal section of the pact involved a commitment to collective self-defense against foreign invasion. The treaty was actively supported by the United States, who had promised limited aid in the form of arms and other equipment. The Europeans, however, soon made it clear that the military credibility of their pact required more from the United States than simply surplus arms and ammunition. They desired American participation in a treaty that would bind the United States to the defense of Europe against a Soviet attack.

Almost nothing is known about the decisions the Administration made concerning its relations with the Brussels Treaty Powers from March to June, 1948. Our feeling is, however, that the decisions to proceed with the agreements that emerged the following year as the North Atlantic Treaty were made prior to June, 1948. The significant event was the passage of Senate Resolution 239 on June 11, 1948. This so-called Vandenberg Resolution, which received the overwhelming support of the Senate (64–4), was a reaction to the Soviet abuse of the veto in the Security Council of the United Nations, which had crippled that organization's ability to act. More basic, however, were three sections of the resolution that dealt with the question of collective security in general. These urged that it ought to be the policy of the United States to seek

(2) progressive development of regional and other collective arrangements for individual and collective self-defense in accordance with the purposes, principles, and provisions of the Charter;

(3) association by the United States, by constitutional process, with such regional and other collective arrangements as are based on continuous and effective self-help and mutual aid, and as affect its national security;

(4) contributing to the maintenance of peace by making clear its determination to exercise the right of individual or collective self-defense under Article 51 should any armed attack occur affecting its national security.

When the United States began to discuss collective security with the Brussels Treaty states in the fall of 1948, it did so under the authority granted it by the Vandenberg Resolution.

Whether this was Vandenberg's intent is not clear. The degree to which the resolution was the brain child of the State Department rather than of Vandenberg is also unresolved. What does seem apparent is that the Administration's repeated injunction that the resolution had invited the United States to begin negotiations for a regional collective security pact committed Vandenberg to the support of the program lest he wish to repudiate his role in the passage of S. Res. 239.

The development of the North Atlantic Treaty was another milestone in the United States' involvement in the world arena. For the first time in its history the United States was prepared to negotiate a peacetime military alliance with Western European states that committed it to the principle of collective security.

The Europeans arrived in Washington desirous of a firm and absolute commitment to respond in kind to any external attack. In preliminary discussions with Under Secretary of State Robert Lovett, the foreign leaders seemed to want an ironclad agreement that any attack on one would mean an attack on all and the response would be military and other appropriate action. Lovett, knowing full well that the Senate would never allow such an infringement on Congress' war powers, appears to have limited the American commitment to taking military *or* other appropriate action. This was unsatisfactory to the Europeans, but such was the state of the treaty when Dean Acheson was selected by President Truman to be his Secretary of State after his surprise election. Acheson's first duty was the negotiation of the North Atlantic Treaty and its implementation with the Military Assistance Program of 1949.

The best single volume on the treaty is Osgood's *NATO: The Entangling Alliance*.[58] Nevertheless, its emphasis is on the development of the alliance from a treaty into a viable and effective collective pact. Of the decisions made at the State Department during the planning and negotiation stage we know very little. We know enough, however, to suggest that the phraseology of Article 5, the operational clause of the

---

[58]Robert E. Osgood, *NATO: The Entangling Alliance.*

treaty, went through a number of drafts. Left by Lovett as reading "to take military *or* other appropriate action," it finally became "to take forthwith . . . such action as it deems necessary, including the use of armed force." What occurred between these two drafts can only be inferred. We know that Acheson met with the members of the Senate Foreign Relations Committee, chaired by Tom Connally. Connally undoubtedly had some reservations; the ranking Republicans, led by Vandenberg, no doubt made other suggestions. Nevertheless, Acheson's previous experience as Assistant Secretary of State for Congressional Relations probably served him well in this capacity. A study is needed of Acheson's dealings with the committee, which wanted a weak commitment, and of his subsequent negotiations with the Europeans, who wanted nothing less than an automatic declaration of action.

During the Senate hearings and debate on the treaty, Administration spokesmen made a forceful case that the European Recovery Program would be jeopardized unless reinforced by the treaty. Unfortunately, the consent to the treaty was one matter; implementing it was quite another. The Administration had originally proposed a 1.3-billion-dollar military assistance program, to be voted on with the treaty. Strong objections from the Senate forces, led by Senator Robert Taft, made separate hearings a requirement. The treaty received the consent of the Senate in July, 1949, by an 82–13 vote, but the Military Assistance Program of 1949 faced a more severe test.

Senate criticism of the military aid program forced the Administration not only to separate it from the North Atlantic Treaty but also to cut the original request, pending development of a unified strategy for the defense of Western Europe. Senator Taft and his colleagues argued that, even as presented by the Administration, the military nature of the program would serve only to provoke the Russians into declaring World War III. Not one to be easily satisfied, he also suggested that if such a program were to be effective it would require much more than the Administration's current request. Thus, for Taft, the proposal was only a small down payment for a multibillion-dollar plan that would extend for twenty years. This of course was fiscally impossible, Taft maintained. All the Administration could do was to suggest that the intent of the program was to make the European military force under the treaty credible and to indicate to the Russians that any Continental adventure would not be worth the inherent risk.

Senate consent to the North Atlantic Treaty and passage in Congress of the Military Assistance Act of 1949 squarely established the United States' stake in the security of Western Europe. To a large degree historic relations had illuminated the United States position vis-à-vis Western Europe and made the series of responses from 1947 to 1949 easier. The clarity of the American interest in Europe and the nature of its response was apparent to all but the most obtuse, but a similar clarity was not to be found regarding American interests in the Far East.

Ironically, the striking success of American foreign policy in Europe was to be contrasted with its seeming failure in Asia. Critics would point to Europe and ask why similar successes had not been forthcoming in Asia. Undoubtedly, the much greater visibility with which the Administration could see how to act effectively in Europe, as contrasted with a lack of clear guidelines in Asia, accounted for the dynamics by which Europe was saved and China foundered.

There is a considerable literature dealing with America's European policy for the period between 1945 and 1949, but by one of those curious quirks, events and developments in American policy after 1949 have been neglected. The Westerfield volume concludes with the ratification of the North Atlantic Treaty, the passage of MAP, and the development of partisan contention over China. After that, the focus of research attention swings to the Far East. True, there are bits and pieces here and there that treat particular elements of policy formation: Paul Hammond's *NSC 68* study, Warner Schilling's "The H-Bomb Decision," and Laurence W. Martin's *American Decision to Rearm Germany*. There is of course an extensive literature on NATO, of which Robert Osgood's *NATO: The Entangling Alliance* is by far the most impressive.

Beyond these, only one analytical study of the development

of United States foreign policy between 1949 and 1953 is available, and that is Coral Bell's *Negotiation from Strength*.[59] Miss Bell provides a brilliantly suggestive study, but it was not intended to be a study in depth. Nevertheless, Miss Bell has raised many of the right questions and therefore ought not to be ignored. Up until 1949 American foreign policy had depended upon a brilliant combination of innovation and improvisation. Miss Bell has rightly pointed out that, for a variety of reasons, by 1950 previous assumptions underlying United States foreign policy were showing themselves to be inadequate. The steadily rising level of Soviet risk-taking, together with the fall of China and the Soviet acquisition of the atomic bomb, raised compelling questions. Was the existing level of Western preparedness sufficient to meet a future challenge without resort to atomic war, and could existing levels produce stability in America's relations with the Communist bloc?

Decisions and recommendations began to be taken within the Administration, calling for a considerably different and greater type of effort. This called forth a reappraisal of previous assumptions underlying the containment doctrine, in part because the situation seemed to call for such a reappraisal and in part because its costs would somehow have to be explained and justified to the American people. It was at this juncture (February 16, 1950) that Dean Acheson advanced the notion of "situations of strength." Miss Bell has attempted to explain the shift as follows:

The most important and substantial difference between the idea of containment and the idea of negotiation from strength is that they offer two alternate notions about a possible end to the power struggle with Russia, which may be called respectively the "domestic change" thesis and the "diplomatic adjustment" thesis. The first holds broadly that abatement of the power struggle is to be looked for only through a process of change within Russia[,][60]

whereas the second envisages inducing a change in Soviet behavior by convincing the Kremlin that its efforts to upset the balance or extend its sphere of power are doomed to failure.

---

[59]Coral Bell, *Negotiation from Strength*.
[60]Bell, *Negotiation from Strength*, 24.

The two theses are distinguished by a number of differing assumptions and consequences. *Containment* implies a rather passive holding at a low level of power, whereas *negotiation from strength* implies an active campaign to alter Soviet perspectives at a considerably higher level of political and diplomatic activity.

No one has subjected this shift to a systematic analysis. It clearly implied that, rather than waiting for or seeking to impose a transformation upon the Soviet system, the United States would do better to conduct an active strategy and diplomacy looking to a transformation of the international system in America's favor. By the logic of its assumptions, *situations of strength* eschews placing the struggle in a moralistic context of the "good guys" against the "bad guys." It also postulates a definite but ambiguously distant point in time at which the Soviet Union would cease and desist from attempting to transform the *status quo* by force and *détente* would emerge. Miss Bell argues that "containment is clearly a *status quo* concept; it aims to keep the situation from deteriorating. Negotiation from strength is *prima facie* a revisionist one: it aims to improve things—for instance to negotiate the Russian troops in Europe back behind the Russian frontier."[61]

The public presentation of *situations of strength* was never fully successful because it was overtaken, first by McCarthyism and then by the war in Korea. Nevertheless, it constituted the essential philosophy and logic behind United States diplomacy in parts of the world after 1950.

The military significance of NATO has obscured its importance to the whole question of European and American relations. Except for Osgood's *NATO: The Entangling Alliance* and a few memoirs, the historic political significance—the ethos and the diplomatic and political effort both within the United States and in Europe that made NATO possible—has hardly been touched.

There is a revolutionary quality and a grandeur, too, about

---

[61]Bell, *Negotiation from Strength*, 23.

the idea of linking the United States and Europe in a common destiny only five years after the war's end. No such perspective existed in American thinking in 1945. As a result of the war some thoughtful Europeans deemed or considered some form of unity to be the only alternative to the eclipse of European culture and influence, but the mingling of the two continents was wholly unanticipated. It is easy to understand that the weakness of Europe in the face of the Soviet colossus created a relationship of dependence on the United States, but that it should develop such creative potential was wholly unanticipated. Because the significance of the achievement has been lost from sight, no major effort to investigate and to understand what was accomplished between 1949 and 1953 has ever been made. The military significance of NATO has pre-empted its study at the expense of the larger political and psychological significance of the factors that were involved. In this regard, Truman's NATO policy has been criticized for its alleged militarization of containment, an excessively delicate view in the light of what was at stake. Sometimes with the support of events, but often against the full weight of nationalism and bureaucratic inertia, political and diplomatic action gave a politico-military form to the North Atlantic Community.

NATO could never have achieved its institutional growth had statesmen not woven a political and diplomatic fabric strong enough to support it. No one Gulf Stream brought life to the North Atlantic Community. Many dreams went into its composition—the dreams and goals of Monnet and Schuman, of Adenauer and De Gasperi, of Paul Hoffman and Lord Franks—and sometimes the synchronization and orchestration were faulty, as perhaps in the case of EDC. These faults notwithstanding, somehow all sought to realize their own goals through something larger. Even the British, for all of their obstinate fears of Continental unity, did not absolutely obstruct or sabotage it. The lesson NATO can give to the relationship of statecraft to the development of regional and supranational entities has not even begun to be explored.

NATO's political significance, first as a demonstration of

the fatuity of the Communist claim that democratic capitalist states are incapable of working together, and secondly as a means of managing the North Atlantic Community's extra-European problems, has not been examined. NATO gave incontrovertible lie to the Communist claim that the West must collapse of its own internecine quarrels at a time when the West needed to renew its self-confidence. NATO also encouraged the British and Dutch, if not the French, to be reasonable in their colonial relations and brought the United States into a constructive relationship to Europe's extra-European problems. The Truman Administration's role in the Anglo-Iranian crisis and in France's troubles with its North African protectorates are in striking contrast to the Eisenhower Administration's handling of the Suez crisis.

Other developments connected with the North Atlantic Community at this time also invite investigation. Both Coral Bell and Marshall Shulman[62] argue that, such was the success of NATO and of American rearmament, in the course of 1951–1952 Western strength achieved an optimal relationship vis-à-vis the Soviet Union and that then was the best time for the United States to have negotiated. Instead, the Truman Administration treated Soviet overtures not as genuine negotiating bids but as delaying bids aimed primarily at slowing down and aborting the consummation of EDC and German rearmament. This is a topic that needs considerable examination. While no final judgment is possible until the nature of Soviet motivation and intentions are more clearly known, the subject raises interesting questions. In and of itself the Soviet note of March, 1952, calling for a neutral, unified Germany with its own national army, represented less of an attempt to find a basis for agreement than a bid for German rejection of its Western attachment. As happened so often to Soviet diplomacy this particular bid misfired because it offended the French.

Soviet diplomacy appears to have constantly overrated its capacity to influence or detach West Germany from its Western orientation. If it had wished to avoid the reconstitution

---

[62]Marshall D. Shulman, *Stalin's Foreign Policy Reappraised.*

and rearmament of Germany it did almost everything wrong. The very situation it ought to have wished to avert was consummated in full. This failure must be regarded as a defeat for Soviet diplomacy. Perhaps Western commitments to Bonn were a price that had to be paid to accomplish this goal. Nevertheless, it has burdened Western and especially United States diplomacy with an obligation to pursue and achieve not only the unity of Germany but also revision of the Oder-Neisse frontier in favor of Germany.

One of the most frequent criticisms leveled against NATO was that it led to an overmilitarization of containment. There is probably no better example of the tendency of many American scholars to generalize without paying sufficient attention to the external demands upon United States foreign policy. Before one can generalize about United States militarization of containment one must first understand the nature of the demands being made upon the United States by its European partners. Without exception, the European governments were insistent upon receiving the maximum in military support and assistance. They desperately wanted United States forces in Europe. When the North Atlantic Treaty was being negotiated, French neutralist newspapers like *Le Monde* ran banner headlines "The Yanks Aren't Coming," in hopeful anticipation that the treaty would not contain a sufficiently reassuring automatic guarantee. It was the European critics of the North Atlantic Treaty who deliberately sought to undermine confidence in the treaty by playing upon the notion that, as in 1940, Europe would be overrun before the Americans arrived and Europe would have to be liberated all over again. In order to respond to these charges the Truman Administration was forced to consider ways and means of making the American guarantee credible. How better could good faith be demonstrated than by the emplacement of American forces in Europe in advance of attack?

Later, when EDC was proposed, British and French governments alike feared that it would provide the United States with an excuse to reduce its military commitments in Europe. The

French feared that, if they ratified EDC and made it work, the United States would no longer feel the same obligation to tie up its forces in Europe. Paradoxically, Frenchmen argued that by defeating EDC they would be assuring the indefinite continuance of the American presence in Europe. Similarly, America's military presence was indispensable to the restitution and rearmament of Germany. It was the cement, so to speak, for any building of community in Europe. NATO also enabled the United States to soften British opposition to EDC and to insulate tentative European moves toward economic and political unity against British wrecking operations. Reducing British opposition entailed acquiescence in Britain's claim to a "special relationship" with the United States.

Negotiation for West German support, on the other hand, built a rigidity into the Western diplomatic position that was characteristic of the alliance so far as extra-alliance relations were concerned. Each partner's commitment to NATO was based on a cost-gain calculus. The force levels and intrusions on individual sovereignty were exceedingly high for a military alliance. The greatly enhanced security that NATO afforded, as well as contributions to their military prowess, made its costs worthwhile, but the reduced perception of the Soviet threat after 1951 lowered the gain value. The only way for the Administration to have accommodated to this shift would have been to lower the costs to its European partners or else to have increased the gain side for them. The Administration attempted to do the latter through military aid, offshore purchases, etc. and by adopting a solicitous attitude toward Europe's overseas problems, but with only limited success. We suggest that only the transformation of the North Atlantic community into an organic political federation could have overcome the inevitable tendency of NATO partners to calculate their interests on a national abacus. Dissolving United States sovereignty in a NATO pool was not feasible, given the climate of opinion in the United States of America.

The obvious importance Europe assumes in our remarks is indicative of the greater importance that Europe has assumed in United States policy making. Why this was so has not been the subject of any single study, although Tang Tsou's *America's Failure in China: 1941–1950* treats it implicitly.[63]

Tang's study represents the most comprehensive and painstaking effort to get to the bottom of what he terms "the American failure in China." Tang concludes that it was due to a lack of genuine understanding of American national interest in China; the outcome of generations of viewing China in sentimental and romantic terms rather than in terms of hardheaded realism; the result of legalistic-moralistic scruples about intervening in a civil war in which the Communists, contrasted with the corrupt and inept Nationalists, did not appear an entirely illegitimate force. Finally, Tang stresses the lack of will on the part of the United States Government to become involved to the degree that would have enabled it to have brought pressure on the Nationalist regime to reform its ways. The weight of expert opinion at the time was against the view that the United States' intervention could affect the outcome of the struggle in China. Aside from charges and allegations leveled against the China experts, both those within and without the State Department, no authoritative study has been made of the way in which the views of the experts influenced the Administration. Did their judgments and conclusions run parallel, or did the experts play a formative role in shaping Administration perspectives about China? Decision making about China may have been, indeed was, plagued by emotionalism and an inability to see consequences clearly, but it was shaped also by a serious concern that America could not influence the decision in China even if it had had the resources that it lacked at the time.

Was the State Department's Far Eastern Division completely close-minded? Was the weight of informed opinion convinced that Chiang's regime had reached a degree of political and social sclerosis that totally inhibited the kind of reform the situation demanded? It is doubtless true that the China policy suffered because of the lack of any great public debate. In part this lack was due to the Administration's unwillingness

---

[63]Tang Tsou, *America's Failure in China: 1941–1950.*

to jeopardize its preferred focus of action—Europe—by exciting a debate over the relative importance of China. In part, too, it was due to the lack of incentive within the Republican party to stimulate a debate that, while it might have forced the Administration to reconsider its China policy, might also have led to greater involvement and greater expenditures—something the Republican party in Congress did not want. Hence, they had no incentive to reorient the Administration's China policy and, by and large, made an issue of it only after China had fallen.

Aside from ignorance, prejudice, or faulty judgment, the Administration's decision to limit the United States' involvement in China and concentrate on Europe must be studied in the context of the limits domestic forces imposed upon the Administration's freedom of action and capability.

No one has thoroughly explored the assumptions and validity of the policy the Administration attempted to adopt toward the Far East in the winter of 1949–1950. Acheson's speech on January 12 is scanned almost entirely for its famous perimeter statement. Its broader policy implications are invariably overlooked. Yet, it was the authentic expression of a new policy approach to Asia. It took as its basic assumption that the strongest counteragent to communism was nationalism and that the United States must not appear to thwart Asian nationalism (or Chinese for that matter). To this end the State Department (following Jessup's trip to the Far East) recommended that the United States adopt a hands-off policy regarding Chiang Kai-shek's regime on Formosa and concentrate on supporting nationalist movements, provided they were not Communist dominated. In his statement, Acheson laid down the caveat that the United States could not hope to supply the newly formed Asian states with the indispensable ability to govern nor to guarantee them the loyalty of their people. The United States, Acheson said, could supply only the missing component of economic assistance and backing against external aggression. The insight into the limits of American power revealed by the speech has not always been adequately appreciated. Unfortunately, the conditions if not the assumptions underlying this policy approach were thrown into question by the North Korean aggression of June 26, 1950.

The Korean War has provided material for some of the most interesting examples of the new style of experimentally oriented research. In the first place it was the third largest of our foreign wars. Second, the MacArthur Hearings (*The Military Situation in the Far East*) provided testimony based on documents and archival material that would not normally have become available until some years later. Third, the fact that the conflict was kept limited has suggested to researchers that the war has something important to tell us about the assumptions and processes under which post-World War II international negotiations are being conducted.

The Korean War has occasioned several striking studies designed to test hypotheses concerning the role of the President and his staff as well as the role of limited war. The most striking examples of the former are, of course, Glenn Paige and Richard Snyder's "The United States Decision to Resist Aggression in Korea,"[64] Richard E. Neustadt's *Presidential Power*,[65] and Morton H. Halperin's *Limited War in the Nuclear Age*.[66] The last is an effort to explore the conditions under which military power may be employed as part of a consciously controlled political strategy or, war having broken out, how force may be kept geographically or militarily limited by processes of mutual self-denial.

It must be said that the American people found this self-denial so painful that it brought the Administration under the most powerful attack since the days of the Civil War and Reconstruction. Insufficient study has been devoted to the challenge to American political institutions posed by General Mac-Arthur's dismissal and the adverse consequences, fed back from the MacArthur crisis, upon America's over-all foreign policy.

---

[64]Richard Snyder and Glenn Paige, "The United States Decision to Resist Aggression in Korea," in Richard C. Snyder and others, *Foreign Policy Decision Making: An Approach to the Study of International Politics*, 206–49.

[65]Richard E. Neustadt, *Presidential Power: The Politics of Leadership*.

[66]Morton Halperin, *Limited War in the Nuclear Age*. Besides being an excellent analysis of limited war, Halperin's study includes the most exhaustive bibliography on the subject thus far compiled.

The study of the Korean War has resulted in a number of outstanding histories. Among the most significant are John Spanier's *The Truman–MacArthur Controversy,*[67] Trumbull Higgins' *Korea and the Fall of MacArthur,*[68] Allen S. Whiting's *China Crosses the Yalu,*[69] Leland Goodrich's *Korea: A Study of U. S. Policy in the United Nations,*[70] and, above all, David Rees's *Korea: The Limited War.*[71] While the military aspects of the Korean War have been exhaustively treated and the war itself has given rise to an important body of theoretical literature on limited war, the political and diplomatic aspects have not been thoroughly explored.

The Administration's rather brilliant handling of the United Nations situation that followed in the wake of MacArthur's recall has been barely touched upon, nor has the lack of insight into Communist political behavior betrayed by the Administration's failure to keep the pressure upon the Chinese after they had become interested in, but had not yet signed, an armistice. This aspect of the Administration's performance has been rather brutally summed up by Bernard Brodie in the following terms:

At lower levels we were learning from interrogation of Chinese prisoners that the Chinese Communist Army morale was in a state of collapse. Chinese troops were defecting and surrendering to us in quite unprecedented numbers, despite the great physical difficulties in doing so. That was why the Chinese had become interested in an armistice. However, we stopped the offensive that produced that result, thus permitting their armies to recover and also relieving them of all pressure to come to terms. I do not suppose our political leaders knew how historically novel their action was, but they wanted to make a gesture of good will, something that would presumably produce a friendlier atmosphere for ensuring negotiations. As a result the negotiations dragged on for over two years, and finally, after the Eisenhower Administration had been helped to power by the electorate's disgust at

[67]John W. Spanier, *The Truman-MacArthur Controversy and the Korean War.*

[68]Trumbull Higgins, *Korea and the Fall of MacArthur: A Précis in Limited War.*

[69]Allen S. Whiting, *China Crosses the Yalu: The Decision to Enter the Korean War.*

[70]Leland M. Goodrich, *Korea: A Study of U. S. Policy in the United Nations.*

[71]David Rees, *Korea: The Limited War.*

the previous Administration's inability to terminate the war conclusively, we settled for terms that were far from being as satisfactory as we could have got earlier.[72]

Beyond this military and political failure, the terrible impact of the Korean War upon our relations with Red China in particular and with Asia in general has not been studied. American eagerness to negotiate an armistice with Peking contrasted strangely with our inclination to isolate them politically and diplomatically. What part did the febrile state of American opinion produced by the virus of McCarthyism play in fixating American foreign policy in a catatonic state so far as Red China is concerned? What role did the implied threat of a direct and possibly nuclear riposte against Red China play in deterring Peking from renewing a major offensive backed by air power in Korea after armistice negotiations had begun?

The Truman Administration has not lacked for interest in its military policies and strategic decisions. The Korean War was the third largest foreign war in the nation's history. The strategy under which that war was conducted became one of the most controversial issues of the Truman years and a much-studied model of limited war.

Prior to 1950 American strategy was geared to defeating the Soviet Union in a general war. It was therefore heavily weighted toward United States air and nuclear superiority. NSC 68 raised more complex considerations of strategy to the level of governmental awareness and in a form that would eventually have gained presidential acceptance had the Korean War not broken out. For the first time United States strategy was discussed in terms of Soviet intentions and capabilities, and there began to develop a view of the purpose of military power that was related to diplomacy and that took into account the possibilities and function of deterrence and limited war.

United States military goals after the onset of the Korean War raised many questions that have not been effectively explored. The Administration put enormous emphasis upon the

---

[72]Bernard Brodie, *The Communist Reach for Empire*, 6.

building up of American and Allied conventional strength. The United States added to its own conventional power substantially, partly by being the only one of the NATO Powers that introduced a two-year term for conscription, and partly by spending a great deal of money for the extra capability. Did the Administration, as a result of the Korean War, develop "an exaggerated preoccupation with a presumed Russian and Chinese urge to territorial conquest?"[73] or was the build-up of American and Allied forces part of a more calculated strategy? If the latter is the case, then it would seem to justify the rather divisive impact that the call for greatly increased European force levels had upon the Alliance.

The war in Korea certainly gave greater substance to the Truman Administration's pressure for a greatly augmented conventional force in Europe. In defending its demands, Acheson envisaged the possibility not only of indirect aggression on the Czech model but also of direct military incursions by Soviet satellites for which the Soviet Union would disclaim responsibility; "in the absence of defense forces-in-being, satellites might be used for such disguised aggression in the hope that they could get away with it, since the free nations could respond only with the weapons of all-out general war, or not at all."[74] Now, there is an undeniable element of prudence in such a statement that must be recognized. On the other hand, how many divisions would have been necessary to deter or defeat a limited probing action or third-party aggression by a satellite? Thirty divisions, sixty, ninety? The first appears the most likely figure unless the United States contemplated that a NATO riposte would be followed by a general war. Why, then, was the emphasis placed on a much higher goal?

In the first place, most of the Administration leaders, including the Joint Chiefs, were convinced that a threat of general war was imminent. We know from open hearings before committees of Congress that the Administration actually construed the Korean attack as being a *ruse de guerre* to entice us into that far-off peninsula while the Russians prepared their

---

[73]Brodie, *Communist Reach*, 14.
[74]Osgood, *NATO*, 79–80.

attack in Europe. We do not know on what basis the assumption was made that the Russians were about to attack. It is easy to say now that "that assumption was completely wrong,"[75] but the United States had experienced such a series of shocks to its expectations since 1945, including the Korean aggression, that one can understand such a misjudgment. Why were estimates of a Soviet attack not revised downward after it became apparent in 1951 that Moscow was undertaking a serious revision of its European policy? Here the importance of a large conventional force to Acheson's "situations of strength" strategy must be taken into account. If, as seems apparent, Acheson viewed the *status quo* along the East-West demarcation line as essentially unstable and therefore requiring modification in a direction favorable to the West, then the extreme emphasis upon a massive conventional build-up makes sense. Acheson, if not the Administration, perceived that only the retraction of Soviet power would solve the political and security dilemma of a divided Europe. He has never been clear on how he expected NATO to accomplish this, although a test of will and strength, say in the wake of an East German or Hungarian-type uprising, presumably was not ruled out. However, this was not something that could be stated openly.

Nevertheless, after 1951 a reduction in perception of the Soviet threat occurred. In the face of this perception of a reduced threat from the Soviet Union, the United States either had to lower costs, that is, cut back on NATO force levels, or else increase the gain side. But here the Administration was up against the limits of sovereignty and of economy. It attempted to enhance the political value of NATO to its European allies by pay-offs outside Europe—aid to the French in Vietnam and to the British in their struggle with Mossadegh. But there were limits to how far the United States could go in supporting its European partners in these directions without compromising itself in the eyes of the emerging, third-force nations.

Even had the Korean War not elevated strategic and military affairs to the front rank, they would still figure promi-

---

[75]Brodie, *Communist Reach,* 15.

nently because of the greatly enhanced relationship that war, preparation for war, and military strategy have had in the conduct of postwar foreign relations. War has become one of the principal facts of international relations in the twentieth century. There is no need to go into the reasons for this situation here. The United States came to world leadership as a result of the greatest war in history. Significantly, that war was ended by the application of an entirely new weapon of mass destruction—the A-bomb—the magnitude of which was destined to give to war an entirely new dimension.

The Truman Administration faced a double task with regard to military and strategic matters, first, of assimilating the requirements of military policy to its conduct of foreign relations and, second, of meeting the challenge to human understanding and control of the new weapons. For the first time since the founding of the Republic, the United States was forced to prepare for military action in advance of war. It fell to the Truman Administration to confront the adjustment to this situation in its most complete and drastic form.

The Truman Administration had to assume responsibility for adjustments in the basic relations between the executive and the Congress with respect to military policy on a scale greater than the accumulation of all previous change in the nation's military history. In many instances military and political imperatives called for changes in strategy with which the traditional institutional arrangements and processes were not equipped to cope. This was true of the executive as well as of the Congress. As a result severe crises of adjustment were experienced all along the line.

A considerable literature exists that treats the various problems and crises connected with the shock of military and strategic imperatives upon the traditional institutional arrangements.[76] The requirements of maintaining and employing the new military establishment in the setting of the Cold War drastically increased the executive's power at the expense of

---

[76]See, for example, Huntington's *The Common Defense* and Schilling and others, *Strategy, Politics, and Defense Budgets*.

the Congress. With the problems of national security policy being so much more complex and more fundamental than those of the past, it was inevitable that traditional processes would be subject to intense, and in some respects intolerable, strains. The issues are so important that in a very real sense the life and vitality of American political democracy is at stake.

The basic issue has been that of relating the nation's military power resources and its institutional mechanisms to the achievement of its objectives in foreign policy. To achieve this balance has challenged traditional institutional arrangements, including the innovation of civilian control over the military. As a result the Truman Administration was beset by a series of controversies—some within the executive between contending branches of the military, or between the military point of view and that of the State Department, and others between the President and the Congress. The unification of the armed services, the B-36 controversy, the fiscal 1950 military budget, NSC 68, and the Korean War have all provided case studies that exemplify the stresses and strains within the Administration and between the Administration and the Congress as the bureaucratic struggle has spilled over into the public domain.

Case studies of these specific problems have enabled Samuel Huntington in *The Common Defense* to produce a brilliant synthesis and analysis of the transformation in strategic policy making. Perhaps not enough has been done to study the role of the Joint Chiefs of Staff. The organization of this advisory group was an innovation of major importance. It is questionable whether the Truman Administration would have been able to persevere in its Korean policy or to weather the MacArthur storm had it not been for the character and role assumed by the Joint Chiefs of Staff. The study of the Joint Chiefs calls for the application of both Huntington's institutional-and-process approach and Janowitz's sociological insights.

More study is needed also on the impact military judgment and formal military requirements had upon the outcome of specific strategic decisions. We have studies of the Berlin Blockade[77] and Laurence Martin's[78] study of the decision to

---

[77] Walter Phillips Davison, *The Berlin Blockade: A Study in Cold War Politics.*

[78] In Stein, ed., *American Civil-Military Decisions*, 643–65.

rearm Germany, and Hammond's[79] delineation of the military point of view in the NSC 68 deliberations. But what about the decisions regarding aid to Nationalist China, the policies toward Formosa and Korea, and the implementation of NATO and EDC? Given the autonomy of the American military within its sphere of competence, it appears to have been exceedingly difficult to break down traditional military attitudes in order to achieve the best political solutions.

Pressure for change also produced convulsions in executive–legislative relations. Never before had military costs in peacetime assumed such a magnitude. This factor alone prompted a much greater interest in Congress. The kinds of problems involved in modern military technology and strategy were hardly ones to which Congress was accustomed. New demands and old attitudes mingled in an explosive mixture. Congress quickly sensed itself at a disadvantage and responded accordingly.

With the end of the Second World War, the consciously isolationist forces reasserted themselves. The Republican victory in the 1946 election reflected a combination of forces that were carrying the American people back to isolationism. For a time bipartisanship between the Democratic Administration and Republican internationalists led by Senator Vandenberg succeeded in producing the support necessary to secure passage of important foreign policy measures. To understand the 1950–1953 period a sequel to Westerfield's *Foreign Policy and Party Politics*[80] is needed.

The continued importance that foreign policy assumed in American national life after 1945 was galling to powerful isolationist and nationalist forces in the Congress—first, because they opposed international involvement in principle and, second, because foreign affairs, being an executive preserve, derogated authority from Congress. Congressional forces—especially the isolationist and Republican—resented the public attention that foreign affairs focused upon the President and on his concomitant monopoly over policy presentation. Many Republicans objected to Truman's 1948 victory because he had seemed to

---

[79]In Schilling and others, *Strategy, Politics, and Defense Budgets*, 267–378.
[80]Westerfield, *Foreign Policy and Party Politics*.

reap the benefit of policies they had either supported or not opposed but with which they were not in agreement. As a result, beginning in 1949, Republicans in Congress, with an occasional Democratic maverick like Pat McCarran, began to take advantage of the fall of China to regain congressional initiative.

What had in fact happened was that the focus of public attention shifted from the White House to the Committee rooms of Congress. Prior to 1950, the major events of government attracting the public attention included the Truman Doctrine, the Marshall Plan, Point Four, the Berlin Blockade, and the North Atlantic Treaty Organization . . . all executive inspired and carried out with the advice and consent of Congress. Then, in June 1950, there was the President's decision to send American troops to Korea.[81]

The circumstances surrounding this presidential interregnum have been presented by Bradford Westerfield[82] and Richard Neustadt.[83] While these writers do not purport to present a complete account of the dynamics of presidential leadership, public support, and congressional acquiescence, they are suggestive.

But even before this display of Presidential initiative, there had commenced on Capitol Hill a series of spectacles the effect of which was to make Congress, not the President, the principal source of news and explanation and opinion. In any news man's book the major Washington stories from 1950 to 1953 would include the Tydings investigation of the McCarthy charges, the MacArthur dismissal inquiry, the McCarran hearings, and Senator McCarthy's continuing war against the State Department.[84]

The dynamics and significance of McCarthyism have barely begun to be studied. Eric Goldman's *Crucial Decade*,[85] Richard Rovere's *Senator Joe McCarthy*,[86] and a handful of scholarly and monographic studies of the McCarthy phenomenon are almost all we have.

---

[81]Douglass Cater, "The Fourth Branch of Government," in Andrew M. Scott and Raymond D. Dawson, eds., *Readings in the Making of American Foreign Policy,* 122.

[82]Westerfield, *Foreign Policy and Party Politics.*

[83]Neustadt, *Presidential Power.*

[84]Cater, "The Fourth Branch of Government."

[85]Eric F. Goldman, *The Crucial Decade: America 1945–1955.*

[86]Richard H. Rovere, *Senator Joe McCarthy.*

It would be a mistake to suggest, as Dean Acheson does, that the witch hunting and anti-Communist attacks upon the State Department and upon foreign policy were without significant impact. One merely has to mention the Jessup Hearings or the Hearings of the McCarran Subcommittee of the Senate Judiciary Committee, to cite but two instances, to appreciate the damage that was being done to American foreign policy.

Nevertheless, all things considered, the main thrust of American foreign policy maintained its direction amazingly well. While much of the public inveighed against the Administration's foreign policy, the policy itself remained surprisingly immune. Troops-to-Europe, the dismissal of MacArthur, and limited war in Korea were all sustained in the face of unprecedented attacks upon the executive. This adherence to policy was due in part to the fact that the critics had little to offer as an alternative, while the Administration managed to retain something of an initiative by anticipating problems, defining the issues, and engaging in the process of building a consensus among wider publics early enough for an informed opinion to develop.

The period from 1945 to 1953 was an era of maximum challenge to the Administration's capacity to relate the nation's power and its institutional mechanisms to the achievement of its foreign policy objectives. In the course of 1950–1953 the Cold War and the war in Korea raised innumerable challenges both to rationality and to the viability or tenability of the constitutional and institutional relationship of Congress to the executive. While the relationships that emerged were not completely satisfactory, they set the pattern for the subsequent development of American foreign policy.

Bibliography
Books

Acheson, Dean G., *Morning and Noon*. Boston, Houghton Mifflin Company, 1965.

Albion, Robert G., and Robert H. Connery, *Forrestal and the Navy*. New York, Columbia University Press, 1962.

Alperovitz, Gar, *Atomic Diplomacy: Hiroshima and Potsdam*. New York, Simon and Schuster, Inc., 1965.

Barber, James D., *Political Leadership in American Government*. Boston, Little, Brown and Company, 1964.

Bell, Coral, *Negotiation from Strength*. New York, Alfred A. Knopf, Inc., 1963.

Brodie, Bernard, *The Communist Reach for Empire*. Santa Monica, Rand, P-2916, 1964.

Burton, John W., *International Relations: A General Theory*. Cambridge, Cambridge University Press, 1965.

Byrnes, James F., *All in One Lifetime*. New York, Harper & Row, Publishers, 1958.

———, *Speaking Frankly*. New York, Harper & Row, Publishers, 1947.

Curry, George, *James F. Byrnes*. New York, Cooper Square Publishers, 1965.

Davison, Walter Phillips, *The Berlin Blockade: A Study in Cold War Politics*. Princeton, Princeton University Press, 1958.

Elder, Robert E., *The Policy Machine*. Syracuse, Syracuse University Press, 1960.

Feis, Herbert, *Between War and Peace: The Potsdam Conference*. Princeton, Princeton University Press, 1960.

———, *Japan Subdued*. Princeton, Princeton University Press, 1961.

———, *The China Tangle*. New York, Atheneum Publishers, 1965.

Flash, Edward S., Jr., *Economic Advice and Presidential Leadership*. New York, Columbia University Press, 1965.

Fleming, D. F., *The Cold War and Its Origins, 1917–1960*. Garden City, N. Y., Doubleday & Company, Inc., 1961.

Freymond, Jacques, *Western Europe Since the War*. New York, Frederick A. Praeger, Inc., 1964.

Goldman, Eric F., *The Crucial Decade: America 1945–1955*. New York, Alfred A. Knopf, Inc., 1956.

Goodrich, Leland M., *Korea: A Study of U. S. Policy in the United Nations*. New York, Council on Foreign Relations, 1956.

Grosser, Alfred, *La IVᵉ Republique et sa Politique Exterieure*. Paris, Colin, 1961.

Halperin, Morton, *Limited War in the Nuclear Age*. New York, John Wiley & Sons, Inc., 1963.

Hammond, Paul Y., *Organizing for Defense*. Princeton, Princeton University Press, 1961.

Healey, Denis, ed., *The Curtain Falls*. London, Lincolns-Prager, 1951.

Hewlett, Richard G., and Oscar E. Anderson, Jr., *A History of the United States Atomic Energy Commission*. University Park, The Pennsylvania State University Press, 1962.

Higgins, Trumbull, *Korea and the Fall of MacArthur: A Précis in Limited War*. New York, Oxford University Press, 1960.

Huntington, Samuel P., *The Common Defense: Strategic Programs in National Politics*. New York, Columbia University Press, 1961.

Jones, Joseph M., *The Fifteen Weeks*. New York, The Viking Press, Inc., 1955.

Latham, Earl, *The Communist Controversy in Washington*. Cambridge, Harvard University Press, 1966.

Lilienthal, David E., *The Journals of David E. Lilienthal*. New York, Harper & Row, Publishers, 1964. 2 vols.

Lukacs, John A., *A History of the Cold War*. Garden City, N. Y., Doubleday & Company, Inc., 1961.

McCamy, James L., *The Conduct of the New Diplomacy*. New York, Harper & Row, Publishers, 1964.

Millis, Walter, *Arms and the State*. New York, The Twentieth Century Fund, 1958.

——, ed., *The Forrestal Diaries*. New York, The Viking Press, Inc., 1951.

Morgenthau, Hans J., *Politics Among Nations: The Struggle for Power and Peace*. New York, Alfred A. Knopf, Inc., 1948.

Mosely, Philip E., *The Kremlin and World Politics*. New York, Vintage Books, 1960.

Neustadt, Richard E., *Presidential Power: The Politics of Leadership*. New York, John Wiley & Sons, Inc., 1960.

Northedge, F. S., *British Foreign Policy*. New York, Frederick A. Praeger, Inc., 1962.

Osgood, Robert E., *NATO: The Entangling Alliance*. Chicago, University of Chicago Press, 1962.

Rees, David, *Korea: The Limited War*. New York, St. Martin's Press, Inc., 1964.

Rogow, Arnold A., *James Forrestal: A Study of Personality, Politics and Policy*. New York, The Macmillan Company, 1963.

Rostow, Walt W., *The United States in the World Arena*. New York, Harper & Row, Publishers, 1960.

Rovere, Richard H., *Senator Joe McCarthy*. New York, Harcourt, Brace & World, Inc., 1959.

Russell, Ruth B., *A History of the United Nations Charter: The Role of the United States, 1940–1945*. Washington, D. C., The Brookings Institution, 1958.

Sanford, Fillmore H., *Psychology: A Scientific Study of Man*. Belmont, Calif., Wadsworth Publishing Co., Inc., 1965.

Schilling, Warner R., Paul Y. Hammond, and Glenn H. Snyder, *Strategy, Politics, and Defense Budgets*. New York, Columbia University Press, 1962.

Scott, Andrew M., and Raymond D. Dawson, eds., *Readings in the Making of American Foreign Policy*. New York, The Macmillan Company, 1965.

Shulman, Marshall D., *Stalin's Foreign Policy Reappraised*. Cambridge, Harvard University Press, 1963.

Snyder, Richard C., H. W. Bruck, and Burton Sapin, eds., *Foreign Policy Decision Making: An Approach to the Study of International Politics*. New York, The Free Press, 1962.

Spanier, John W., *The Truman–MacArthur Controversy and the Korean War*. Cambridge, Harvard University Press, 1959.

Stein, Harold, ed., *American Civil-Military Decisions: A Book of Case Studies*. University, Alabama, University of Alabama Press, 1963.

Stimson, Henry L., and McGeorge Bundy, *On Active Service in Peace and War*. New York, Harper & Row, Publishers, 1948.

Tang Tsou, *America's Failure in China, 1941–1950*. Chicago, University of Chicago Press, 1963.

Truman, Harry S., *Memoirs*. Garden City, N. Y., Doubleday & Company, Inc., 1955, 1956. 2 vols.

Tucker, Robert W., *The Just War: A Study in Contemporary American Doctrine*. Baltimore, The Johns Hopkins Press, 1960.

Werth, Alexander, *France: 1940–1955*. London, Robert Hale, 1957.

Westerfield, H. Bradford, *Foreign Policy and Party Politics*. New Haven, Yale University Press, 1955.

Whiting, Allen S., *China Crosses the Yalu: The Decision to Enter the Korean War*. New York, The Macmillan Company, 1960.

Williams, William A., *The Tragedy of American Diplomacy*. New York, Dell Publishing Co., Inc., 1961.

Woodhouse, C. M., *British Foreign Policy Since the Second World War*. New York, Frederick A. Praeger, Inc., 1962.

Xydis, Stephen G., *Greece and the Great Powers: 1944–1947*. Thessaloniki, Institute for Balkan Studies, 1963.

Public Documents

U. S. Congress, Senate Committee on Armed Services, *General of the Army Douglas MacArthur and the American Policy in the Far East*. Washington, D. C., Government Printing Office, 1951.

Articles and Book Reviews

The American Review, 2:4 (March, 1963).

Gallois, Pierre M., "U. S. Foreign Policy: A Study in Military Strength and Diplomatic Weakness." *Orbis*, 9:2 (Summer, 1965), 342–43.

Kennan, George F. ("Mr. X"), "The Sources of Soviet Conduct." *Foreign Affairs* (July, 1947), 566–82.

Schilling, Warner R., "The H-Bomb Decision: How to Decide Without Actually Choosing." *Political Science Quarterly* (March, 1961), 24–26.

Schlesinger, Arthur M., Jr., and Gar Alperovitz, "Letters." *New York Review of Books,* 7 (October 20, 1966), 37–38.

Snell, John L., "The Cold War: Four Contemporary Appraisals." *American Historical Review,* 68 (October, 1962), 69–75.

Steel, Ronald, "Review of *Atomic Diplomacy: Hiroshima and Potsdam* by Gar Alperovitz," *New York Review of Books,* 5 (November 25, 1965), 9.

Watt, D. C., "American Diplomatic History." *The Review of Politics* (October, 1965), 556.

Wright, Theodore P., "The Origins of the Free Elections Dispute in the Cold War." *Western Political Quarterly,* 14:4 (December, 1961), 850–64.

Economic Policies*

✦

BARTON J. BERNSTEIN

THOUGH THIRTEEN YEARS HAVE PASSED since President Harry S Truman retired from the White House, historians have generally neglected the domestic activities of his Administration. In contrast, within an equal period following the death of Franklin D. Roosevelt, substantial volumes on his government had appeared. For many who lived through Roosevelt's Presidency, the vigor of reform and the boldness of experimentation seemed to mark a departure in the patterns of American life, and perhaps the need to come to terms with the recent past, seemingly characterized by great events, impelled men to examine the political experience. To them the challenge the nation had faced was clear and inescapable—the struggle against depression. Economic progress, when wedded to reform,

*I wish to express my gratitude to the participants in the Institute's conference for their suggestions, particularly to Professor Allen J. Matusow of Rice University and Professor Alan D. Harper of Queens College (New York) for compelling a reappraisal of liberalism and of business-military relations and to Professor Donald C. Swain of the University of California at Davis of his invaluable guidance to the literature on conservation, science, and public policy.

This bibliographic essay does not analyze foreign economic policies, including the activities of the International Monetary Fund and the Export-Import Bank, which seem to fall more appropriately within the domain of the paper on foreign policy, nor does it analyze such economic welfare measures as public housing, social security, aid to migratory labor, and un-

87

was the theme that shaped most histories of the New Deal.[1] While the Cold War may seem to possess equal drama and even greater significance, historians have been slow to study the domestic, and particularly the economic, policies of the Truman Administration. There are many reasons for their reluctance. Truman's Government, particularly its leading personnel, suffers by contrast with Roosevelt's Administration. In retrospect, as in their own day, they seem less dynamic and vital, as men of smaller scale and limited vision. Unlike the Cold War or the New Deal, the domestic events of the postwar years do not constitute a watershed. They are less interesting and their themes less clear, not susceptible to presentation as history on a large canvas. Certainly, economic policies are not central. The result is that most subjects—legislation and executive decisions, government leaders and federal agencies,

---

employment compensation, which are more appropriate to the discussion of the Administration's welfare policies.

[1]The main popular studies of the Truman Administration are generally unsatisfactory. Tris Coffin, *Missouri Compromise*, is a harsh indictment of the Government's early floundering, and Jonathan Daniels, *The Man of Independence*, is generally sympathetic, rather uncritical, and frequently unreliable. Alfred Steinberg, *The Man from Missouri: The Life and Times of Harry S Truman*, is careless, superficial, and devotes nearly half the volume to the pre-Presidential years. Unfortunately, the best study is Cabell Phillips, *The Truman Presidency: The History of a Triumphant Succession*, which Bernstein criticizes in "Truman's Record," *Progressive*, 30 (October, 1966), 46–48.

By 1958 the scholarly literature on the New Deal included: Basil Rauch, *The History of the New Deal, 1933–1938;* Arthur M. Schlesinger, *The New Deal in Action, 1933–1939;* and James MacGregor Burns, *Roosevelt: The Lion and the Fox.* In addition, Frank Freidel had already published the first three volumes of his multivolume biography, *Franklin D. Roosevelt,* and Arthur Schlesinger, Jr.'s first volume of *The Age of Roosevelt* had also appeared. (Since only twenty-one years have passed since Truman entered the White House, perhaps it would be more meaningful to look at the volumes on FDR that had appeared after a like span—two on his Government by Rauch and Schlesinger and one scholarly biography by Freidel.) A considerable literature by Roosevelt's friends and associates had appeared, whereas there are only a few volumes from the Truman years and, aside from his *Memoirs,* only five on domestic policy: Edwin G. Nourse, *Economics in the Public Service: Administrative Aspects of the Employment Act;* Marriner B. Eccles, *Beckoning Frontiers: Public and Personal Recollections,* Sidney Hyman, ed.; Cyrus S. Ching, *Review and Reflection: A Half-Century of Labor Relations;* George E. Allen, *Presidents who Have Known Me;* Alben W. Barkley, *That Reminds Me.* It is hoped that someone will edit the diary of Harold Smith, the director of the Bureau of the Budget. The diary is available in manuscript at the Bureau of the Budget Library and at the Franklin D. Roosevelt Library.

interest groups and economic thought—await investigation. The historical writing on the period has been occasional and generally narrow—a handful of articles, a few unpublished manuscripts, and some dissertations, but no broad and penetrating analysis. Consequently, scholars must depend for details and generalizations upon the guidance of economists and political scientists, who have explored more aspects of the Truman years.

During Truman's years in the White House the American economy was described in many ways—as "people's capitalism," "the welfare state," "creeping socialism," "a mixed economy," "monopoly capitalism," and "state capitalism." Despite widespread disagreement about the character of the economy, most scholars would acknowledge that, as groups came to rely increasingly upon federal funds, the economy became increasingly a mixture of public and private ownership, of public and private rights and obligations.[2]

---

[2]Victor Perlo, "People's Capitalism and Stock Ownership," *American Economic Review*, 47 (June, 1958), 333–47; Andrew Schonfield, *Modern Capitalism: The Changing Balance of Public and Private Power;* Daniel Bell, *The End of Ideology: On the Exhaustion of Political Ideas in the Fifties;* Friedrich A. Hayek, *The Road to Serfdom;* Joseph A. Schumpeter, *Capitalism, Socialism and Democracy;* Paul A. Baran, *The Political Economy of Growth;* Maurice H. Dobb, *Studies in the Development of Capitalism;* Paul A. Baran and Paul M. Sweezy, *Monopoly Capital: The American Economic and Social Order;* Paul K. Crosser, *State Capitalism in the Economy of the United States.* By state capitalism, Dobb, 384, means the "coexistence of capitalist ownership and operation exercised by the State, which pursues ends that are not identical with those of an individual firm." The type of state capitalism, he explains, depends on the form of the state, the classes and their relations, and the interests served by the state. Crosser, 5, explains that "the continuous transfer of fiscal funds for use by individual entrepreneurs and corporations in industry, farming, and foreign commerce, constitutes state capitalism practice *in substance.* The continuous utilization of public controls by either business or labor groups constitutes, in turn, state capitalist practice *in form."* Though concluding that private enterprise became, in its most significant phase—the phase of capital formation—a state-financed enterprise, he unfortunately does not consider the structure of power. Andrew Hacker, *The Corporate Take-Over,* 10, concludes that the American economic system "continues, in major outlines, to be capitalist in structure. Talk of a welfare state, of a mixed economy, even of a managerial revolution is of limited utility, for the fact remains that major decisions in the economy are private. They are made in the confines of closed circles, and public agencies may not intrude in any effective way."

In the largest sense, America under Truman was a broker state. Within the general acceptance of changing corporate capitalism, becoming more dependent on the state and modified by growing union power, interest-group politics continued to operate. The happy faith in countervailing power, however, has distorted understanding, for not all interests possessed equal power. America was basically a business society, and businessmen exercised disproportionate political power. Undoubtedly, large corporations continued to be the major beneficiaries of the government's widespread and energetic activities.[3]

In the Truman years, large business, along with smaller firms, and organized labor and agriculture, continued to seek government assistance. Through tariffs and regulations, subsidies and contracts, they sought a larger share of the expanding national income and solutions to their problems. Restrictions on imports constituted an indirect subsidy to industries as well as to the workers and communities that depended upon these businesses. The powerful oil industry, as Robert Engler has established, still influenced foreign policy, received favorable tax advantages, and used federal regulations to restrict competition, which would have unsettled prices and disrupted markets. The merchant marine and commercial airlines, as well as farmers, were recipients of direct bounties. In other industries, particularly among producers of aircraft and other military goods, the major firms and their congressmen and unions needed contracts for survival, and they therefore lobbied vigorously for larger defense appropriations.[4]

---

[3]John K. Galbraith, *American Capitalism: The Concept of Countervailing Power;* David Riesman and others, *The Lonely Crowd,* 239–59; David B. Truman, *The Governmental Process: Political Interests and Public Opinion.* See also Henry S. Kariel, *The Decline of American Pluralism;* Samuel P. Huntington, "Clientalism: A Study in Administrative Politics"; and Grant McConnell, *Private Power and American Democracy.*

[4]Crosser, *State Capitalism;* Robert Engler, *The Politics of Oil: A Study of Private Power and Democratic Directions; The International Petroleum Cartel,* staff report to the Federal Trade Commission submitted to the Subcommittee on Monopoly of the Select Committee on Small Business of the Senate, 82nd Congress, 2nd Session; Wayne A. Leeman, *The Price of Middle East Oil: An Essay in Political Economy.* Unfortunately, there has been no adequate study of the tariff. Despite the tariff advantages secured by particular interests, the prevailing belief was that national prosperity depended upon international prosperity, and that required a relaxation of trade barriers.

Laissez-faire rhetoric, despite its frequency, often cloaked behavior and concealed deeper interests. It was the demands of organized interests that largely shaped the interventionist economic policies of the Truman Administration. In addition to wanting the government to advance their specific welfare, groups increasingly expected the President to act as the "Manager of Prosperity," to promote economic growth and stability. Through nearly eight years, as Truman moved along uncharted courses between the pressures of rival interests and struggled with inflation, the maintenance of prosperity contributed to new views of, and enriched hopes for, the economy. For many Americans the postwar experience reduced to foolish fantasies the differing apocalyptic visions of Friedrich Hayek and Joseph Schumpeter and slowly banished the problems of the thirties. For American liberals the postwar years, with their large defense budgets, marked the general success of fiscal policy— that the government could regulate prosperity—and reshaped their faith. Extolling the abundance of American capitalism, liberals denied the existence of widespread poverty, commended the achievements of progressive taxation, and celebrated the more equitable redistribution of income and wealth; they lost their fear of the large corporation, lauded corporate bigness, and praised political pluralism. Unfortunate captives of this restrictive, and sometimes myopic, liberalism, scholars have dwelled on rhetoric and process, have neglected behavior, and have minimized the use of power and its consequences in the war and postwar economy.[5]

---

[5]Clinton L. Rossiter, *The American Presidency*, 33–36. Unfortunately, Francis X. Sutton and others, *The American Business Creed*, by dwelling on rhetoric and neglecting nonverbal behavior and private activities, concentrate on deceptive issues and construct a thesis of limited value for understanding the political behavior of businessmen. Cf. David M. Potter, *People of Plenty: Economic Abundance and the American Character.* For reconsideration of traditional interpretations of business-government relations in the Progressive era, see: Gabriel Kolko, *The Triumph of Conservatism: A Reinterpretation of American History, 1900–1916;* and Robert H. Wiebe, *Businessmen and Reform: A Study of the Progressive Movement.* Also, see Robert E. Lane, *The Regulation of Businessmen.* In 1946 and again in 1949, Schumpeter had reaffirmed suspicion expressed earlier that capitalism might endure for about another fifty years. However, he warned that "price controls might hasten the surrender of private enterprise by the bureaucracy—the resultant friction and deadlocks being attributed to private enterprise and used as

Properly, any analysis should begin in the war years, but unfortunately, scholars have generally neglected the larger issues of this period—stabilization of the economy, mobilization and production for the war, demobilization, and reconversion. With few exceptions, most political studies of wartime stabilization concentrate on particular agencies or on specific studies of wartime specific interest groups. The outstanding exception is Philip Coombs's "The Strategy of Stabilization," which incisively analyzes the political struggle to achieve stabilization. An unpublished and unedited work in political economy, it investigates the early failures, the political challenges, and the skirmishes with major interest groups—oil producers, textile manufacturers, farm organizations, and labor unions. In a brief manuscript on Chester Bowles, the head of the Office of Price Administration (OPA), Bernstein, following Coombs, has explained the uneasy participation of the major interest groups in stabilization and the successful efforts of Bowles in forging a temporary alliance. Joel Seidman's *American Labor* is a fine survey of organized labor's great contributions to defense production, its uneasy participation in stabilization, and its anxious cooperation with management. Appraising wartime stabilization and mobilization, Paul Koistinen, in an unpublished study, "The Hammer and the Sword," concludes, "With few exceptions throughout [these] years, labor, not management, made the sacrifices when sacrifices were necessary." Though the war brought prosperity and may have spawned greater reforms than did the New Deal, the Congress continued to be suspicious of the Administration and hostile to labor. Unfortunately, wartime politics remain largely unexamined. Roland Young mechanically surveys congressional activity during the war, but neglects most of the interesting questions—the structure of politics, the expectations of the Administration, and the operation of the conservative alliance.[6]

arguments for further restrictions and regulations." On liberalism, see Alonzo Lee Hamby, "Harry S. Truman and American Liberalism, 1945–1948."

[6]Philip Coombs, "The Strategy of Stabilization"; Bernstein, "Chester Bowles: A Liberal Businessman as Protector of the Public Interest"; Joel I. Seidman, *American Labor: From Defense to Reconversion;* Paul A. C. Koistinen, "The Hammer and the Sword: Labor, the Military, and Industrial

Looking at the impact of federal taxation, Gabriel Kolko emphasizes that wartime measures, by extending the income tax to low- and middle-wage earners, imposed a new burden on these groups. The most thorough analyses of wartime fiscal policy, by A. E. Holmans and Lester V. Chandler, criticize the nation for not endorsing the increased taxation necessary to sop up more of the inflationary surplus. In contrast, Henry C. Murphy praises the tax policy for meeting a higher percentage of expenditures than in earlier wars. A history of the money supply by Milton Friedman and Anna Schwartz as well as studies by Murphy and Chandler emphasize the inflationary impact of the Federal Reserve's policy of supporting Treasury obligations at par and monetizing the federal debt. Appraising this relationship, which continued with modification until 1951, Chandler concludes, "It is more than half true that in monetary management the Treasury wielded power without responsibility while the Federal Reserve had responsibility without power."[7]

Mobilization, 1920–1945," 2 vols., quote on 143; Roland A. Young, *Congressional Politics in the Second World War*. John K. Galbraith, *A Theory of Price Control*, has contributed a penetrating analysis of the theory of price control. Undoubtedly the best source on OPA, despite the uncomfortable prose that characterizes most government efforts, is the multivolume official history; it focuses on legal and administrative problems and sporadically discusses the political struggle to impose and maintain price restrictions. Office of Temporary Controls, *Historical Reports on War Administration: Office of Price Administration*. The official history of the War Labor Board (WLB), Department of Labor, *National War Labor Board Termination Report*, is disappointing. Largely a collection of documents, it eschews interpretation but provides information about the clashes with management and organized labor. A useful, but very uneven supplement is a collection of essays: Colston E. Warne and others, eds., *Yearbook of American Labor*, I, *War Labor Policies*. For organized labor's assault on the cost-of-living index, the basis for the Little Steel Formula which limited wage raises, see Kathryn Arnow, "The Attack on the Cost-of-Living-Index," in Harold Stein, ed., *Public Administration and Policy Development*, 775–854. Politics and achievements of the farmers are treated by Walter W. Wilcox, *The Farmer in the Second World War*, and Dean Albertson, *Roosevelt's Farmer: Claude R. Wickard in the New Deal*. Koistinen, 824, concludes that the war meant the end of reform. "By seeking a rapprochement with the business community, the President signalled that the New Deal was officially ended." For a different view, see Mary H. Hinchey, "The Frustration of the New Deal Revival, 1944–1946." On labor and the draft, see Albert A. Blum, "Deferment from Military Service: A War Department Approach to the Solution of Industrial Manpower Program."

7Gabriel Kolko, *Wealth and Power in America: An Analysis of Social Class and Income Distribution*, 1–45; J. Keith Butters and others, *Effects*

Though there are government histories of mobilization agencies, scholars know little about their actual structure of power, the activities of businessmen on their staffs, their relations with the military, and their associations with industry and finance. Clearly, the war marked the open *rapprochement* of government and Big Business, the temporary abandonment of antitrust activities, and the beginning of an enduring, close relationship between important executives and the federal government. Michael Reagan looks briefly at businessmen in the wartime government and emphasizes that they sometimes served their own purposes (frequently those of their firm or industry), but his dissertation neglects many of the wartime disputes. Unfortunately, the studies of the Truman Committee, the watchdog committee on defense, which at times restrained the military and assisted small business, are disappointing, and there are no studies of the competition for military contracts. So far, the examination of small business, its participation in the war, its struggles and aspirations, is inadequate.[8]

---

of Taxation: Investments by Individuals, particularly 29; A. E. Holmans, *United States Fiscal Policy, 1945–1959: Its Contribution to Economic Stability,* 14–44; Lester V. Chandler, *Inflation in the United States, 1940–1948,* 61–202; Henry C. Murphy, *The National Debt in War and Transition;* Milton Friedman and Anna J. Schwartz, *A Monetary History of the United States, 1867–1960,* 546–91; cf. James Tobin, "The Monetary Interpretation of History," *American Economic Review,* 4 (June, 1965), 464–85. Also see Charles C. Abbott, *The Federal Debt: Structure and Impact,* and Ralph Freeman, "Postwar Monetary Policy," Robert M. Solow, "Income Inequality Before the War," and E. Cary Brown, "Federal Fiscal Policy in the Postwar Period," in Ralph E. Freeman, ed., *Postwar Economic Trends in the United States,* 51–189; Bureau of the Census, *Income Distribution of the United States,* 2–27.

[8]On the early mobilization, see: Eliot Janeway, *The Struggle for Survival,* LIII in Allan Nevins, ed., *The Chronicles of America;* I. F. Stone, *Business As Usual: The First Year of Defense;* Gabriel Kolko, "American Business and Germany, 1930–1941," *Western Political Quarterly,* 15 (December, 1962), 713–28; Bernstein, "The Automobile Industry and the Coming of the Second World War," *Southwestern Social Science Quarterly,* 46 (June, 1966); Michael Reagan, "Serving Two Masters: Problems in the Employment of Dollar-a-Year and Without Compensation Personnel"; Donald H. Riddle, *The Truman Committee: A Study in Congressional Responsibility;* Sister M. Patrick Ellen Maher, "The Role of the Chairman of a Congressional Investigating Committee: A Case Study of the Special Committee of the Senate to Investigate the National Defense Program, 1941–1948"; Matthew Yung-chun Yang, "The Truman Committee." Roger Willson has recently completed at Harvard a doctoral thesis on the Truman Committee.

Industrial Mobilization for War, the official history of the War Production Board (WPB), as well as the agency's special monographs, notes conflicts within the WPB and between its members and representatives of the military, but denies that ideology or self-interest determined the positions of adversaries. In contrast, the history by the Bureau of the Budget, *The United States at War,* generally agrees with the postwar reflections of Donald Nelson, the deposed head of the WPB, and of Bruce Catton, his assistant, that the military tried to take over the war economy. Basing his judgment partly on these studies, C. Wright Mills concludes that during the war "the merger of the corporate economy and the military bureaucracy came into its present-day significance"—the basis of the "power elite." This wartime alliance, contends Mills, was "most dramatically revealed in their agreement" in 1944 to block industrial reconversion. In close studies of this episode, Jack Peltason, Koistinen, and Bernstein agree that some Big Businessmen on the board and military leaders opposed any shift to production of more consumer goods, and they allied to thwart reconversion. Peltason largely documents their arguments but is reluctant to appraise motives. Bernstein and Koistinen, however, examine motives and conclude that some military chiefs not only dreaded the ebbing of civilian sacrifices but wished to direct the economy, and that industrial and financial executives feared that the earlier entry of small producers into lush markets would upset the prewar oligopolistic patterns.[9]

On small business, see: Harmon Zeigler, *The Politics of Small Business;* and John H. Bunzel, *The American Small Businessman.* There is a general need for a large and careful study of business-government relations, 1939–1945. See Arthur M. Johnson, "Continuity and Change in Governmen-Business Relations," in John Braeman, and others, *Change and Continuity in Twentieth-Century America,* 191–219, and for useful interpretations, also Kolko's *Triumph* and Wiebe's *Businessmen.*

[9]James W. Fesler and others, *Industrial Mobilization for War,* 717–862 and 987–92 for special studies. Bureau of the Budget, *The United States at War: Development and Administration of the War Program by the Federal Government,* 467–502. Donald M. Nelson, *Arsenal of Democracy: The Story of American War Production,* xv, 410, denies that business biases were responsible for opposition to reconversion, but charges that the military wanted to take control of the economy. Bruce Catton, *The War Lords of*

By 1945, as the war was ending, major producers conveniently returned to the rhetoric of *laissez faire*, however, and urged the prompt lifting of WPB controls. While many large companies anticipated some shortages, with their superior market power they expected to corner scarce supplies. Small businessmen, captives of a *laissez-faire* ideology and generally puzzling to scholars, acquiesced in, or endorsed, relaxation of controls. The significant opposition came from OPA: As the representative of unorganized consumers, the agency lacked the political power to reverse a decision urged by WPB, desired by leading businessmen, and supported by the President's close friend and adviser, John Snyder, director of the Office of War Mobilization and Reconversion (OWMR). The removal of WPB controls, concludes the OPA historians and Bernstein, weakened OPA's capacity to suppress inflationary pressures. For many, however, including liberals who expected construction to soften the anticipated economic decline, forecasts justified the easing of some restrictions.[10]

During the war, most economists had predicted a huge postwar depression unless the government acted to increase aggregate demand. Fortunately, the bleak predictions were erroneous; they exaggerated the time required for physical conversion and

Washington; C. Wright Mills, *The Power Elite,* particularly 212–13; Jack Peltason, "The Reconversion Controversy," in Harold Stein, ed., *Public Administration and Policy Development,* 215–84; Koistinen, "Hammer and the Sword," 720–27; Bernstein, "The Debate on Industrial Reconversion: The Protection of Oligopoly and Military Control of the War Economy," scheduled for *American Journal of Economics and Sociology* (April, 1967). Cf. Daniel Bell, *The End of Ideology,* 47–74; William Kornhauser, " 'Power Elite' or 'Veto Groups'?" in Seymour M. Lipset and Leo Lowenthal, eds., *Culture and Social Character: The Work of David Riesman Reviewed,* 252–67; Talcott Parsons, "The Distribution of Power in American Society," *World Politics,* 10 (October, 1957), 123–43; Richard H. Rovere, "The Interlocking Overlappers," *Progressive,* 20 (June, 1956), 33–35. Also see: Samuel P. Huntington, *The Soldier and the State: The Theory and Politics of Civil-Military Relations,* 336–44; John Brigante, *The Feasibility Dispute,* prepared for *Cases in Public Administration,* 1950; Blum, "Deferment from Military Service"; and Harold L. Ickes, *Fightin' Oil.*

[10]Harvey Mansfield and others, *A Short History of the O.P.A.,* 82–94; Bernstein, "The Removal of War Production Board Controls on Business, 1944–1946," *Business History Review,* 39 (Summer, 1965), 243–60; Herman Somers, *Presidential Agency: The Office of War Mobilization and Reconversion,* 90–93.

severely underestimated the private capital formation and the pent-up demand for consumer goods. Perhaps, surprisingly, most Keynesians were wildly wrong, while some orthodox economists were more nearly accurate. Among the many post-mortem analyses, probably the most revealing are by Everett E. Hagen, W. S. Woytinsky, and Michael Sapir, and they constitute an excellent introduction for a neglected, and difficult, study—a history of wartime and postwar economic thought.[11]

Had the dark forecasts not proved wrong, many Americans would have condemned the Roosevelt and Truman administrations, as well as the Democratic congresses, for not developing adequate programs to offset the depression. Though some economists still quarreled about the validity of Keynesian economics, many, including those within the Bureau of the Budget, recommended large public-works projects. Partly as an anti-depression strategy, Harold Ickes, the Secretary of the Interior, planned for river-valley development, but Congress rebuffed Roosevelt when he submitted the proposal. Blocked on this measure, the Roosevelt Administration asked the obdurate legislature for such economic reforms as a full-employment law and higher unemployment compensation but seldom moved beyond these requests to vigorous executive planning. Curiously, while some government officials foresaw the great need for postwar housing, during the war few considered federal housing construction as a way to soften the anticipated economic decline. So far, scholars have neither examined the reasons for inadequate planning (why preparations did not follow economic advice) nor investigated the efforts of the short-lived National Resources Planning Board. Nor have they looked

11Everett E. Hagen, "The Reconversion Period: Reflections of a Forecaster," *Review of Economics and Statistics,* 29 (May, 1947), 95–101; W. S. Woytinsky, "What Was Wrong in Forecasts of Postwar Depression?" *Journal of Political Economy,* 55 (April, 1947), 142–51; Michael Sapir, "Review of Economic Forecasts for the Transition Period," *Studies in Income and Wealth,* 11 (1947), 275–352. On the eve of V-J Day, the Committee for Economic Development, a liberal business group, announced, on the basis of its survey of Big Business' plans for investment and production, that the economy would achieve full employment. For the CED, see Karl Schriftgeisser, *Business Comes of Age,* a light, chatty survey. While there was consideration of foreign trade to offset depression, economists did not emphasize it.

98 | BARTON J. BERNSTEIN

closely at the activities of OWMR directors—James Byrnes, Fred Vinson, and John Snyder. In his fine administrative history of OWMR, Herman Somers unfortunately does not probe the assumptions of the directors and skims over the challenge of the predicted depression.[12]

Probably the most serious effort to avoid depression was the ill-fated Full Employment bill, which did not detail or effect programs but empowered the government to provide adequate investment for continuing full employment. Inspired by the Bureau of the Budget and emerging from a group of labor leaders, liberal congressmen, and other liberals, the proposal received Roosevelt's endorsement and Truman's sporadic support. As Stephen Bailey shows in his model study, the measure fell before its enemies. Under their assault, the act that emerged was simply a pious expression of hope that the nation could avoid the perils of the business cycle. Though authorizing three institutions—the Council of Economic Advisers, an annual economic report by the President, and the Joint Congressional Committee on the Economic Report—the act did not change economic thought or policy. While institutionalizing a new source of economic advice for the President, the measure did

---

[12]Bureau of Reclamation, Missouri River Basin, *Conservation, Control, and Use of Water Resources of the Missouri River Basin in Montana, Wyoming, Colorado, North Dakota, South Dakota, Kansas, Iowa, and Missouri.* Hinchey, "The Frustration of the New Deal Revival," 1–55, is not generally critical of the efforts of the Roosevelt Administration, but skims over the question of postwar planning (for example, public works) and emphasizes the struggle for new reforms. However, she does note that Byrnes "interpreted his assignment [for postwar planning] in a severely restricted sense" and points for additional evidence to the report by Bernard Baruch and John Hancock on postwar readjustment. On Truman's campaign promises on planning, in particular on the Missouri Valley Authority, as well as for his later actions, see: Hinchey, "The Frustration of the New Deal Revival," 106–8; and Hamby, "Truman and American Liberalism," 48–50. On housing, see: Richard O. Davies, *Housing Reform During the Truman Administration,* Chaps. I-IV; Bernstein, "Reluctance and Resistance: Wilson Wyatt and Veterans' Housing in the Truman Administration," *Register of the Kentucky Historical Society,* 65 (January, 1967), 47–66. Charles Merriam, "The National Resources Planning Board, A Chapter in America's Planning Experience," *American Political Science Review,* 38 (December, 1944), 1075–88. Also see John D. Millett, *The Process and Organization of Government Planning.* Philip Warken, a Ph.D. candidate in history at Ohio State, is preparing a thesis on the NRPB. There is also need for a study of the guaranteed annual wage, a proposal explored by a committee of the OWMR.

not mark a new point in the murky dialogue on fiscal policy, nor did it even foreclose the continued use of outmoded and ill-conceived arguments. Herbert Stein, however, accords some importance to the law, because it confirmed "the existing state of affairs," represented what he regards as a postwar consensus, and "permitted us to move on." However, Edward S. Flash, Jr., along with many others, concludes that the act made "explicit the federal government's responsibility for using its resources to help avoid recession . . . and transformed the issue of conscious governmental intervention in the nation's welfare from 'whether' to 'how.' "[13]

Before passage of the bill, proponents of compensatory fiscal policy found the Administration endorsing a tax cut that nearly all congressmen and the major interest groups supported. Holmans surveys the debates and traces the bill through revisions, and Bernstein emphasizes that, in practice, many so-called conservatives no longer feared annual deficits. His conclusion that the yearly balanced budget had a very low priority among their valued public policies suggests the need for a re-examination of the ideology of fiscal orthodoxy and may explain the nation's later conversion in practice to Keynesian policies.[14]

When Congress passed the tax cut, experts were still fearful of depression, but Bowles suspected that the real menace might be inflation. Unprepared to loosen controls, the OPA's Chief, as Allen J. Matusow and Bernstein show, first simply coun-

---

[13]Stephen K. Bailey, *Congress Makes A Law: The Story Behind the Employment Act of 1946;* Herbert Stein, "Twenty Years of the Employment Act," 4; Edward S. Flash, Jr., *Economic Advice and Presidential Leadership: The Council of Economic Advisers,* 9. Among others, Walter Reuther makes this claim in "The Employment Act of 1946—Future Tasks," Gerhard Colm, ed., *The Employment Act: Past and Future: A Tenth Anniversary Forum,* 58. In a limited sense, Flash is correct, but the legislation begged the questions, What federal resources? What new federal powers? What likely federal efforts? Flash, 9–17, retreats in places to a more cautious position.

[14]Holmans, *Fiscal Policy,* 30–55; Bernstein, "Charting a Course Between Inflation and Depression: Secretary of the Treasury Fred Vinson and the Truman Administration's Tax Bill"; Carl S. Shoup, "The Revenue Act of 1945," *Political Science Quarterly,* 60 (December, 1945), 481–91; Hinchey, "The Frustration of the New Deal Revival," 114–16, 161–67. See also Robert Leckachman, *The Age of Keynes.*

seled caution. While the farm bloc expressed its fear of economic disaster and demanded consideration, Bowles resisted these demands: he delayed reducing agricultural subsidies and letting food prices rise. Fearing famine in Europe, he opposed the termination of meat rationing. In Clinton Anderson, the new Secretary of Agriculture, OPA faced an able foe. When the stabilization program or larger needs threatened his constituents or his reputation, Anderson acted to protect farm interests and his political future, concludes Matusow in a critical study of the Secretary's policies. Anderson was slow to acknowledge the famine abroad, joined many in the government who were unsympathetic to India's starving millions, and did not go on a wheat crusade until he discovered that America might not meet its earlier commitment to Europe. Through the winter and spring, while farmers criticized the Administration for showing favoritism to labor, Anderson and Bowles scrapped about price controls, subsidies, and incentives for luring from the farms the grain needed to save Europe. Ultimately, the Administration was compelled to yield to the demands of farmers and raise prices. By retreating, the government reinforced what the interest groups were learning—resistance to the stabilization program could be successful and profitable.[15]

The difficulties Truman encountered in his early years as President resulted from more than the shifting economic predictions that left the Administration unprepared for inflation. The sources of trouble were deeper, and the evidence is abundant. Though most historical studies of Truman's first two years in office present evidence of errors and ineptitude, of drift and disaster, only Matusow and Bernstein have followed contemporary observers and have so characterized the early government. They have attributed the difficulties to Cabinet

[15]Matusow, "Food and Farm Policies of the First Truman Administration: 1945–1948," Chaps. I-III; Bernstein, "The Postwar Famine and Price Control, 1946," *Agricultural History,* 38 (October, 1964), 235–40, and "Clash of Interests: The Postwar Battle Between O. P. A. and Agriculture," *Agricultural History,* 41 (January, 1967), 45–57. On the response to India's famine, see M. S. Venkataramani, *Undercurrents in American Foreign Relations: Four Studies,* 43–95.

government, incompetent advisers, factionalism, and the politics of inflation.[16]

The new politics created problems that might have thwarted even a better staffed and bolder administration. Whereas the politics of depression generally allowed the Roosevelt Administration, by bestowing benefits, to court interest groups and contribute to an economic upturn, the politics of inflation required a responsible government like Truman's to curb wages, prices, and profits and to deny the growing expectations of rival groups. While wartime patriotism had temporarily suppressed hostility and delayed clashes, peace unleashed anxieties and hopes. First fearful of depression and suspicious that the government would sacrifice their interests and then eager for the benefits of inflation, farmers assailed federal restrictions on their prices and accused the government of favoritism to labor. As businessmen realized they would be facing a seller's market, they attacked curbs on prices and profits and yelped about red tape. While organized labor supported price controls, it wanted the government to withdraw wage restrictions and to permit free collective bargaining. Hostility to wage controls during the war had spurred rank and file in some militant CIO locals to topple the leadership and had provoked the heads of internationals to withdraw the no-strike pledge.[17]

---

[16]Among contemporary observers, see Tris Coffin, *Missouri Compromise.* For similar judgments, see: Samuel Lubell, *The Future of American Politics,* 1–59; and Charles A. Madison, *Leaders and Liberals in 20th Century America,* 412–62. For recent studies, see: Robert Branyan, "Antimonopoly Activities During the Truman Administration"; R. Alton Lee, "Harry S Truman and the Taft-Hartley Act"; Richard O. Davies, *Housing Reform,* Chaps. I-V; John R. Waltrip, "The Public Power Program of the Truman Administration"; William C. Berman, "The Politics of Civil Rights in the Truman Administration." Cf. Bernstein, "The Ambiguous Legacy: The Truman Administration and Civil Rights," and "Reluctance and Resistance"; Matusow, "Food and Farm Policies," Chaps. I-IV; and Bernstein, "The Truman Administration and the Politics of Inflation," and "The Presidency Under Truman," *Yale Political Review,* 4 (Fall, 1964), 8 ff. Two more recent theses—Hinchey, "The Frustrations of the New Deal Revival," and Hamby, "Truman and American Liberalism"—are gently critical of the Administration.

[17]John Dunlop, "The Decontrol of Wages and Prices," in Colston E. Warne and others, eds., *Labor in Postwar America,* 3–24.

John Dunlop suggests that the Administration was helpless before the demands of union leaders and had to relax wage restraints or face an open rebellion. Harry Millis and Emily Clark Brown, however, imply that the situation was more tractable. They blame the government for short-sightedness and contend that it could have planned a more effective postwar policy. Coombs and Bernstein are even more critical of the government and believe that Truman, by acting more wisely and decisively, could have won a renewal of labor's wartime no-strike pledge. But the President's misunderstanding of possibilities, his unwillingness to deal directly with labor leaders, and his enthusiasm for letting the Secretary of Labor conduct negotiations—all made the pact impossible. When Truman blundered again, the War Labor Board resigned. Dependent upon the unsuccessful labor-management conference, which has never been closely examined, the Administration was forced again to revise its policies, and its new formula sparked more discontent.[18]

Confronted by strikes, the government seized oil refineries and meat-packing plants, but balked at the challenge of the steel industry and sought briefly to avoid the General Motors dispute. Irving Howe and B. J. Widick emphasize the radicalism of the United Automobile Workers' demand that prices and, indirectly, profits be subjects of collective bargaining. While escaping serious embroilment in that conflict, the Administration could not remain aloof from the steel strike, which was hobbling reconversion. In entering the fray, the President, according to Coombs and Bernstein, first damaged his prestige when the industry rebuffed him and then further weakened his power by yielding to its excessive demands: He thus disclosed to other groups that the government would retreat under pressure.[19]

[18]Dunlop, "Decontrol"; Harry A. Millis and Emily C. Brown, *From the Wagner Act to Taft-Hartley: A Study of National Labor Policy and Labor Relations*, 311–15; Coombs, "Strategy of Stabilization," Chap. XVIII; Bernstein, "The Truman Administration and Its Reconversion Wage Policy," *Labor History*, 6 (Fall, 1965), 214–31.

[19]Irving Howe and B. J. Widick, *The U.A.W. and Walter Reuther*, 126–48; cf. Bernstein, "Walter Reuther and the General Motors Strike of 1945–

Though the decision weakened stabilization and disclosed cleavages within the Administration, this strike, as well as others, was significant for another reason: There was no violence. Less than a decade had passed since the CIO had battled against Pinkertons and tear gas to organize mass-production industries. Since collective bargaining had lapsed during the war years, the postwar struggles constituted the test of union strength and of management's willingness to accept unions and collective bargaining. The results dramatically confirmed industry's acceptance of organized labor.

The challenge of strikes and federal intervention, the theme of maturity and adjustment, the drama of brewing passion and inflated rhetoric, have attracted scholars to this period, but there are still gaps in our information. The Administration's relations with labor leaders, its understanding of union expectations, and its doubts about the union-management struggle for power remain unclear. Arthur McClure, in evaluating Truman's liberalism, concludes that his Government was impartial in its treatment of labor. Any appraisal of the Administration's attitudes must rely heavily upon an examination of the railroad and coal strikes. In an unpublished essay, Bernstein is critical of the Administration and suggests that Truman knew that the railroad settlement was in process when he

1946," *Michigan History*, 49 (September, 1965), 260–77. Coombs, "Strategy of Stabilization," Chap. XIX; Bernstein, "The Truman Administration and the Steel Strike of 1946," *Journal of American History*, 52 (March, 1966), 791–803; Frederick H. Harbison and Robert C. Spencer, "The Politics of Collective Bargaining: The Postwar Record in Steel," *American Political Science Review*, 48 (September, 1954), 705–20. Albert Rees concludes that "collective bargaining in the basic steel industry during the first three rounds of postwar wage increases did not significantly affect general wage levels." The tight labor market, even without union organization, reasons Rees, might have encouraged similar increases, and he notes that the average percentage of the increase unorganized workers gained exceeded those of organized labor. In addition, the wage raises in steel "had little to do with the amount of price increases, although they had a great influence on their timing." Albert E. Rees, "The Economic Impact of Collective Bargaining in the Steel and Coal Industries During the Post-War Period," *Industrial Relations Research Association Proceedings*, 3 (December, 1950), 201–12, and discussion, 213 ff.; Rees, "Wage Price Relations in the Basic Steel Industry, 1945–1948," *Industrial and Labor Relations Review*, 3 (January, 1953), 195–205; Rees, "Postwar Wage Determination in the Basic Steel Industry," *American Economic Review*, 41 (June, 1951), 389–404.

asked Congress for authority to draft strikers. Robert Dishman, who is studying federal seizures, is more favorable in his view of the President's actions and admires Truman's exercise of presidential power. There is still need for a good biography of the mine workers' chieftain, John L. Lewis, that would include accounts of his frequently bitter relations with Truman, but until that appears the best sources on the coal strikes are only adequate—Saul Alinsky's enthusiastic biography and Bernstein's unpublished essay.[20]

Embattled on the labor front and rejected by New Dealers, the government also floundered in the struggle against inflation. Without adequate support from the President, OPA succumbed to mutilation by amendment. The OPA history sketches these events, and Matusow and Bernstein believe that Anderson contributed to the debacle, first by weakening OPA and then by undermining the agency when Congress restored controls. Ultimately, a cattlemen's strike created meat shortages, antagonized consumers, and forced the President shortly before the election to abolish price controls on meat. It was too late. By then the Administration had estranged most groups. Farm-

---

[20]Some gaps may remain until key collections are available—the files of major unions and leaders, the records of struck companies and executives, and the oral history memoir of John Steelman, Truman's labor adviser. Unfortunately, the papers of William Green at Cornell University, of Philip Murray at Catholic University, and of Lewis Schwellenbach at The Library of Congress are very thin and contain nothing of value for this period; the memoir of Steelman will be closed until 1985. Files of the Department of Labor at the National Archives are open, but they are not very useful for an analysis of policy formation or personal relations. Arthur F. McClure, II, "The Truman Administration and Labor Relations, 1945–1948," is happier about the Department's records. For the strikes of the spring, see: Bernstein, "The Estrangement of Labor"; Robert Dishman, "President Truman and the Engineers' and Trainmen's Strike of 1946"; Saul David Alinsky, *John L. Lewis: An Unauthorized Biography.* R. Alton Lee, "Taft-Hartley," and Millis and Brown, *Taft-Hartley,* examine the antilabor bills of 1964. Along with other scholars, they also focus on these stoppages as major sources of irritation with labor and of the movement for revision of the Wagner Act. Also see: Philip Taft, *The A. F. of L. from the Death of Gompers to the Merger;* George W. Taylor, *Government Regulation of Industrial Disputes;* Colston E. Warne, ed., *Labor in Postwar America;* Neil W. Chamberlain and James M. Schilling, *The Impact of Strikes: Their Social and Economic Costs;* and Myron Hoch, "The Oil Strike of 1945," *Southern Economic Journal,* 15 (October, 1948), 117–33; Philip D. Bradley, *The Public Stake in Union Power;* David M. Wright, ed., *The Impact of the Union.*

ers were bitter about price curbs and resented Anderson's plans for reorganizing his department; organized labor could not forgive the President for his strike-breaking; businessmen had chafed under price controls; and consumers, with more money in their pockets, grumbled about black markets and shortages.[21]

Though seeking legislative authorization to extend New Deal programs, Truman was more cautious than Roosevelt, and his Administration was staffed by conservatives and moderate liberals who undercut the plans he sporadically endorsed. He seemed unsympathetic to new ideas and hostile to old New Dealers. Unable to lead and buffeted by events, he could not mend the tattered Democratic coalition or reverse the growing legislative-executive antagonism, and his Government could not cope with the problems unleashed by peace and prosperity. With the nation deeply ambivalent—both wanting the benefits of the New Deal and responsive to the GOP rhetoric promising a partial repeal of the New Deal—Truman's party went down to defeat in the congressional elections of 1946.

It was a chastened and repudiated President who awaited the new and predictably hostile Republican Congress. In the interim he jettisoned the remaining wage controls and nearly all price regulations, ended the Veterans' Emergency Housing Program, and lashed out at a persistent tormentor—John L. Lewis. To regain national respect and to assert his authority, Truman had determined to resist Lewis: First, the government enjoined the UMW from striking, and then it brought an action against Lewis and the union for violating the court order.

It was the Congress and foreign policy which consumed most of Truman's energy. Undoubtedly the most important

---

21Harvey Mansfield, *A Short History of the O.P.A.*, 88–101; Matusow, "Food and Farm Policies," Chaps. I-IV; Bernstein, "Clash of Interests." Mary Hinchey, "The Frustration of the New Deal Revival," studies this period, and Hamby, "Truman and American Liberalism," analyzes the estrangement of liberals, but there is still need for a study of the politics of reconversion and the election of 1946. Though the available materials are skimpy, analyses of party organization and structure are also necessary and possible. On the party's relationship with the South, see: V. O. Key, Jr., *Southern Politics in State and Nation;* and Dewey W. Grantham, Jr., *The Democratic South,* 42–99.

postwar legislature, the Eightieth Congress is only now being studied in monographic detail, and the conservative alliance as well as the brilliant Robert A. Taft still merit close examination. On domestic issues, the Eightieth Congress, led in the Senate by Taft, meant a limited Republican assault on the New Deal, a series of battles, many vetoes, numerous defeats for the President, and ultimately a valuable record for his campaign in 1948. Both parties knew that the presidential election could be won or lost in Congress, but scholars have neglected the GOP's strategy and disagreed on Truman's plan. Richard O. Davies concludes that Truman sought to cooperate with Taft to secure public housing and implies that the President tried to minimize his differences with Congress. In contrast, Lee concludes that the necessity of creating a record compelled Truman from the opening of the session to oppose the Republican program. Bernstein, however, suggests that after a brief period, when Truman may have earnestly sought compromise, the President moved to build a record for re-election. By blocking his attempts and thwarting his will, the GOP-dominated legislature allowed him the luxury of urging legislation he knew he could not secure—civil rights and price controls. By appearing irresponsible in domestic policy, by passing Taft-Hartley over Truman's veto, the Republicans enabled him to regain the support of labor leaders.[22]

---

[22]Susan Hartmann has written a dissertation at the University of Missouri on the Eightieth Congress, and Travis Adams, a graduate student at Vanderbilt, is writing a thesis on the conservative bloc. At the Southern Historical Association's meeting in 1966 the conservative coalition was the subject of one session. John R. Moore gave a paper on "The War Years" and Adams on "The Postwar Years." On the New Deal years, see James T. Patterson's fine study, *The Conservative Coalition in Congress, 1933–1939*, which emphasizes the political maneuvering and denies the existence of a formal structure. On the differences between the Executive's urban-based constituency and the Congress' rural-based constituency, see Stephen K. Bailey and Howard D. Samuel, *Congress at Work*, 414; and for the use of the concept, Lee, "Taft-Hartley," Chap. I. William S. White's *The Taft Story* is full of flourish but weak on analysis. The Taft papers, still in control of his family, probably will not be open to scholars before completion of an authorized biography. Davies, *Housing Reform*, Chap. V; R. Alton Lee, "Mr. Veto in the White House: President Truman's Rejection of a Tax Reduction Program in 1947"; Bernstein, "Challenge and Responsibility."

Perhaps Truman's earlier actions had kindled antilabor antagonism, but the major works on Taft-Hartley, by Lee and Millis and Brown, attribute the labor-management act of 1947 largely to the disruptive strikes during reconversion. Had there been better planning by the Administration in formulating earlier wage-price policies, argue Millis and Brown, "the long-range legislation [might have] developed with less heat and anger and more real statesmanship." Abuses under the Wagner Act, according to these authors, "brought a need for certain checks upon union activities," and they survey the earlier movements for reform in the states. Both studies document the sentiments of major groups demanding revision of the Wagner Act. Contending that unions had gained excessive power and lacked responsibility and that they received privileges under existing law, business groups, such as the NAM and the Chamber, campaigned openly for a new measure but argued that they were protecting the public welfare. Unfortunately, neither work closely examines these business organizations, and there are no adequate analyses of their structure and ideology.[23]

In vetoing Taft-Hartley, Truman moved into clear opposition to the Congress, and for the next year their impasse continued in domestic affairs. Much of their early antagonism grew out of differences on the budget and tax reduction. The initial measure the President vetoed, just a few days before Taft-Hartley, was the first of three Republican-sponsored tax cuts. Lee contends that political necessity compelled Truman to distinguish his position from the Republican program, and that when the GOP announced that it would slice taxes, Truman had to oppose the effort. Placing Truman's behavior in a larger context, Bernstein stresses that the Administration still feared inflation, tried sporadically to formulate rough guidelines for prices (but not wages), uneasily watched rising administered prices, and was alarmed that the tax reduction would spawn more inflation and weaken the economy. It was not that Truman and Snyder, his Secretary of the Treasury, were afraid that inflation would redistribute national income,

---

[23]Millis and Brown, *Taft-Hartley*, 314; Lee, "Taft-Hartley."

but rather that it might catapult the nation into depression by widening the gap between prices and demand. They were also apprehensive lest unbalanced budgets sap the nation's strength, create doubts about the economy, and ultimately ruin it.[24]

These fears also constricted the debate on military budgets. *The Forrestal Diaries,* masterfully edited by Walter Millis, record the struggles of the Secretary of Defense to secure what he deemed an adequate budget. Compelled by Truman ("a hard money man," as Forrestal described him) to cut his requests, Forrestal chafed under the restraints but failed to move Truman. Warner Schilling and Bernstein analyze the skirmishes over the military budget for fiscal 1949. Focusing on the political process, Schilling concludes that the Congress made decisions in ignorance: It did not consider the strategic assumptions behind the Administration's proposals or underlying alternatives that the services advanced. Leaning on Schilling's study, Bernstein finds that all important participants in the debate accepted orthodox economics and maneuvered within its narrow limits. The factors that separated Truman and Forrestal, then, were not their unexamined economic premises nor their evaluations of military need but their judgments of competing risks to national security—weakening the military or endangering the economy.[25]

---

[24]Lee, "Mr. Veto"; Bernstein, "Challenge and Responsibility," and "The Struggle Against Wage-Price Rises"; Holmans, *Fiscal Policy,* 56–101. On the relationship of union wage demands to full employment and a (more or less) constant price level, see: Melvin W. Reder, "The General Level of Money Wages," *Industrial Relations Research Proceedings,* 3 (December, 1950), 186–202; Walter A. Morton, "Trade Unionism, Full Employment and Inflation," *American Economic Review,* 40 (March, 1950), 13–39, and replies of Martin Bronfenbrenner and David Lapkin, *ibid.* (September, 1950), 622–27. Morton concludes that "wages as a cost did not markedly influence market prices of goods sold under competition" and that many large producers were selling at less than equilibrium prices, which the appearance of gray markets emphasized. Also see: Morton, "Keynesianism and Inflation," *Journal of Political Economy,* 59 (June, 1951), 258–65; Martin Bronfenbrenner, "Postwar Political Economy: The President's Reports," *ibid.,* 55 (October, 1948), 382–85; and Henry C. Simons, *Economic Policy for a Free Society.*

[25]James Forrestal, *The Forrestal Diaries,* Walter Millis, ed.; Warner R. Schilling, "The Politics of National Defense: Fiscal 1950," in Schilling and others, *Strategy, Politics, and Defense Budgets,* 1–266; Bernstein, "Military Budgets and Economic Policy." So far, there has been no study of the

Truman's fears of unbalanced budgets and his anxieties about inflation suggest some of the weaknesses of the "open door" thesis argued by William Appleman Williams in *The Tragedy of American Diplomacy*. American policy, according to Williams, was based on the belief that expansion abroad was the key to domestic prosperity: The Marshall Plan was devised in large measure to restore needed markets upon which the American economy had traditionally depended. Williams is correct that some businessmen and labor leaders responded to appeals couched in these terms and that many Americans still expected a depression in the next few years, but he overlooks the fact that few in the executive anticipated an imminent decline. For them, large-scale foreign aid was likely to widen the inflationary gap and endanger the economy. However misguided the Administration's analyses of Russian expansion, the Marshall Plan, as Joseph Jones argues, was largely a response to political challenges and human needs. Yet, in a larger context, in which government officials defined peace in terms of international prosperity and viewed domestic prosperity as dependent in the long run upon the international economy, Americans were also accepting short-run economic risks for long-run economic gains. It is in this framework that the Williams thesis merits closer examination for its judgment of the aims of interest groups in the postwar period.[26]

Budget Bureau's specific influence on legislation, executive decisions, or formation of economic policy during the Truman years. Richard E. Neustadt's "Presidential Clearance of Legislation" and a revised portion, "The Presidency and Legislation: The Growth of Central Clearance," *American Political Science Review*, 48 (September, 1954), 641–71, concentrate on structural relations. Arthur Smithies, *The Budgetary Process in the United States*, focuses on the general process, and Aaron B. Wildavsky, *The Politics of the Budgetary Process*, emphasizes the political and tactical maneuvers in executive creation and legislative consideration of the budget. John Ramsey, a graduate student at the University of Missouri, is working on a doctoral dissertation on the Bureau of the Budget as a policy-making agency in the Truman Administration.

[26]William A. Williams, *The Tragedy of American Diplomacy*, particularly 1–50, 229–89; also see the weak essay by Clarence Geiger, "The Marshall Plan and American Prosperity: A Study in the Economic Motivation Behind the Foreign Aid Assistance Act of 1948." For some support for the Williams thesis, see the discussion by Forrest Pogue and Dexter Perkins, in *Conference of Scholars on the European Recovery Program, March 20–21, 1964, at the Harry S. Truman Library*, 13. Cf. Bernstein, "Challenge and Responsibility";

The magnitude of Truman's achievements may ultimately rest on his foreign policy; yet, it was neither victory nor vision in that realm, but economic problems at home and Congress' failure in domestic policy that greatly assisted the President in his uphill struggle for re-election. The battles with the Eightieth Congress—its obdurate resistance to welfare legislation and its slashing of appropriations for agriculture and reclamation—dramatized for many the dangers of a Republican administration. To emphasize the shortcomings of the "Do-Nothing" Congress, Truman called the special Turnip Session and challenged the GOP to enact its program. When the Republicans failed to grant standby price and wage controls he had requested (but did not want) and blocked other measures, he blamed them for high prices, inadequate housing, and stingy welfare benefits and effectively fastened on Thomas Dewey responsibility for the "Neanderthal men" in the GOP.[27]

By courting Western farmers, Northern Negroes, and urban workers, Truman reshaped the faltering Democratic coalition. To each group he promised benefits. He played skillfully on

Joseph M. Jones, *The Fifteen Weeks;* and Harry Bayard Price, *The Marshall Plan and Its Meaning.* Had the nation not been exporting goods in 1948–1950 under the plan, the first postwar recession would have been more severe, or it would have required more vigorous federal activity. Unfortunately, there is no careful study of the plan's operation, its assistance to particular industries and firms, and their attempts to influence purchases or European development. Thomas Patterson, a doctoral candidate at the University of California at Berkeley, is working on a thesis on American businessmen and foreign policy, 1945–1950. Among other subjects meriting attention are: the Export-Import Bank, on which congressional hearings are a rich source; the loan to Britain, which is analyzed in Richard N. Gardner, *Sterling-Dollar Diplomacy: Anglo-American Collaboration in the Reconstruction of Multilateral Trade,* and on which sources are available in hearings and in the Baruch Papers at Princeton; Reciprocal Trade Agreements; and the World Bank and the International Monetary Fund. Certainly there is room for a study of the ideology of expansion in the postwar years; presumably the forthcoming volume by Walter La Feber on the Cold War will consider these issues. Also see *Report to the President on Foreign Economic Policies* and Ilse Mintz, *American Exports During Business Cycles.* Matusow, "Food and Farm Policies," Chaps. V-VI, carefully investigates the earlier export policy of the Department of Agriculture and criticizes Anderson and Truman for their slow response in the spring and summer of 1947 to Europe's immediate needs.

[27] R. Alton Lee, "The Turnip Session of the Do-Nothing Congress: Presidential Campaign Strategy," *Southern Social Science Quarterly,* 43 (December, 1963), 256–67.

painful memories of Hoovervilles and bread lines and warned that a Republican triumph would plunge farmers and workers into poverty. The fear of depression, what Galbraith derisively calls the "depression psychosis," shaped many votes. In the West, particularly in the grain belt, collapsing prices thrust many voters into the Democratic column. Elsewhere, especially in the cities, discontent with gnawing inflation also cost the GOP support. Called upon to vote for the party of Hoover, which had freed prices, and pledged sometimes to repeal the New Deal, Americans were unwilling to trust the GOP with the economy. They would not gamble on endangering their gains and risk a return to the despair and deprivation of the depression years.[28]

Elected in his own right, as the confident recipient of the popular mandate, Truman acted to fulfill his campaign pledges (largely the promises of earlier years) and officially launched the Fair Deal. Despite the Democratic majority, the Eighty-first Congress continued its independence of the Executive and remained in the clutches of the conservative coalition. Granting him only public housing, a higher minimum wage, extension of social security, and more funds for ambitious reclamation and public-power projects, the Congress blocked most of his program—medical care, regional development (like TVA), civil rights, aid to agriculture, price and wage controls, and repeal of Taft-Hartley. Though David Truman selected this Congress for his useful analysis of the anatomy and physiology of *The Congressional Party,* and there are individual studies of particular legislation, unfortunately there is no general history of the Congress, of the conservative coalition, or of the

---

[28]Among the many sources on the election, see: Jules Abels, *Out of the Jaws of Victory;* Samuel Lubell, *The Future of American Politics;* Bernard R. Berelson and others, *Voting: A Study of Opinion Formation in a Presidential Campaign.* An impressionistic examination of the results suggests that local candidates may have carried Truman to victory. The surprisingly small vote suggests that party regulars constituted an unusually large proportion of the vote. Also see: Samuel J. Eldersveld, "The Influence of Metropolitan Party Pluralities in Presidential Elections Since 1920: A Study of Twelve Key Cities," *American Political Science Review,* 43 (December, 1949), 1189–1206; V. O. Key, Jr., assisted by Milton C. Cummings, Jr., *The Responsible Electorate.*

Administration's legislative strategy and tactics, its expectations and priorities.[29]

In studying the movement against Taft-Hartley, Lee contends that the Administration wanted sincerely to fulfill its pledge and win repeal of the measure. He attributes failure to the refusal of Administration supporters to compromise. Gerald Pomper, following a brief study by Benjamin Aaron, notes that those who had voted for Taft-Hartley still constituted a majority in each house, but ascribes the defeat to organized labor—its lack of unity, poor alliances, and resistance to compromise. While labor's mandate was geographically narrow and its allies without great strength, splits among union leaders on tactics and differences with the Administration on substance and strategy weakened the effort. By becoming more

[29]David B. Truman, *The Congressional Party: A Case Study.* So far there is almost nothing available on conservation policy, and it does not seem to have been of great concern to the President or to his advisers. As a result, the departments seem to have formulated most policies and carried them out with only occasional glances from the White House. Donald C. Swain of the University of California at Davis is working on a study, "Federal Conservation Policy, 1933–1953," which will focus on the resource agencies of the Department of Agriculture and the Department of Interior. For studies of conservation, see: Judson King, *The Conservation Fight: From Theodore Roosevelt to the Tennessee Valley Authority,* 277–96; Alfred R. Golze, *Reclamation in the United States;* Gordon B. Dodds, "The Historiography of American Conservation: Past and Prospects," *Pacific Northwest Quarterly,* 52 (April, 1965), 75–81; Arthur A. Maas, *Muddy Waters: The Army Engineers and the Nation's Rivers;* and also see President's Water Policies Commission, *A Water Policy for the American People.* On public power, see the small study by John Waltrip, "The Public Power Program of the Truman Administration." On river-valley authorities and regional development, see: William E. Leuchtenburg, *Flood Control Politics: The Connecticut River Valley Problem, 1927–1950;* Henry C. Hart, "Valley Development and Valley Administration in the Missouri Basin," *Public Administration Review,* 7 (Winter, 1948), 1–11, and *The Dark Missouri;* Wesley C. Clark, "Proposed Valley Authority Legislation," *American Political Science Review,* 40 (February, 1946), 62–70; Marion E. Ridgeway, *The Missouri Basin's Pick-Sloan: A Case Study in Congressional Determination;* Bureau of Reclamation, *Conservation, Control and Use of Water Resources of the Missouri River Basin;* Missouri Basin Inter-Agency Committee, *The Missouri River Basin Development Program;* Missouri River States Committee, *The Future Development of the Missouri River Valley, A Report on the Program and Activities of the Missouri River Valley Committee;* "A Symposium on Regional Planning," *Iowa Law Review,* 32 (January, 1947), 193–406. On migratory labor, see: Ellis W. Hawley, "The Politics of the Mexican Labor Issue, 1950–1955," *Agricultural History,* 40 (July, 1966), 157–76; and *Migratory Labor in American Agriculture: Report of the President's Committee on Migratory Labor.*

firmly committed to the Administration, which could offer Southern Democrats concessions on labor policy, union chiefs "limited their own freedom of action," concludes Pomper. His analysis follows Richard Neustadt's suggestion that the Fair Deal sometimes yielded to the exigencies of foreign policy and to the need for support from Southern Democrats.[30]

The Congress also rebuffed Truman's agricultural program —the Brannan Plan. Long a sick industry, first rescued by wartime demand and then briefly sustained by foreign need, agriculture by 1949 seemed in danger of succumbing to its earlier malaise. Designed to encourage abundant production and consumption, the plan, whose history Reo Christenson examines, carried the name of Truman's Secretary of Agriculture, Charles Brannan, who unveiled it in April, 1949. Featuring subsidies and emphasizing assistance to the small family farm, it seemed at first a political triumph. By promising farmers prosperity and consumers low prices, the plan heartened Democratic politicians, who welcomed its contribution to the revived labor-farmer coalition. However, the program, under scrutiny, proved economically vulnerable, as Matusow explains in his analysis of its defects and demise; it soon lost its attractiveness and enraged the powerful Farm Bureau and the Grange. Within a few months the proposal became a political liability, and Congress passed a more traditional farm bill that primarily benefited large commercial farms. Despite defeat, Truman continued to campaign for Brannan's measure until the Korean War rendered it irrelevant.[31]

---

[30]Lee, "Taft-Hartley"; Gerald Pomper, "Labor and Congress: The Repeal of Taft-Hartley," *Labor History*, 2 (Fall, 1961), 323–43; Benjamin Aaron, "Amending the Taft-Hartley Act: A Decade of Frustration," *Industrial and Labor Relations Review*, 11 (April, 1958), 327–38; Sumner H. Slichter, "The Taft-Hartley Act," *Quarterly Journal of Economics*, 43 (February, 1949), 1–31; Neustadt, "Congress and the Fair Deal: A Legislative Balance Sheet," in Carl Friedrich and John K. Galbraith, eds., *Public Policy*, 5 (1954), 351–58. Also see H. Bradford Westerfield, *Foreign Policy and Party Politics: From Pearl Harbor to Korea.*

[31]Reo M. Christenson, *The Brannan Plan: Farm Policies and Policy;* Matusow, "The Brannan Plan"; also see William E. Hendrix, "The Brannan Plan and Farm Adjustment Opportunities in the Cotton South," *Journal of Farm Economics*, 31 (August, 1949), 487–96. Grant McConnell's *The Decline of Agrarian Democracy* is a fine study of the Farm Bureau.

Though prices had started to decline in early 1949, the Administration was slow to abandon its request for standby controls and to recognize that the threat of inflation had turned into the menace of recession. In part, the President was a captive of the past and, in part, a victim of poor advice. Dependent upon his Council of Economic Advisers, which was torn by a long-standing dispute, he received conflicting analyses; opposing controls and finding evidence of readjustment (*disinflation* was his term) was the chairman, Edwin G. Nourse. A respected professional economist of orthodox views, he had hoped to establish the council as a nonpolitical ("scientific") adviser to the President, but Truman frequently disregarded him and liberal White House advisers rebuffed him. Nourse's own reflections on these years express disappointment with Truman, naïveté about the political process, and annoyance with his ambitious, very political, and staunchly liberal vice-chairman, Leon Keyserling. Separating these men of different personalities, commitments, and aspirations, as Corinne Silverman explains in her case study, was a basic institutional issue—the role of the council and, specifically, whether members should testify before congressional committees.[32]

Keyserling triumphed in this squabble, and he enjoyed his activities as the Administration's economic advocate. Backing the President's quest for increased taxes and controls, the Vice-Chairman was slow to discern, or at least to acknowledge, the end of inflation and the onset of recession. When the government finally backed away from these measures, it was slow to

Charles Hardin's *The Politics of Agriculture: Soil Conservation and the Struggle for Power in Rural America* and William J. Block's *The Separation of the Farm Bureau and the Extension Service* are useful analyses of limited problems. But there are no adequate studies of the Farmers Union or the National Grange and nothing of value on the unorganized farmers, the sharecroppers, or the migrant workers. John A. Crampton's *The National Farmers Union: Ideology of a Pressure Group* is mechanical and narrow, in most ways unsatisfactory.

[32]Nourse, *Economics in the Public Service*, particularly 209–71; Corinne Silverman, *The President's Economic Advisers*. On the council there is also a very bad book by E. Ray Canterbery, *The President's Council of Economic Advisers: A Study of Its Functions and Its Influences on the Chief Executive's Decisions*, which is mechanical in interpretation and emphasizes as a standard for judgment the test, How Keynesian was the council?

take action against recession. At the time and on the basis of available evidence, the efforts seemed inadequate, although they were ultimately sufficient for what proved to be an inventory recession. The Administration's program included mild stimulants to investment, some planning for public works, credit expansion, and a small deficit, but Congress was unsympathetic to most of these plans. A. E. Holmans criticizes the Congress and charges the White House with complacency, but Wilfred Lewis is more charitable to the Administration. He emphasizes "the important break with tradition" when Truman decided to tolerate a budget deficit, and he praises the President's public explanation of this policy.[33]

Despite these economic analyses and Lee's examination of aid to depressed areas, there remains a need for a full study of the government's belated and groping responses to the recession. The economic downturn provides an excellent opportunity for investigating the attitudes of interest groups and the quality of economic thought within the profession and in different sectors of the government. Such a monograph should also consider the unsuccessful efforts of Senator James Murray and Representative Wright Patman to secure an economic expansion measure. The measure would have authorized the government, when private enterprise lagged, to construct needed industrial plants and to plan public works. The bill, despite Keyserling's enthusiasm, received no support from the White House and never reached a vote. In Congress many were still suspicious of planning and feared that development of fed-

[33]Holmans, *Fiscal Policy*, 102–31, and "The Eisenhower Administration and the Recession, 1953–1955," *Oxford Economic Papers*, 10 (February, 1958), 34–54; Wilfred Lewis, Jr., *Federal Fiscal Policy in the Postwar Recessions*, 91–130. Also see Bert G. Hickman, *Growth and Stability of the Postwar Economy*, 51–78; R. Alton Lee, "Federal Assistance to Depressed Areas in the Postwar Recessions," *Western Economic Journal*, 2 (Fall, 1963), 1–23. For earlier views on inflation, see "Ten Economists on the Inflation," *Review of Economics and Statistics*, 30 (February, 1949), 1–29. In 1948 the UAW and General Motors concluded a new contract that soon became a model for many labor agreements. By providing for an increment for productivity and also for adjustments for increases in the cost of living, it seemed to protect organized labor from the threat of inflation and to promise steady increase in real wages. See Howe and Widick, *The U.A.W. and Walter Reuther*, 175–85.

erally owned production facilities would lead to socialism. Throughout these years the Administration apparently believed that economic growth would persist, with occasional urging, and it concentrated on restraining inflation.[34]

Until the Korean War the President struggled to restrict military spending, which threatened to unbalance the budget. Even after acknowledging the recession, Truman, as Schilling and Bernstein establish, resisted many of the military's demands. During these years the Air Force was clearly most successful, as the legislature and executive succumbed to the charms of the atomic bomb. But when Congress granted the Air Force larger appropriations than Truman had approved, he refused to spend the additional funds. Though Paul Hammond investigates some aspects of the interservice rivalry for shares of the budget, and Fred Cook's *The Warfare State* is replete with information and insights, suggestions, and suspicions, there is still need for a careful study of the influence of the services, their new industrial and scientific allies, and organizations of retired officers, on the size and composition of the military budget.[35]

---

[34]William Wagnon, a Ph.D. candidate at the University of Missouri, is preparing a thesis on the recession. For a study of the steel industry, see Henry W. Broude, *Steel Decisions and the National Economy*, 207–307.

[35]Schilling, "Fiscal Year 1950"; Bernstein, "Military Budgets and Economic Policy"; Hammond, "Super Carriers and B-26 Bombers: Appropriations, Strategy and Politics," in Harold Stein, ed., *American Civil-Military Decisions: A Book of Case Studies*, 465–568; Fred J. Cook, *The Warfare State.* Also see: Samuel P. Huntington, *The Soldier and the State*, 315–564, and *The Common Defense: Strategic Programs in National Politics;* Paul Y. Hammond, *Organizing for Defense: The American Military Establishment in the Twentieth Century*, 107–287; Walter Millis and others, *Arms and the State: Civil-Military Elements in National Policy*, 139–333; Harold Lasswell, "The Garrison State Hypothesis Today," in Huntington, ed., *Changing Patterns of Military Politics*, 51–70; Elias Huzar, *The Purse and the Sword: Control of the Army by Congress Through Military Appropriations, 1933–1950.* For the best bibliography, see Huntington, "Recent Writing in Military Politics—Foci and Corpora," in *Changing Patterns of Military Politics*, 235–66; and for Lasswell's earlier work on the garrison state, see Huntington, *Soldier and the State*, 506n1. On the aircraft industry, see Gene R. Simonson, "Economics of the Aircraft Industry."

Only in recent years have scholars started examining the effect of scientists (and science) on the formulation of federal policy, particularly on military strategy and expenditures, and on economic growth: For the wartime period, see: James P. Baxter, *Scientists Against Time;* Irvin Stewart, *Organizing Scientific Research for War: The Administrative History of the Office of Scientific Research and Development;* Alice K. Smith, *A Peril and a Hope: The Scientist's Movement in America, 1945–47;* Robert Gilpin, *American Scientists and Nuclear Weapons Policy;* Richard G. Hewlett and Oscar E. Anderson, Jr., *The New World, 1939–46,* Vol. I, *A History of the United States Atomic Energy Commission.* Emerging from the Second World War were a more complex technology and the recognition by the government and industry of the increased importance of scientific research to armaments and profits and, later, of the contributions of science and technology to the economy. The results have been dramatic—national and regional economic growth, higher profits, and the appearance (sometimes through indirect subsidy) of new industries; more devastating weapons; increased prestige, power, and income for physical scientists and engineers; intimacy of government and business with the university; creation and growth of research institutions (for example, Rand, Lincoln Laboratory, Stanford Research Institute); and the close relationship of Big Business and the federal government. On postwar science and public policy, see: Vannevar Bush, *Science, the Endless Frontier: A Report to the President on a Program for Postwar Scientific Research,* and *Modern Arms and Free Men: A Discussion of the Role of Science in Preserving Democracy;* Smith, *A Peril and a Hope;* F. Stefan Dupre and Sanford A. Lakoff, *Science and the Nation: Policy and Politics;* National Academy of Sciences, Committee on Science and Public Policy, *Federal Support of Basic Research in Institutions of Higher Learning;* A. Hunter Dupree, "Central Scientific Organization in the United States," *Minerva,* 1 (Summer, 1963), 453–69; Gilpin, *American Scientists and Nuclear Weapons Policy;* Gilpin and Christopher Wright, eds., *Scientists and National Policy Making;* President's Scientific Research Board, *Science and Public Policy;* Don K. Price, *Government and Science: Their Dynamic Relation in American Democracy,* and *The Scientific Estate;* Dael Wolfle, *Science and Public Policy.* On the impact of technology and organization on the new character of contracts, and for the difficulty of asserting effective federal control over research and development, see: H. L. Nieburg, *In the Name of Science;* Richard J. Barber, *The Politics of Research;* and Bruce L. R. Smith, *The Rand Corporation: Case Study of a Nonprofit Advisory Corporation.* For the Truman years, the best congressional source on the relationship of the military and science is probably Senate, Subcommittee on the Committee on Military Affairs, *Hearings on Science Legislation,* 79th Congress, 1st Session. A. Hunter Dupree is preparing what will probably be the definitive work on science and the federal government, 1940–1960, but there still may be room for a study relating science and technology to general or particular (regional or industrial) economic growth. For years American intellectuals have sought to guide or reshape their society, and the appointment of scientists, as well as economists and other academic experts, as consultants or employees in the federal government during and after the war fulfilled some of their earlier hopes for recognition, prestige, and influence. This development, a continuation of earlier aims articulated by reformers from at least Robert LaFollette's governorship and continuing through the New Deal, has raised basic questions about the freedom of intellectuals and the role of universities and about the allocation of intellectual resources and the distribution of rewards. Clearly, the reliance of the government and industry upon the universities and their faculties has created new constituencies and greatly altered higher education. Probably the best discussion of the service university is Clark Kerr, *The Uses of the University,* and see 127–35 for additional sources.

When the State Department doubted the adequacy of the military budget, it formed a special study group with Defense, as Hammond shows, to consider budgets three times (to $50 billion) above prevailing levels. The expansionary economics of Keyserling provided the economic rationale for large deficits and justified the policies they were considering. While the group was conferring, Louis Johnson, the new Secretary of Defense, was transforming the President's hopes for budget trimming into a crusade. A self-designated advocate of economy, a foe of waste and extravagance, Johnson was slicing authorized military expenditures. Had the Korean War not erupted, Johnson's economy drive might have advanced his political hopes and won accolades from scholars. Instead, though he was following the President's policies, the nation blamed Johnson for military weaknesses, and Truman sacrificed him on the altar of political necessity.[36]

So far, there has been no thorough study of mobilization —no examination of the impact on particular firms and industries, no scrutiny of businessmen in government, no probing of earlier planning, no analysis of the influence of military leaders. Robert Branyan and Harmon Zeigler skim over the ineffectual Smaller Defense Plants Administration. Reagan's dissertation focuses on legal restrictions designed to restrain industrial executives in government service. Herbert Rosenberg's unpublished thesis, a revised official history of the top mobilization agency, the Office of Defense Mobilization, is thin and neglects interesting structural issues in civil-military relations. Harry Yoshpe's *A Case Study in Peacetime Mobilization Planning: The National Security Resources Board* exhibits the limitations of most official histories. These studies are useful primarily as guides to research. Though the files of some federal agencies are still closed, much of the story can be pieced together from magazines and newspapers, congressional hearings and debates, and the published reports of agencies.[37]

---

[36]Hammond, "NSC-68: Prologue to Rearmament," in Schilling and others, *Strategy, Politics, and Defense Budgets*, 267–378.

[37]Branyan, "Antimonopoly Activities"; Zeigler, *Politics of Small Business,*

In examining the battle against inflation, scholars have been more active. While there are no evaluations of the impact of wartime tax increases on the distribution of income and wealth, Holmans and Flash survey the history and examine the politics of these measures. As an anti-inflation policy, increased taxation supplemented the Federal Reserve Board's restrictions on consumer credit. Until the Accord of 1951, however, the Federal Reserve was unable to use open-market operations to control the money supply and restrain inflationary pressures. Monetary policy could have been more restrictive, explains Chandler, if less importance had been attached to restraining service charges on the federal debt, to easing Treasury refundings, to protecting the credit of the government and investors against capital depreciation. Long chafing under an informal agreement to support government securities at par, the Reserve Board earlier had withdrawn support for some short-run issues but had continued to back long-run obligations. Spurred by the Joint Economic Committee, the Federal Reserve in late 1950 again withdrew support from some securities and clashed with the Treasury. Before Truman could arrange a settlement, the agencies reached an accord that allowed the Federal Reserve discretion in permitting fluctuations in the yields and prices of marketable federal securities and restored its monetary power. Despite the many surveys of events and analyses of these economic issues, there is no political examination of the banking communities or of this conflict. Probably the best study of the accord is Flash's very brief discussion, which concludes that "the conflict was not a battle between traditional enemies [but] . . . a strain *en famille,* as painful to one member as to the other."[38]

87–135; Reagan, "Serving Two Masters"; Herbert Rosenberg, "ODM: A Study of Civil-Military Relations During the Korean Mobilization"; Harry Yoshpe, *A Case Study in Peacetime Mobilization Planning: The National Security Resources Board, 1947–1953.* In the library of the Office of Emergency Planning there are some useful case studies. For a general survey of mobilization and stabilization, see Donald H. Wallace, *Economic Controls and Defense.*

[38]Holmans, *Fiscal Policy,* 132–94; Flash, *Economic Advice,* 30–81; Lester V. Chandler, "The Place of Monetary Policy in the Stabilization Program," *Review of Economics and Statistics,* 33 (August, 1951), 184–86. Discussions of the Federal Reserve's postwar activities are also available in:

Despite the restoration of its monetary powers, the Federal Reserve remained cautious in their exercise. Writing at that time, Seymour Harris cynically concluded that the general failure to use monetary policy to combat inflation was not primarily the result of pressure from the Treasury. "Much more important" was the unwillingness among the powerful interests —labor, farmers, and business—to combat inflation. "They all give lip service to the fight, but in their activities they are highly inflationary." Though Harris was correct in saying that groups continued to seek benefits that contributed to inflation, he overemphasized their influence on the Federal Reserve. The failure to move to a highly restrictive monetary policy, as Chandler explained, was the result of pressure from the Treasury and of problems in federal debt management.[39]

To restrain these interest groups the government also relied on direct controls. Gardner Ackley, then a government adviser, prepared the most thorough account of price controls. Based upon his own experience near the vortex of decisions and relying upon agency files and unpublished reports, the manuscript is a detailed, but unedited, history. Endorsing Ackley's conclusions, Matusow and Bernstein suggest that under partial mobilization direct controls proved economically unnecessary and provoked political conflicts the government might otherwise have avoided. They acknowledge that the events of the first fall and winter of war—the Chinese invasion, the second round of scare buying, the new wage increases, the demands of a fearful nation and disgruntled labor—forced the Administration to impose controls. Flash, Ackley, and Bernstein adequately investigate the interest-group pressures and the in-

---

Chandler, "Federal Reserve Policy and the Federal Debt," *American Economic Review*, 39 (March, 1949), 405–29; James L. Knipe, *The Federal Reserve and American Dollar: Problems and Policies, 1946–1964*, 38–62; Daniel S. Ahearn, *Federal Reserve Policy Reappraised, 1951–1959;* and J. S. Fforde, *The Federal Reserve System*. Unfortunately, there is no political examination of the Federal Reserve System for this period, no analysis of its personnel and their relations with constituencies of the federal government.

[39]Seymour E. Harris, "The Controversy Over Monetary Policy," *Review of Economics and Statistics*, 33 (August, 1951), 179–84; Chandler, "The Place of Monetary Policy."

decision and division within the government. Unfortunately, aside from brief surveys, there has been no study of the later discontent of labor and its brief withdrawal from the stabilization program. However, Matusow, in a model study, analyzes the farmers' assault on the stabilization programs and the concessions they wrung from the Congress.[40]

By the autumn of 1951, inflation had waned and military production schedules were lagging. While bottlenecks might have required some rescheduling, when Truman reviewed military programs, he resolved for other reasons to "stretch out" production and to postpone reaching recently planned levels of military preparedness. Truman's decision, Rosenberg emphasizes, was based primarily on the assumption that a large war was unlikely in the next fiscal year. Forced to choose among cutting the budget, or seeking an extension of the statutory debt limit, or additional taxes, he found the "stretch-out" decision most attractive. It "gave mobilization feasibility and politics a common bond—the art of the practicable."[41]

Truman's decision, according to Flash, also marked the end of the "period of influence" and the beginning of the "period of frustration" for the Council of Economic Advisers. Though Flash overemphasizes its influence after Nourse's departure and Keyserling's promotion—and he particularly exaggerates the council's role in the early stages of mobilization—the "stretch-out" decision was the *coup de grâce* to the expansionary economics of Leon Keyserling. By focusing on expansionary economics earlier, the Keyserling council "had provided the economic rationale for the . . . Fair Deal." But expansion never achieved a high priority, and the Administration soon succumbed to more orthodox considerations. Though Truman

---

[40]Gardner Ackley, "Selected Problems of Price Control Strategy, 1950–1952," and also available on microfilm, on Roll 1 of T-460, Defense History Program Studies Prepared During the Korean War, Publication of the National Archives; Flash, *Economic Advice*, 35–75; Bernstein, "Stabilization During the Korean War"; Matusow, "The Korean War." Almost nothing is available on the Wage Stabilization Board. On inflation, see also George Katona and Eva Mueller, *Consumer Attitudes and Demand, 1950–1952.*

[41]Rosenberg, "ODM," 164–69; Flash, *Economic Advice*, 85–95.

seemed intuitively to recognize the advantages of slight inflation and the politics of major economic groups may have demanded it, he was primarily interested in stability, not growth.
Offered programs that would expand the industrial plant at
the cost of diverting materials from production and of probably adding to inflationary pressures, Truman would not yield.
"His coolness to expansion policies," concludes Flash, "was
reinforced by antipathy towards economic expertise." Some
later observers, as does Flash, suggest that it was one of the
serious shortcomings of Truman that he was not more concerned about general growth, that he was not more visionary,
that he would not sacrifice stability to growth.[42]

Despite these criticisms, perhaps the larger failure of his
Administration, as well as of liberal thought, was its limited
view of the structure of the economy—the growing neglect of
poverty, great inequality in income, and federal contributions
to business power. Because the poor were unorganized and not
conveniently visible, Americans could disregard them, and the
government, which was battling inflation, slowly concluded
by the fifties that poverty was vanishing, that the nation was
becoming an affluent society. Persuaded that federal taxation
was very progressive, and minimizing the regressive quality of
state and local levies, the Administration believed that America
was still undergoing a silent revolution and achieving a more
equitable distribution of income and wealth. In large measure,
the reform and welfare programs that Truman requested would
have benefited the organized sectors of society, including skilled
workers and many members of the middle classes, but his
proposals generally would not have significantly aided the
numerous poor, whom the nation thought were advancing into
the middle class. Though Robert Bremner has briefly discussed
the periodic rediscovery of poverty, there has been no adequate
explanation of its waning visibility to government leaders,
liberal social scientists, and middle-class Americans. Perhaps
their observations reinforced values they cherished, but main-

---

[42]Flash, *Economic Advice*, 85–99. On inflation and growth, also see John
K. Galbraith, *The Affluent Society*, 189–98.

tained uneasily, as they sought respite from reform and grew complacent about the power of business.[43]

---

[43]For literature reflecting the theme of abundance, which became popular after the nation avoided a serious postwar downturn, see: David M. Potter, *People of Plenty;* Riesman and others, *The Lonely Crowd;* Simon S. Kuznets, *Shares of Upper Income Groups in Income and Savings;* Shepard B. Clough, *The American Way: The Economic Basis of Our Civilization.* Robert H. Bremner, "Poverty in Perspective," in Braeman and others, eds., *Change and Continuity,* 263–80. Also see: Kolko, *Wealth and Power;* Baran and Sweezy, *Monopoly Capital;* Robert J. Lampman, *The Share of the Top Wealth-Holders in National Wealth, 1922–56.* Truman was a victim of the defective liberal analysis, which suggested that poverty was disappearing and that welfare (and some reform) programs would greatly assist the marginal people, who were assumed to be few. While public housing was designed to rescue and speed the redemption of the poor, Truman indicated that he had little understanding of the magnitude of the problem and of the extent of distress. In 1949 he asserted that only five million were living in slums and firetraps, thus greatly understating the nation's need. *Public Papers of the Presidents: Harry S. Truman, 1949,* 6. He requested funds for 1,000,000 units, to be built over a seven-year period, received congressional approval for 810,000 units over a six-year period, but virtually ended the program a year later in order to halt inflation during the war. His occasional calls for slum-clearance programs, even if approved by the Congress and successful, would have only slowed the urban rot and certainly would not have ended the misery of the underprivileged in cities. Though he had requested a medical program in 1945 to aid the very needy, by 1948 he minimized the problems of the poor: "There are only two classes of people that can get the proper medical care nowadays, and that is [*sic*] the indigent and the very rich." *Public Papers, 1945,* 481–83; *1948,* 351. While proposing a great extension of the social security program and some improvement in benefits, the Administration seemed generally willing to settle for those reforms that would benefit the middle sectors of society. *Public Papers, 1949,* 5; *1950,* 600. Even the much-heralded Brannan Plan was designed to aid small family farms, but there was no provision for the really marginal people—agricultural laborers, migrant workers, sharecroppers. In summary, then, Truman's proposed reforms, as the accomplishments of the New Deal, would have primarily continued the "half-way revolution" initiated under Franklin Roosevelt. William E. Leuchtenburg, *Franklin D. Roosevelt and the New Deal,* particularly 326–48; Carl Degler, *Out of Our Past: The Forces That Shaped Modern America,* 379–416; Frank Freidel, *The New Deal in Historical Perspective.* Davies, at least in his thesis "The Truman Housing Program," was more optimistic than Bernstein about the aims, perceptions, and accomplishments of the Administration. Monte M. Poen has just completed a doctoral dissertation at the University of Missouri on the Administration's efforts for national health insurance. Of course, many of the other reform proposals have not been examined, and little is known about the forces within the Administration that sponsored them or the priorities Truman assigned. Studies of these measures should wisely go beyond the issues of endorsements and priorities as well as the political struggles that were frequently rural-urban conflicts, to appraise what changes the plans might have fostered, what groups the programs would actually have benefited, and whether the aims and rhetoric of the Administration and other groups indicate that they accurately foresaw the likely consequences of reform measures. Among

In these years, leading liberals, once fearing the excessive power of Big Business, were moving to celebrate its achievements. David Lilienthal, formerly an enthusiastic Brandeisian, extolled the large corporation, neglected its efforts to prevent many technological advances, and even praised it for technological contributions. Adolf Berle, Jr., previously troubled by the great unchecked power of managers of giant corporations, commended them for developing a corporate conscience and lauded their social responsibility. Adding to the comforting ideology, John K. Galbraith's theory of countervailing powers, offered as description and prescription, reconciled Americans to the waning of competition and the increasing size of large firms.[44]

Though concentration did not increase during these years, Galbraith and many other contributors to the complacent liberal faith overlooked the government's assistance to concentration. As economic power increases and gains greater social acceptance, argues Walter Adams and Horace Gray, "the federal government becomes more subservient to it, more dependent on it, more disposed to favor it with grants of privilege,

---

the published sources meriting attention are: *Migratory Labor in American Agriculture;* and the study by the staff of the Joint Committee on the Economic Report, *Underemployment of Rural Families,* 82nd Congress, 1st Session, which reveals some awareness of rural poverty.

[44]David E. Lilienthal, *Big Business: A New Era;* Adolf Berle, Jr., *The 20th Century Capitalist Revolution;* Galbraith, *American Capitalism.* Hard-pressed for evidence, Berle relies heavily upon the low-price policies of the automobile industry in 1947 and 1948, when the companies could have charged higher prices. What he does not emphasize is that dealers, who had suffered during the war, were frequently receiving more than list price for their cars and that the industry did not curtail this practice. By letting dealers recoup earlier losses, the industry was strengthening itself, and perhaps its behavior can be explained most adequately by a theory of long-run profit maximization. Galbraith acknowledges that countervailing powers will not operate effectively during inflationary periods when demand exceeds supply, because the resistance of purchasers cannot be effective, but he does not recognize that administered-price increases or generally level prices during periods of deflation discredit his theory as an adequate description of economic behavior. For the literature on admininstered prices, see: Gardiner C. Means, *The Corporate Revolution in America: Economic Reality vs. Economic Thought,* and his *Price Power and the Public Interest;* William E. Strevig, "Administered Prices: A Review and Appraisal," *Southwestern Social Science Quarterly,* 42 (September, 1961), 135–47, and *Business Concentration and Price Policy.*

protection, and subsidy." Many factors have shaped the government's efforts: the necessity of war and national defense; error and disregard of principle; "political pressures from business unmatched by equivalent political pressures from antimonopoly forces"; and "public reluctance to allow the government to intervene on behalf of monopoly under the guise of promoting private enterprise."[45]

Even in the disposal of federally owned war plants, particularly in aluminum and steel, where the government might have extended competition, efforts were not very successful. In aluminum, which Robert Branyan, Harold Stein, and Adams and Gray study more fully, the Administration's actions were faltering, often confused, and sometimes contradictory. By forcing Alcoa to share patents and by providing subsidies to new rivals, the government reached a limited goal—the conversion of a monopoly into a sturdy oligopoly. During the Korean War, the Administration endorsed expansion by the three producers and sought to encourage the entry of some smaller competitors, but instead lured giant firms that were seeking diversification. According to Branyan, creation of this oligopoly "was the high spot in the Truman Administration's resistance to concentration through nonlitigative techniques." The record in steel is less happy. By selling a West Coast plant to U. S. Steel, despite the opposition of the Antitrust Division, the government almost doubled the company's share (to nearly 50 per cent) of the area's ingot capacity. Aside from the brief discussion by Branyan and Adams and Gray, there is no study of the disposal of steel plants nor of the War Assets Administration, which sold war equipment, nor of the Reconstruction Finance Corporation.[46]

---

[45]M. A. Adelman, "The Measurement of Industrial Concentration," *Review of Economics and Statistics*, 33 (November, 1951), 169–96. Also see the exchange *ibid.* (February, 1951), 63–76. Walter Adams and Horace M. Gray, *Monopoly in America: The Government as Promoter*, quotations on 1 and 2.

[46]Branyan, "Antimonopoly Activities"; Stein, "The Disposal of Aluminum Plants," in Stein, ed., *Public Administration*, 313–62; Adams and Gray, *Monopoly in America*, 120–35. The only substantial consideration of the RFC is Jules Abels' *The Truman Scandals*, which focuses on the corruption and mistakes. The larger and more interesting issues of the agency's policies and activities remain unexamined. So far, there has been no study of the

Paradoxically, though the antitrust movement was "one of the faded passions of American reforms," as Richard Hofstadter remarks, the Administration prosecuted many companies; earlier, there had been a movement but fewer prosecutions. Despite the increased activity, antitrust was not an important theme of the Administration, and the President seemed largely unaware of the efforts. While he occasionally assailed Big Business during the 1948 campaign and may have even been suspicious of major, Eastern-based corporations, Truman was not particularly interested in resisting concentration or in opposing unfair business practices. Presumably, most litigation can be attributed to the Department of Justice, particularly to its Antitrust Division, but unfortunately there has been no study of the men and ideas shaping these decisions. Despite Simon N. Whitney's two volumes on the impact of antitrust efforts on major industries, Herbert Packer's fine survey of research in antitrust law, and Ralph Nelson's examination of the merger movement, scholars know very little about antitrust policy during the Truman years. Branyan's thesis on antimonopoly activities is thin, narrow, and unimaginative, and it neglects the regulatory commissions (except FTC). Lamentably, there has been no probing analysis of these agencies, which were usually captured by the interests they were empowered to direct.[47]

disposal of surplus property (largely military goods) in the postwar years. George Steinmeyer, a Ph.D. candidate in history at the University of Oklahoma, is writing a thesis on the disposition of government-owned industrial facilities after the Second World War.

[47]Hofstadter, "What Happened to the Antitrust Movement? Notes on the Evolution of a Creed," in Earl F. Cheit, ed., *The Business Establishment*, 113–51. Hofstadter attributes the new popular acceptance of the corporation to the success of the postwar economy, but neglects remarking that the rate of unemployment has been higher in the past two decades than during the first three of the twentieth century. Citing William H. Whyte, Jr., *Is Anybody Listening?* for evidence of business' failure to sell free enterprise, Hofstadter also overlooks the more subtle, and more substantial, influence of business and other prominent institutions in advancing the notion that American business is socially responsible and contributes greatly to the public welfare. Simon N. Whitney, *Antitrust Policies: American Experience in Twenty Industries;* Herbert L. Packer, *The State of Research in Anti-Trust Law;* Ralph L. Nelson, *Merger Movements in American Industry, 1895–1956.* Probably the best general work on the sad state of these commissions is James M. Landis, *Report on Regulatory Agencies to the President-Elect,*

In the legislative area the Administration pursued anti-monopoly policies sporadically, and it was neither bold nor unsuccessful. The executive seldom cooperated effectively with congressional committees studying concentration and monopoly. The Administration, however, did gain measures that tightened the Clayton Act to bar some mergers (prohibiting purchase of the assets of one corporation by another if the effect was likely to be reduced competition) and that reinstated fair-trade pricing after judicial assault on the practice. Despite the President's veto, Congress exempted railroads (Reed-Bulwinkle) from anti-trust restrictions, but he was more successful in blocking the cement industry's attempt to restore basing-point pricing, which the Supreme Court had struck down. Earl Latham closely investigates the industry's efforts, and Fritz Machlup analyzes the economics of the basing-point system. Latham and Zeigler, as well as Branyan, also examine the Administration's occasional unsuccessful efforts before the Korean War to assist small business, which its representatives opposed.[48]

Many important subjects have been disregarded. Surprisingly, there has been no consideration of the Department of Commerce, the views of its secretaries, its relations with business constituencies, and its attempts to advance the interests of business both at home and abroad. Though some of the department's records are open and considerable information is available in published sources, scholars have been unexpectedly reluctant to probe into these activities. For a thorough analysis of business-government relations, what is ultimately needed is a broad investigation that would also include the impact and intent of policies on general economic and regional development. Such a study would also consider the relations of the

---

which raises numerous questions useful to scholars of the Truman Administration. On the ICC and CAB, see Huntington, "Clientalism"; and also see Henry J. Friendly, *The Federal Administrative Agencies*. For a historical sketch and interpretation of the problems, see Marver H. Bernstein, *Regulating Business by Independent Commission*.

[48]Branyan, "Antimonopoly Activities"; Earl Latham, *The Group Basis of Politics: A Study of Basing-Point Legislation*; Fritz Machlup, *The Basing-Point System: An Economic Analysis of a Controversial Practice*; Zeigler, *Politics of Small Business*, 78–115.

Department of the Interior to mining, oil, and lumber interests and the Paley Commission's (President's Materials Policy Commission) recommendations to domestic and foreign economic policy.[49]

As part of its efforts to maintain a strong capitalist structure, Truman's Government not only conducted a vigorous foreign policy, sometimes shaped by the quest for materials and markets, and assisted corporations in their venture to achieve stability and rationalization, but it also aided organized labor and protected its gains. While not creating in labor an effective countervailing power to business, the government did advance the welfare of organized workers and increase the prestige of labor leaders. As allies of the Democratic party, they received recognition and some political support. Because labor's chiefs never challenged the basic assumptions of the capitalist system, they achieved a *modus vivendi* with the giant corporations, which knew that they could pass on wage increases to consumers and slowly learned to appreciate the stability union organization provided. As a result, the Administration was able to operate comfortably within a narrow framework, and neither its actions nor those of labor threatened to redistribute economic power or to reshape the social structure. While disputes

---

[49]Edward S. Mason, *Economic Concentration and the Monopoly Problem,* 221–326. The President's Materials Policy Commission, *Resources for Freedom.* On regional development, see: n. 29; Martin G. Glaeser, *Public Utilities in American Capitalism,* particularly 445–73; William R. Willoughby, *The St. Lawrence Waterway: A Study in Politics and Diplomacy.* Probably the most significant federal influences on regional development were not conservation and related activities but other policies and programs—for example, benefits to particular firms or industries, allocation of contracts, and farm subsidies—which may not have been intended primarily for regional development. In many cases, the policies and programs were probably a response to the political power of strong firms and interest groups that were regionally based, but even their aims may have been far more narrow than regional economic expansion. Also, see: Gerald D. Nash, "Western Economic History as a Field for Research," *Western Economic Journal,* 3 (Fall, 1964), 86–98, for a survey of some materials and some suggestions for research. Generally, there has been no study of state-federal government relations in the postwar years or of the impact of decisions in these realms upon industrial development and economic growth. James Patterson of the University of Indiana is studying state-federal government relations during the New Deal, and his efforts to assess the impact of the New Deal are taking him into the war and postwar years.

over wages or welfare provisions sometimes provoked the passions of labor and management and stoppages occasionally compelled federal intervention, neither these quarrels nor the government's intrusion endangered the systm. To retain labor's loyalty, Truman generally avoided invoking Taft-Hartley; he sometimes supported labor rhetorically and even occasionally chided industry for raising prices beyond the levels required by wage raises. Despite charges by management, the President was not seeking to weaken private enterprise but to protect the economy from the perils of inflation.[50]

Though many of the labor-management disputes of these years await examination, the steel strike of 1952 has attracted considerable scholarly attention. It was probably Truman's last major defeat. According to Rexford Tugwell, the unsuccessful steel seizure "bulks very large in the later history of the Presidency, perhaps the most serious setback it has ever suffered." Students of the Constitution have analyzed the Supreme Court's decision that the seizure was unconstitutional, that the President lacked the "inherent powers" a federal attorney had invoked to justify Truman's action. That argument was a costly blunder, resulting from the failure of White House assistants to check the government's brief in advance. His excessive claim distressed many sincere constitutionalists and permitted many of the President's enemies, who accused Truman of dictatorial ambition, to lash him savagely.[51]

---

[50]On organized labor and its leaders, see: C. Wright Mills, *The New Men of Power: America's Labor Leaders,* and *The Power Elite,* particularly 262–63. On the growth of unions, see Irving Bernstein, "The Growth of American Unions, 1945–1960," *Labor History,* 2 (Spring, 1961), 131–57, and replies, *ibid.* (Fall, 1961), 361–80. For a summary of experiences under Taft-Hartley, see Sumner Slichter, "Revision of the Taft-Hartley Act," *Quarterly Journal of Economics,* 67 (May, 1953), 149–80. For a survey of scholarship, see Neil W. Chamberlain and others, eds., *A Decade of Industrial Relations Research 1946–1956.*

[51]Rexford G. Tugwell, *The Enlargement of the Presidency,* 55. Alan F. Westin, ed., *The Anatomy of a Constitutional Law Case.* The political studies of federal intervention are limited—brief summaries in general volumes on labor, Harbison and Spencer, "The Politics of Collective Bargaining," and Bernstein, "The Struggle Against Wage-Price Rises." In particular, there is need for a study of the 1949 steel strike and the prolonged dispute over welfare measures. Samuel Hand of the University of Vermont, in his work on a biography of Samuel Rosenman, a member of the President's board in the steel dispute, has been gathering materials on the strike.

The most detailed studies of the 1952 debacle are by Harold Enarson and Grant McConnell. They conclude that the President's tactics were careless and that his staff handled negotiations poorly and failed to consider alternatives until the week of the strike. Poor communications with the tripartite Wage Stabilization Board, divisions between stabilization officials, and the resistance of the Secretary of Commerce to presidential orders contributed to the disaster. Richard Neustadt uses the seizure as a test case for studying the limitations of presidential power—the dependence upon assistants, their power to resist or to reshape policies, and the restricted sanctions available for securing compliance. By emphasizing that the capacity for persuasion is central to presidential power, Neustadt has illuminated a critical weakness of the Truman Administration, and Bernstein has followed this analysis closely in his study of the politics of the dispute.[52]

Defeated by the Court and rejected by the nation, Truman in his last years was a hapless figure, without prestige or great influence. Republicans condemned him for being soft on communism, and Senator Joseph McCarthy harassed his government. Truman's popularity had plunged to disastrous levels, and many blamed him for the war in Korea. After the Democratic setback in the 1950 elections, Congress had turned even further right and obdurately opposed his will. Differences on domestic policy had extended to basic disputes on foreign policy, and the President in his last years was a discredited man, moving from political defeat to defeat—from the outcry over the dismissal of General Douglas MacArthur to the Court's opposition to the steel seizure.

Had the Administration relaxed controls when inflationary pressures waned, it could have avoided the steel seizure and freed itself of an unnecessary political liability. But neither

---

[52]Harold Enarson, "The Politics of an Emergency Dispute," in Irving Bernstein and others, eds., *Emergency Disputes and National Policy;* Grant McConnell, *The President Seizes the Steel Mills;* Richard E. Neustadt, *Presidential Power: The Politics of Leadership;* Bernstein, "The Steel Seizure of 1952." Also see Mary K. Hammond, "The Steel Strike of 1952," *Current History,* 23 (November, 1952), 285–90, who concludes that the only loser was the public.

controls nor economic policies, even broadly defined, were significant issues in the election of 1952. Repudiating Truman, Americans elected Dwight D. Eisenhower, who did not seem to threaten the economic gains of twenty years. To a nation seeking leadership, Eisenhower seemed to offer new hopes, medicine for festering sores—Korea and China, communism and corruption. The issues had changed.[53]

Seymour M. Lipset, Daniel Bell, and others have sought to explain the new politics as status politics. Unfortunately, it is adequate neither as description nor explanation. Status politics exaggerates the irrationality of the fifties, misunderstands the sources of protest, neglects the continuity with earlier periods, and minimizes the efforts and passions of economic-interest groups in their struggle to wrest additional benefits from the state. (Were Texas millionaires who assailed the income tax in the fifties more irrational than corporate executives in the thirties who accused FDR of plotting the destruction of American capitalism?) The skirmishes over economic controls, the inflated rhetoric that characterizes American political dispute, and the continuing battles over extension of welfare measures were also part of the 1950's. Politics were angrily partisan and frequently savage. During these rancorous years, Harry S Truman acted to preserve a modified capitalism and struggled to maintain economic stability. The economy over which he presided had become increasingly reliant upon the state, but continued under the domination of big businesses that received the greatest benefits. Though other groups could sometimes impose their demands, and commercial farmers and organized workers received rewards, Big Business, while not a monolith, exercised the most power. Most Americans never severely challenged this system. Popular theories of pluralism partly cloaked it, and Truman and other leaders, endorsing pluralism, accepted it and contributed to the restricted political dialogue.[54]

---

[53]On the election also see n. 28. Though Taft-Hartley no longer seemed as critical, there were attempts to use it as an issue. Lee, "Taft-Hartley." Also see Lubell, *The Future of American Politics*, on Taft's 1950 victory over labor opposition that tried to make Taft-Hartley the issue.

[54]On status politics, see the essay in Daniel Bell, ed., *The Radical Right*.

BIBLIOGRAPHY

Books and Pamphlets

Abbott, Charles C., *The Federal Debt: Structure and Impact*. New York, The Twentieth Century Fund, 1953.

Abels, Jules, *Out of the Jaws of Victory*. New York, Henry Holt Company, 1959.

———, *The Truman Scandals*. Chicago, Henry Regnery Company, 1956.

Adams, Walter, and Horace M. Gray, *Monopoly in America: The Government as Promoter*. New York, The Macmillan Company, 1955.

Ahearn, Daniel S., *Federal Reserve Policy Reappraised, 1951–1959*. New York, Columbia University Press, 1963.

Albertson, Dean, *Roosevelt's Farmer: Claude R. Wickard in the New Deal*. New York, Columbia University Press, 1961.

Alinsky, Saul David, *John L. Lewis: An Unauthorized Biography*. New York, G. P. Putnam's Sons, 1956.

Allen, George E., *Presidents Who Have Known Me*. New York, Simon and Schuster, Inc., 1950.

Apter, David E., ed., *Ideology and Discontent*. Glencoe, Ill., The Free Press, 1964.

Bailey, Stephen K., *Congress Makes a Law: The Story Behind the Employment Act of 1946*. New York, Columbia University Press, 1950.

———, and Howard D. Samuel, *Congress at Work*. New York, Holt, Rinehart & Winston, Inc., 1952.

Baran, Paul A., *The Political Economy of Growth*. New York, Monthly Review Press, 1966.

———, and Paul M. Sweezy, *Monopoly Capital: The American Economic and Social Order*. New York, Monthly Review Press, 1966.

Many who use the concept of status politics confuse history and simplify analysis by exaggerating the issues of the thirties, attributing class politics to that period and then neglecting the concept of interest-group politics. See Seymour M. Lipset, "The Sources of the Radical Right," in Bell, ed., *Radical Right*, particularly 307–9. C. Vann Woodward, in discussing Hofstadter's analysis of Populism, makes a similar criticism of his use of status politics: *The Burden of Southern History*, 141–66. For criticisms of status politics and status anxiety as explanations of right-wing political behavior, see: Nelson W. Polsby, "Towards an Explanation of McCarthyism," *Political Studies*, 7 (1960), 250–71; Martin Trow, "Small Businessmen, Political Tolerance and Support for McCarthy," *American Journal of Sociology*, 64 (November, 1958), 270–81; and on the Birch society, Raymond E. Wolfinger and others, "America's Radical Right: Politics and Ideology," in David E. Apter, ed., *Ideology and Discontent*, 262–93. Also see Hofstadter, *The Paranoid Style in American Politics and Other Essays*, 66–92.

Barber, Richard J., *The Politics of Research*. Washington, D. C., Public Affairs Press, 1966.

Barkley, Alben W., *That Reminds Me*. Garden City, N. Y., Doubleday & Company, Inc., 1954.

Baxter, James P., *Scientists Against Time*. Boston, Little, Brown and Company, 1946.

Bell, Daniel, *The End of Ideology: On the Exhaustion of Political Ideas in the Fifties*. New York, The Crowell-Collier Publishing Company, 1962.

———, ed., *The Radical Right*. Garden City, N. Y., Doubleday & Company, Inc., 1964.

Berelson, Bernard R., and others, *Voting: A Study of Opinion Formation in a Presidential Campaign*. Chicago, University of Chicago Press, 1954.

Berle, Adolf A., *The 20th Century Capitalist Revolution*. New York, Harcourt, Brace & World, Inc., 1954.

Bernstein, Irving, and others, eds., *Emergency Disputes and National Policy*. New York, Harper & Row, Publishers, 1955.

Bernstein, Marver H., *Regulating Business by Independent Commission*. Princeton, Princeton University Press, 1955.

Block, William J., *The Separation of the Farm Bureau and the Extension Service*. Urbana, University of Illinois Press, 1960.

Bradley, Philip D., *The Public Stake in Union Power*. Charlottesville, The University Press of Virginia, 1959.

Braeman, John, and others, eds., *Change and Continuity in Twentieth Century America*. Columbus, Ohio State University Press, 1964.

Brigante, John, *The Feasibility Dispute*. Cases in Public Administration, 1950.

Broude, Henry W., *Steel Decisions and the National Economy*. New Haven, Yale University Press, 1963.

Bunzel, John H., *The American Small Businessman*. New York, Alfred A. Knopf, Inc., 1961.

Burns, James MacGregor, *Roosevelt: The Lion and the Fox*. New York, Harcourt, Brace & World, Inc., 1956.

Bush, Vannevar, *Modern Arms and Free Men: A Discussion of the Role of Science in Preserving Democracy*. New York, Simon and Schuster, Inc., 1949.

———, *Science, the Endless Frontier: A Report to the President on a Program for Postwar Scientific Research*. Washington, D. C., Government Printing Office, 1945.

Butters, J. Keith, and others, *Effects of Taxation: Investments by Individuals*. Boston, Division of Research, Graduate School of Business Administration, Harvard University, 1953.

Canterbery, E. Ray, *The President's Council of Economic Advisers: A*

Study of Its Functions and Its Influences on the Chief Executive's Decisions. New York, Exposition Press, 1961.

Catton, Bruce, *The War Lords of Washington.* New York, Harcourt, Brace & World, Inc., 1948.

Chamberlain, Neil W., and James M. Schilling, *The Impact of Strikes: Their Social and Economic Costs.* New York, Harper & Row, Publishers, 1954.

————, and others, eds., *A Decade of Industrial Relations Research, 1946–1956.* New York, Harper & Row, Publishers, 1958.

Chandler, Lester V., *Inflation in the United States, 1940–1948.* New York, Harper & Row, Publishers, 1951.

Cheit, Earl F., ed., *The Business Establishment.* New York, John Wiley & Sons, Inc., 1965.

Ching, Cyrus S., *Review and Reflection: A Half-Century of Labor Relations.* New York, B. C. Forbes and Sons, 1953.

Christenson, Reo M., *The Brannan Plan: Farm Politics and Policy.* Ann Arbor, The University of Michigan Press, 1959.

Clough, Shepard B., *The American Way: The Economic Basis of Our Civilization.* New York, Thomas Y. Crowell Company, 1953.

Coffin, Tris, *Missouri Compromise.* Boston, Little, Brown and Company, 1947.

Colm, Gerhard, ed., *The Employment Act: Past and Future: A Tenth Anniversary Forum.* Washington, D. C., National Planning Association, 1956.

Cook, Fred J., *The Warfare State.* New York, The Macmillan Company, 1962.

Crampton, John A., *The National Farmers Union: Ideology of a Pressure Group.* Lincoln, University of Nebraska Press, 1965.

Crosser, Paul K., *State Capitalism in the Economy of the United States.* New York, Bookman Associates, 1960.

Daniels, Jonathan, *The Man of Independence.* Philadelphia, J. B. Lippincott Company, 1950.

Davies, Richard O., *Housing Reform During the Truman Administration.* Columbia, University of Missouri Press, 1966.

Degler, Carl N., *Out of Our Past: The Forces That Shaped Modern America.* New York, Harper & Row, Publishers, 1959.

Dobb, Maurice H., *Studies in the Development of Capitalism.* New York, International Publishers Co., Inc., 1947.

Dupre, F. Stefan, and Sanford A. Lakoff, *Science and the Nation: Policy and Politics.* Englewood Cliffs, N. J., Prentice-Hall, Inc., 1962.

Eccles, Marriner B., and Sidney Hyman, eds., *Beckoning Frontiers: Public and Personal Recollections.* New York, Alfred A. Knopf, Inc., 1951.

Engler, Robert, *The Politics of Oil: A Study of Private Power and Democratic Directions.* New York, The Macmillan Company, 1961.

Ferrell, Robert H., and Jerry N. Hess, eds., *Conference of Scholars on the European Recovery Program.* Independence, Missouri, Harry S. Truman Library Institute, 1964.

Fesler, James W., and others, *Industrial Mobilization for War.* Washington, D. C., Government Printing Office, 1947.

Fforde, J. S., *The Federal Reserve System.* London, Oxford University Press, 1954.

Flash, Edward S., Jr., *Economic Advice and Presidential Leadership: The Council of Economic Advisers.* New York, Columbia University Press, 1965.

Freeman, Ralph E., ed., *Postwar Economic Trends in the United States.* New York, Harper & Row, Publishers, 1960.

Freidel, Frank, *Franklin D. Roosevelt.* Boston, Little, Brown and Company, 1952, 1954, 1956. 3 vols.

————, *The New Deal in Historical Perspective.* Washington, D. C., Service Center for Teachers of History, Publication No. 25, 1959.

Friedman, Milton, and Anna J. Schwartz, *A Monetary History of the United States, 1867–1960.* Princeton, Princeton University Press, 1963.

Friendly, Henry J., *The Federal Administrative Agencies.* Cambridge, Harvard University Press, 1962.

Galbraith, John K., *The Affluent Society.* Boston, Houghton Mifflin Company, 1958.

————, *American Capitalism: The Concept of Countervailing Power.* Boston, Houghton Mifflin Company, 1956.

————, *A Theory of Price Control.* Cambridge, Harvard University Press, 1952.

Gardner, Richard N., *Sterling-Dollar Diplomacy: Anglo-American Collaboration in the Reconstruction of Multilateral Trade.* Oxford, The Clarendon Press, 1956.

Gilpin, Robert, *American Scientists and Nuclear Weapons Policy.* Princeton, Princeton University Press, 1962.

————, and Christopher Wright, eds., *Scientists and National Policy Making.* New York, Columbia University Press, 1964.

Glaeser, Martin G., *Public Utilities in American Capitalism.* New York, The Macmillan Company, 1957.

Golze, Alfred R., *Reclamation in the United States.* Caldwell, Idaho, The Caxton Printers, Ltd., 1961.

Grantham, Dewey W., Jr., *The Democratic South.* Athens, University of Georgia Press, 1963.

Hacker, Andrew, *The Corporate Take-Over*. New York, Harper & Row, Publishers, 1964.

Hammond, Paul Y., *Organizing for Defense: The American Military Establishment in the Twentieth Century*. Princeton, Princeton University Press, 1961.

Hardin, Charles M., *The Politics of Agriculture: Soil Conservation and the Struggle for Power in Rural America*. Glencoe, Ill., The Free Press, 1952.

Hart, Henry C., *The Dark Missouri*. Madison, University of Wisconsin Press, 1957.

Hayek, Friedrich A., *The Road to Serfdom*. Chicago, University of Chicago Press, 1944.

Hewlett, Richard G., and Oscar E. Anderson, Jr., *The New World: A History of the United States Atomic Energy Commission*. University Park, The Pennsylvania State University Press, 1962.

Hickman, Bert G., *Growth and Stability of the Postwar Economy*. Washington, D. C., The Brookings Institution, 1960.

Hofstadter, Richard, *The Paranoid Style in American Politics and Other Essays*. New York, Alfred A. Knopf, Inc., 1965.

Holmans, A. E., *United States Fiscal Policy, 1945–1959: Its Contribution to Economic Stability*. London, Oxford University Press, 1961.

Howe, Irving, and B. J. Widick, *The U.A.W. and Walter Reuther*. New York, Random House, Inc., 1949.

Huntington, Samuel P., *The Common Defense: Strategic Programs in National Defense*. New York, Columbia University Press, 1961.

———, *The Soldier and the State: The Theory and Politics of Civil-Military Relations*. Cambridge, Harvard University Press, 1957.

———, ed., *Changing Patterns of Military Politics*. Glencoe, The Free Press, 1962.

Huzar, Elias, *The Purse and the Sword: Control of the Army by Congress through Military Appropriations, 1933–1950*. Ithaca, Cornell University Press, 1950.

Ickes, Harold L., *Fightin' Oil*. New York, Alfred A. Knopf, Inc., 1943.

Janeway, Eliot, *The Struggle for Survival*. New Haven, Yale University Press, 1951.

Johnson, Allen, and Allan Nevins, eds., *The Chronicles of America*. New York, United States Publishers Association, Inc. 56 vols.

Jones, Joseph M., *The Fifteen Weeks*. New York, The Viking Press, Inc., 1955.

Kariel, Henry S., *The Decline of American Pluralism*. Stanford, Stanford University Press, 1961.

Katona, George, and Eva Mueller, *Consumer Attitudes and Demand, 1950–1952*. Ann Arbor, The University of Michigan Press, 1953.

Kerr, Clark, *The Uses of the University*. Cambridge, Harvard University Press, 1963.

Key, V. O., Jr., *Southern Politics in State and Nation*. New York, Alfred A. Knopf, Inc., 1949.

———, and Milton C. Cummings, Jr., *The Responsible Electorate*. Cambridge, Harvard University Press, 1966.

King, Judson, *The Conservation Fight: From Theodore Roosevelt to the Tennessee Valley Authority*. Washington, D. C., Public Affairs Press, 1959.

Knipe, James L., *The Federal Reserve and the American Dollar: Problems and Policies, 1946–1964*. Chapel Hill, University of North Carolina Press, 1965.

Kolko, Gabriel, *The Triumph of Conservatism: A Reinterpretation of American History, 1900–1916*. New York, Free Press of Glencoe, Inc., 1963.

———, *Wealth and Power in America: An Analysis of Social Class and Income Distribution*. New York, Frederick A. Praeger, Inc., 1962.

Kuznets, Simon S., *Shares of Upper Income Groups in Income and Savings*. New York, National Bureau of Economic Research, 1953.

Lampman, Robert J., *The Share of the Top Wealth-Holders in National Wealth, 1922–1956*. Princeton, Princeton University Press, 1962.

Landis, James M., *Report on Regulatory Agencies to the President-Elect*. Washington, D. C., Government Printing Office, 1960.

Lane, Robert E., *The Regulation of Businessmen*. New Haven, Yale University Press, 1954.

Latham, Earl, *The Group Basis of Politics: A Study of Basing-Point Legislation*. Ithaca, Cornell University Press, 1952.

Leeman, Wayne A., *The Price of Middle East Oil: An Essay in Political Economy*. Ithaca, Cornell University Press, 1962.

Lekachman, Robert, *The Age of Keynes*. New York, Random House, Inc., 1966.

Leuchtenburg, William E., *Flood Control Politics: The Connecticut River Valley Problem, 1927–1950*. Cambridge, Harvard University Press, 1953.

———, *Franklin D. Roosevelt and the New Deal*. New York, Harper & Row, Publishers, 1963.

Lewis, Wilfred, Jr., *Federal Fiscal Policy in the Postwar Recessions*. Washington, D. C., The Brookings Institution, 1962.

Lilienthal, David E., *Big Business: A New Era*. New York, Harper & Row, Publishers, 1953.

Lipset, Seymour M., and Leo Lowenthal, eds., *Culture and Social Character: The Work of David Riesman Reviewed*. Glencoe, Ill., Free Press of Glencoe, Inc., 1961.

Lubell, Samuel, *The Future of American Politics.* Garden City, N. Y., Doubleday & Company, Inc., 1956.

Maas, Arthur A., *Muddy Waters: The Army Engineers and the Nation's Rivers.* Cambridge, Harvard University Press, 1951.

McConnell, Grant, *The Decline of Agrarian Democracy.* Berkeley, University of California Press, 1953.

———, *The President Seizes the Steel Mills.* University, University of Alabama Press, 1960.

———, *Private Power and American Democracy.* New York, Alfred A. Knopf, Inc., 1966.

Machlup, Fritz, *The Basing-Point System: An Economic Analysis of a Controversial Practice.* Philadelphia, Blakiston, 1949.

Madison, Charles A., *Leaders and Liberals in 20th Century America.* New York, Frederick Ungar Publishing Co., Inc., 1961.

Mansfield, Harvey, and others, *A Short History of the O.P.A.* Washington, D. C., Government Printing Office, 1947.

Mason, Edward S., *Economic Concentration and the Monopoly Problem.* Cambridge, Harvard University Press, 1957.

Means, Gardiner C., *The Corporate Revolution in America: Economic Reality vs. Economic Thought.* New York, The Crowell-Collier Publishing Company, 1962.

———, *Price Power and the Public Interest.* New York, Harper & Row, Publishers, 1962.

Millett, John D., *The Process and Organization of Government Planning.* New York, Columbia University Press, 1947.

Millis, Harry A., and Emily C. Brown, *From the Wagner Act to Taft-Hartley: A Study of National Labor Policy and Labor Relations.* Chicago, University of Chicago Press, 1950.

Millis, Walter, and others, *Arms and the State: Civil-Military Elements in National Policy.* New York, The Twentieth Century Fund, 1958.

———, ed., *The Forrestal Diaries.* New York, The Viking Press, Inc., 1951.

Mills, C. Wright, *The New Men of Power: America's Labor Leaders.* New York, Harcourt, Brace & World, Inc., 1948.

———, *The Power Elite.* New York, Oxford University Press, 1959.

Mintz, Ilse, *American Exports During Business Cycles.* Occasional Paper 76, Washington, D. C., National Bureau of Economic Research, 1961.

Murphy, Henry C., *The National Debt in War and Transition.* New York, McGraw-Hill, Inc., 1950.

Nelson, Donald M., *Arsenal of Democracy: The Story of American War Production.* New York, Harcourt, Brace & World, Inc., 1946.

Nelson, Ralph L., *Merger Movements in American Industry, 1895–1956.* Princeton, Princeton University Press, 1959.

Neustadt, Richard E., *Presidential Power: The Politics of Leadership.* New York, John Wiley & Sons, Inc., 1962.

Nieburg, H. L., *In the Name of Science.* Chicago, Quadrangle Books, Inc., 1966.

Nourse, Edwin G., *Economics in the Public Service: Administrative Aspects of the Employment Act.* New York, Harcourt, Brace & World, Inc., 1953.

Packer, Herbert L., *The State of Research in Anti-Trust Law.* New Haven, Walter E. Meyer Institute of Law, 1963.

Patterson, James T., *The Conservative Coalition in Congress, 1933–1939.* Lexington, University of Kentucky Press, 1967.

Phillips, Cabell, *The Truman Presidency: The History of a Triumphant Succession.* New York, The Macmillan Company, 1966.

Potter, David M., *People of Plenty: Economic Abundance and the American Character.* Chicago, University of Chicago Press, 1954.

Price, Don K., *Government and Science: Their Dynamic Relation in American Democracy.* New York, New York University Press, 1954.

———, *The Scientific Estate.* Cambridge, Belknap Press, 1965.

Price, Harry Bayard, *The Marshall Plan and Its Meaning.* Ithaca, Cornell University Press, 1955.

Rauch, Basil, *The History of the New Deal, 1933–1938.* New York, Creative Age Press, 1944.

Riddle, Donald H., *The Truman Committee: A Study in Congressional Responsibility.* New Brunswick, Rutgers University Press, 1964.

Ridgeway, Marion E., *The Missouri Basin's Pick–Sloan: A Case Study in Congressional Determination.* Urbana, University of Illinois Press, 1955.

Riesman, David, and others, *The Lonely Crowd.* Garden City, N. Y., Doubleday & Company, Inc., 1953.

Rossiter, Clinton L., *The American Presidency.* New York, New American Library of World Literature, Inc., 1964.

Schilling, Warner R., and others, *Strategy, Politics, and Defense Budgets.* New York, Columbia University Press, 1962.

Schlesinger, Arthur M., *The New Deal in Action, 1933–1939.* New York, The Macmillan Company, 1940.

Schlesinger, Arthur M., Jr., *The Age of Roosevelt.* Boston, Houghton Mifflin Company, 1957.

Schonfield, Andrew, *Modern Capitalism: The Changing Balance of Public and Private Power.* London, Oxford University Press, 1965.

Schriftgeisser, Karl, *Business Comes of Age.* New York, Harper & Row, Publishers, 1960.

Schumpeter, Joseph A., *Capitalism, Socialism and Democracy.* New York, Harper Brothers, 1950.

Seidman, Joel I., *American Labor: From Defense to Reconversion.* Chicago, University of Chicago Press, 1953.

Silverman, Corinne, *The President's Economic Advisers.* Inter-University Case Study 48. University of Alabama, 1959.

Simons, Henry C., *Economic Policy for a Free Society.* Chicago, University of Chicago Press, 1948.

Smith, Alice K., *A Peril and a Hope: The Scientists' Movement in America, 1945–1947.* Chicago, University of Chicago Press, 1965.

Smith, Bruce L. R., *The Rand Corporation: Case Study of a Nonprofit Advisory Corporation.* Cambridge, Harvard University Press, 1966.

Smithies, Arthur, *The Budgetary Process in the United States.* New York, McGraw-Hill, Inc., 1955.

Somers, Herman M., *Presidential Agency: The Office of War Mobilization and Reconversion.* Cambridge, Harvard University Press, 1950.

Stein, Harold, ed., *American Civil-Military Decisions: A Book of Case Studies.* University, University of Alabama Press, 1963.

———, ed., *Public Administration and Policy Development.* New York, Harcourt, Brace & World, Inc., 1952.

Steinberg, Alfred, *The Man from Missouri: The Life and Times of Harry S. Truman.* New York, G. P. Putnam's Sons, 1962.

Stewart, Irvin, *Organizing Scientific Research for War: The Administrative History of the Office of Scientific Research and Development.* Boston, Little, Brown and Company, 1948.

Stone, I. F., *Business as Usual: The First Year of Defense.* New York, Modern Age Books, 1941.

Strevig, William E., *Business Concentration and Price Policy.* Princeton, Princeton University Press, 1955.

Sutton, Francis X., and others, *The American Business Creed.* Cambridge, Harvard University Press, 1956.

Taft, Philip, *The A. F. of L. from the Death of Gompers to the Merger.* New York, Harper & Row, Publishers, 1959.

Taylor, George W., *Government Regulation of Industrial Disputes.* New York, Prentice-Hall, Inc., 1948.

Truman, David B., *The Congressional Party: A Case Study.* New York, John Wiley & Sons, Inc., 1959.

———, *The Governmental Process: Political Interests and Public Opinion.* New York, Alfred A. Knopf, Inc., 1951.

Truman, Harry S., *Memoirs.* Garden City, N. Y., Doubleday & Company, Inc., 1955, 1956. 2 vols.

Tugwell, Rexford G., *The Enlargement of the Presidency.* Garden City, N. Y., Doubleday & Company, Inc., 1960.

Venkataramani, M. S., *Undercurrents in American Foreign Relations: Four Studies.* New York, Asia Publishing House, 1965.

Wallace, Donald H., *Economic Controls and Defense*. New York, The
Twentieth Century Fund, 1953.

Warne, Colston E., and others, eds., *Labor in Postwar America*. Brooklyn, Remsen Press, 1949.

———, and others, eds., *Yearbook of American Labor:* Vol. 1, *War
Labor Policies*. New York, Philosophical Library, Inc., 1945.

Westerfield, H. Bradford, *Foreign Policy and Party Politics: From
Pearl Harbor to Korea*. New Haven, Yale University Press, 1955.

Westin, Alan F., ed., *The Anatomy of a Constitutional Law Case*.
New York, The Macmillan Company, 1950.

White, William S., *The Taft Story*. New York, Harper & Row, Publishers, 1954.

Whitney, Simon N., *Antitrust Policies: American Experience in Twenty
Industries*. New York, The Twentieth Century Fund, 1958.

Whyte, William H., Jr., *Is Anybody Listening?* New York, Simon and
Schuster, Inc., 1952.

Wiebe, Robert H., *Businessmen and Reform: A Study of the Progressive Movement*. Cambridge, Harvard University Press, 1962.

Wilcox, Walter W., *The Farmer in the Second World War*. Ames,
Iowa State University Press, 1947.

Wildavsky, Aaron B., *The Politics of the Budgetary Process*. Boston,
Little, Brown and Company, 1964.

Williams, William A., *The Tragedy of American Diplomacy*. New
York, Delta Books, 1962.

Willoughby, William R., *The St. Lawrence Waterway: A Study in
Politics and Diplomacy*. Madison, University of Wisconsin Press,
1961.

Wolfle, Dael L., *Science and Public Policy*. Lincoln, University of Nebraska Press, 1955.

Woodward, C. Vann, *The Burden of Southern History*. Baton Rouge,
Louisiana State University Press, 1960.

Wright, David M., ed., *The Impact of the Union*. New York, Harcourt, Brace & World, Inc., 1951.

Yoshpe, Harry, *A Case Study in Peacetime Mobilization Planning: The
National Security Resources Board, 1947–1953*. Washington,
D. C., Government Printing Office, 1953.

Young, Roland A., *Congressional Politics in the Second World War*.
New York, Columbia University Press, 1956.

Zeigler, Harmon, *The Politics of Small Business*. Washington, D. C.,
Public Affairs Press, 1961.

Public Documents

Bureau of the Budget, *The United States at War: Development and
Administration of the War Program by the Federal Government*.
Washington, D. C., Government Printing Office, 1947.

Bureau of Reclamation, Missouri River Basin, *Conservation, Control, and Use of Water Resources of the Missouri River Basin in Montana, Wyoming, Colorado, North Dakota, South Dakota, Kansas, Iowa, and Missouri*. Washington, D. C., Government Printing Office, 1944.

Department of Labor, *National War Labor Board Termination Report*. Washington, D. C., Government Printing Office, 1946. 3 vols.

Missouri Basin Inter-Agency Committee, *The Missouri River Basin Development Program*. Washington, D. C., Government Printing Office, 1952.

Missouri River States Committee, *The Future Development of the Missouri River Valley: A Report on the Program and Activities of the Missouri River Valley Committee*. Chicago, Council of State Governments, 1944.

National Academy of Sciences, Committee on Science and Public Policy, *Federal Support of Basic Research in Institutions of Higher Learning*. Washington, D. C., National Academy of Sciences—National Research Council, 1964.

Office of Temporary Controls, *Historical Reports on War Administration: Office of Price Administration*. Washington, D. C., Government Printing Office, 1947. 15 vols.

President's Committee on Migratory Labor, *Migratory Labor in American Agriculture: Report of the President's Committee on Migratory Labor*. Washington, D. C., Government Printing Office, 1951.

President's Materials Policy Commission, *Resources for Freedom*. Washington, D. C., Government Printing Office, 1952. 5 vols.

President's Scientific Research Board. *Science and Public Policy*. Washington, D. C., Government Printing Office, 1947. 5 vols.

President's Water Resources Policies Commission, *A Water Policy for the American People*. Washington, D. C., Government Printing Office, 1950.

Public Papers of the Presidents: Harry S. Truman. Washington, D. C., Government Printing Office, 1961–1966. 8 vols.

Report to the President on Foreign Economic Policies. Washington, D. C., Government Printing Office, 1950.

U. S. Congress, Joint Committee on the Economic Report, *Underemployment of Rural Families*. Washington, D. C., Government Printing Office, 1951.

U. S. Federal Trade Commission, *The International Petroleum Cartel*. Staff report to the Federal Trade Commission, submitted to the Subcommittee on Monopoly of the Select Committee on Small Business of the U. S. Senate. Washington, D. C., Government Printing Office, 1952.

U. S. Senate, Subcommittee of the Committee on Military Affairs, *Hearings on Science Legislation*. 79th Congress, 1st Session, 1945.

Articles and Book Reviews

Aaron, Benjamin, "Amending the Taft-Hartley Act: A Decade of Frustration." *Industrial and Labor Relations Review,* 11 (April, 1958), 327–38.

Adelman, M. A., "The Measure of Industrial Concentration." *Review of Economics and Statistics,* 33 (November, 1951), 169–96.

Bernstein, Barton J., "The Automobile Industry and the Coming of the Second World War." *Southwestern Social Science Quarterly,* 46 (June, 1966).

———, "Charting a Course Between Inflation and Depression: Secretary of the Treasury Fred Vinson and the Truman Administration's Tax Bill." To be published in *The Register of the Kentucky Historical Society.*

———, "Clash of Interests: The Postwar Battle Between the Office of Price Administration and Agriculture." *Agricultural History,* 41 (January, 1967), 45–57.

———, "Reluctance and Resistance: Wilson Wyatt and Veterans' Housing in the Truman Administration." *The Register of the Kentucky Historical Society,* 65 (January, 1967), 47–66.

———, "The Debate on Industrial Reconversion: The Protection of Oligopoly and Military Control of the War Economy." *American Journal of Economics and Sociology* (April, 1967), 159–72.

———, "The Postwar Famine and Price Control, 1946," *Agricultural History,* 38 (October, 1964), 235–40.

———, "The Presidency Under Truman." *Yale Political Review,* 4 (Fall, 1964).

———, "The Removal of War Production Controls on Business, 1944–1946." *Business History Review,* 39 (Summer, 1965), 243–60.

———, "The Truman Administration and Its Reconversion Wage Policy." *Labor History,* 6 (Fall, 1965), 214–31.

———, "The Truman Administration and the Steel Strike of 1946." *Journal of American History,* 52 (March, 1966), 791–803.

———, "Truman's Record." *Progressive,* 30 (October, 1966), 46–48.

———, "Walter Reuther and the General Motors Strike of 1945–46." *Michigan History,* 49 (September, 1965), 260–77.

Bernstein, Irving, "The Growth of American Unions, 1945–1960." *Labor History,* 2 (Spring, 1961), 131–57.

Bronfenbrenner, Martin, "Postwar Political Economy: The President's Reports." *Journal of Political Economy,* 55 (October, 1948), 382–85.

Chandler, Lester V., "Federal Reserve Policy and the Federal Debt." *American Economic Review,* 39 (March, 1949), 405–29.

———, "The Place of Monetary Policy in the Stabilization Program." *Review of Economics and Statistics,* 33 (August, 1951), 184–86.

Clark, Wesley C., "Proposed Valley Authority Legislation." *American Political Science Review,* 40 (February, 1946), 62–70.

Dodds, Gordon B., "The Historiography of American Conservation: Past and Prospects." *Pacific Northwest Quarterly,* 52 (April, 1965), 75–81.

Dupree, A. Hunter, "Central Scientific Organization in the United States." *Minerva,* 1 (Summer, 1963), 453–69.

Eldersveld, Samuel J., "The Influence of Metropolitan Party Pluralities in Presidential Elections Since 1920: A Study of Twelve Key Cities." *American Political Science Review,* 43 (December, 1949), 1189–1206.

Hagen, Everett E., "The Reconversion Period: Reflections of a Forecaster." *Review of Economics and Statistics,* 29 (May, 1947), 95–101.

Hammond, Mary K., "The Steel Strike of 1952." *Current History,* 23 (November, 1952), 285–90.

Harbison, Frederick H., and Robert C. Spencer, "The Politics of Collective Bargaining: The Postwar Record in Steel." *American Political Science Review,* 48 (September, 1954), 705–20.

Harris, Seymour E., "The Controversy Over Monetary Policy." *Review of Economics and Statistics,* 33 (August, 1951), 179–84.

Hart, Henry C., "Valley Development and Valley Administration in the Missouri Basin." *Public Administration Review,* 7 (Winter, 1948), 1–11.

Hawley, Ellis W., "The Politics of the Mexican Labor Issue, 1950–1955." *Agricultural History,* 40 (July, 1966), 157–76.

Hendrix, William E., "The Brannan Plan and Farm Adjustment Opportunities in the Cotton South." *Journal of Farm Economics,* 31 (August, 1949), 487–96.

Hoch, Myron, "The Oil Strike of 1945." *Southern Economic Journal,* 15 (October, 1948), 117–33.

Holmans, A. E., "The Eisenhower Administration and the Recession, 1953–1955." *Oxford Economic Papers,* 10 (February, 1958), 34–54.

Kolko, Gabriel, "American Business and Germany, 1930–1941." *Western Political Quarterly,* 15 (December, 1962), 713–28.

Lee, R. Alton, "Federal Assistance to Depressed Areas in the Postwar Recessions." *Western Economic Journal,* 2 (Fall, 1963), 1–23.

———, "The Turnip Session of the Do-Nothing Congress: Presidential Campaign Strategy." *Southwestern Social Science Quarterly,* 43 (December, 1963), 256–67.

Merriam, Charles E., "The National Resources Planning Board, A

Chapter in America's Planning Experience." *American Political Science Review*, 38 (December, 1944), 1075–88.

Morton, Walter A., "Keynesianism and Inflation." *Journal of Political Economy*, 59 (June, 1951), 258–65.

———, "Trade Unionism, Full Employment and Inflation." *American Economic Review*, 40 (March, 1950), 13–39.

Nash, Gerald D., "Western Economic History as a Field for Research." *Western Economic Journal*, 3 (Fall, 1964), 86–98.

Neustadt, Richard E., "Congress and the Fair Deal: A Legislative Balance Sheet." *Public Policy*, 5 (1954), 349–81.

———, "The Presidency and Legislation: The Growth of Central Clearance." *American Political Science Review*, 48 (September, 1954), 641–71.

Parsons, Talcott, "The Distribution of Power in American Society." *World Politics*, 10 (October, 1957), 123–43.

Perlo, Victor, "People's Capitalism and Stock Ownership." *American Economic Review*, 47 (June, 1958), 333–47.

Polsby, Nelson W., "Towards an Explanation of McCarthyism." *Political Studies*, 7 (1960), 250–71.

Pomper, Gerald, "Labor and Congress: The Repeal of Taft-Hartley." *Labor History*, 2 (Fall, 1961), 323–43.

Reder, Melvin W., "The General Level of Money Wages." *Industrial Relations Research Proceedings*, 3 (December, 1950), 186–201.

Rees, Albert E., "The Economic Impact of Collective Bargaining in the Steel and Coal Industries During the Post-War Period." *Industrial Relations Research Association Proceedings*, 3 (December, 1950), 201–12.

———, "Postwar Wage Determination in the Basic Steel Industry." *American Economic Review*, 41 (June, 1951), 389–404.

———, "Wage–Price Relations in the Basic Steel Industry, 1945–1948." *Industrial and Labor Relations Review*, 3 (January, 1953), 195–205.

Rovere, Richard H., "The Interlocking Overlappers." *Progressive*, 20 (June, 1956), 33–35.

Sapir, Michael, "Review of Economic Forecasts for the Transition Period." *Studies in Income and Wealth*, 11 (1947), 275–352.

Shoup, Carl S., "The Revenue Act of 1945." *Political Science Quarterly*, 60 (December, 1945), 481–91.

Slichter, Sumner H., "Revision of the Taft-Hartley Act." *Quarterly Journal of Economics*, 67 (May, 1953), 149–80.

———, "The Taft-Hartley Act." *Quarterly Journal of Economics*, 43 (February, 1949), 1–31.

Strevig, William E., "Administered Prices: A Review and Appraisal." *Southwestern Social Science Quarterly*, 42 (September, 1961), 135–47.

"A Symposium on Regional Planning." *Iowa Law Review,* 32 (January, 1947), 193–406.

"Ten Economists on the Inflation." *Review of Economics and Statistics,* 30 (February, 1949), 1–29.

Tobin, James, "The Monetary Interpretation of History." *American Economic Review,* 4 (June, 1965), 464–85.

Trow, Martin, "Small Businessmen, Political Tolerance and Support for McCarthy." *American Journal of Sociology,* 64 (November, 1958), 270–81.

Woytinsky, W. S., "What Was Wrong in Forecasts of Postwar Depression?" *Journal of Political Economy,* 55 (April, 1947), 142–51.

Unpublished Studies

Ackley, Gardner, "Selected Problems of Price Control Strategy, 1950–1952." Washington, Defense History Program, manuscript in the Office of Emergency Planning Library.

Berman, William C., "The Politics of Civil Rights in the Truman Administration." Ph.D. dissertation, Ohio State University, 1963.

Bernstein, Barton J., "The Ambiguous Legacy: The Truman Administration and Civil Rights." Manuscript in author's possession.

———, "Challenge and Responsibility." Manuscript in author's possession.

———, "Chester Bowles: A Liberal Businessman as Protector of the Public Interest." Manuscript in author's possession.

———, "The Estrangement of Labor." Manuscript in author's possession.

———, "Military Budgets and Economic Policy." Manuscript in author's possession.

———, "Stabilization During the Korean War." Manuscript in author's possession.

———, "The Steel Seizure of 1952." Manuscript in author's possession.

———, "The Struggle Against Wage–Price Rises." Manuscript in author's possession.

———, "The Truman Administration and the Politics of Inflation." Ph.D. dissertation, Harvard University, 1963.

Blum, Albert A., "Deferment from Military Service: A War Department Approach to the Solution of Industrial Manpower Programs." Ph.D. dissertation, Columbia University, 1953.

Branyan, Robert L., "Antimonopoly Activities During the Truman Administration." Ph.D. dissertation, University of Oklahoma, 1961.

Coombs, Philip, "The Strategy of Stabilization." Manuscript in author's possession.

Davies, Richard O., "The Truman Housing Program." Ph.D. dissertation, University of Missouri, 1963.

Dishman, Robert, "President Truman and the Engineers' and Trainmen's Strike of 1946." Manuscript in author's possession.

Geiger, Clarence, "The Marshall Plan and American Prosperity: A Study in the Economic Motivation Behind the Foreign Aid Assistance Act of 1948." Master's thesis, University of Wisconsin, 1957.

Hamby, Alonzo L., "Harry S. Truman and American Liberalism, 1945–1948." Ph.D. dissertation, University of Missouri, 1965.

Hartmann, Susan M., "President Truman and the 80th Congress." Ph.D. dissertation, University of Missouri, 1966.

Hinchey, Mary H., "The Frustration of the New Deal Revival, 1944–1946." Ph.D. dissertation, University of Missouri, 1965.

Huntington, Samuel P., "Clientalism: A Study in Administrative Politics." Ph.D. dissertation, Harvard University, 1950.

Koistinen, Paul A. C., "The Hammer and the Sword: Labor, the Military and Industrial Mobilization, 1920–1945." Ph.D. dissertation, University of California, 1965.

Lee, R. Alton, "Harry S. Truman and the Taft-Hartley Act." Ph.D. dissertation, University of Oklahoma, 1962.

———, "Mr. Veto in the White House: President Truman's Rejection of a Tax Reduction Program in 1947." Manuscript in author's possession.

Maher, Sister Patrick Ellen, F.H.M., "The Role of the Chairman of a Congressional Investigating Committee: A Case Study of the Special Committee of the Senate to Investigate the National Defense Program, 1941–1948." Ph.D. dissertation, St. Louis University, 1962.

Matusow, Allen J., "The Brannan Plan." Manuscript in author's possession.

———, "Food and Farm Policies of the First Truman Administration: 1945–1948." Ph.D. dissertation, Harvard University, 1963.

———, "The Korean War." Manuscript in author's possession.

McClure, Arthur F., II, "The Truman Administration and Labor Relations, 1945–1948." Ph.D. dissertation, University of Kansas, 1965.

Neustadt, Richard E., "Presidential Clearance of Legislation." Ph.D. dissertation, Harvard University, 1951.

Reagan, Michael, "Serving Two Masters: Problems in Employment of Dollar-a-Year and Without Compensation Personnel." Ph.D. dissertation, Princeton University, 1959.

Rosenberg, Herbert, "ODM: A Study of Civil-Military Relations During the Korean Mobilization." Ph.D. dissertation, University of Chicago, 1957.

Simonson, Gene R., "Economics of the Aircraft Industry." Ph.D. dissertation, University of Washington, 1959.

Stein, Herbert, "Twenty Years of the Employment Act." Manuscript in author's possession.

Waltrip, John R., "The Public Power Program of the Truman Administration." Ph.D. dissertation, University of Missouri, 1965.

Willson, Roger E., "The Truman Committee." Ph.D. dissertation, Harvard University, 1966.

Yang, Matthew Yung-chun, "The Truman Committee." Ph.D. dissertation, Harvard University, 1947.

Social Welfare Policies

✣

RICHARD O. DAVIES

Social and economic reform provides a useful central theme for interpreting twentieth-century American history. Much of what Americans call *politics* involves the continuing debate over the best means of providing social and economic justice for the American people within the context of a complex urban and industrial society. The shocking paradox of widespread poverty within a nation frequently described as an "affluent society" or a "people of plenty" prompted the development of a reform tradition in the late nineteenth century that is still a fundamental aspect of American politics. This reform movement has attracted the attention of many able historians, and the literature already produced is impressive, both for its quality and for its quantity.[1]

Except for a few isolated exceptions, however, this material does not push beyond the New Deal period. As scholars have begun to study the Truman Administration, their attention has been attracted by the exciting new departures in civil rights, civil liberties, and foreign policy. The seeming reluctance of

---

[1]The origin and evolution of this reform movement is best summarized in the following interpretative works: Samuel P. Hays, *The Response to Industrialism, 1885–1914;* Eric Goldman, *Rendezvous with Destiny;* Henry Steele Commager, *The American Mind;* Russell B. Nye, *Midwestern Progressive Politics;* Richard Hofstadter, *The Age of Reform.*

scholars to research the Truman policies on social welfare is perhaps best explained by the factor that the Administration erected no new monuments to the American reform tradition, but it concentrated upon the more prosaic activities of consolidation and modification. As one views the spate of publications on foreign policy, civil rights, and civil liberties, he is readily convinced that during the Truman years social reform could no longer generate excitement and enthusiasm as it had during the previous decade.

The lack of drama and frenetic action, however, should not imply the absence of historical significance, because the social welfare policies of Harry S Truman were intricately interwoven into the basic fabric of the entire Administration. In addition to the crucial role of preserving the New Deal, Truman's Administration provided the link between it and the New Frontier and the Great Society. More directly, social welfare policies provided a fundamental ingredient of domestic politics from 1945 until 1950.

The history of the Truman policies on social welfare, therefore, is yet to be written. At the present time, only one monograph based upon the Truman Papers has been published,[2] and the number of relevant doctoral dissertations is almost as meager.[3] We know practically nothing about most of his Cabinet members, the composition of the four Congresses,[4] or the White House staff. We need detailed studies of the specific legislative reforms Truman advocated, and we cannot construct sound interpretations until research is conducted upon the administration of programs already in existence. Our understanding of the political structure of the nation is, at best, hazy, and —a most important lack—we do not yet have a biography of Mr. Truman that is based upon the original sources.[5]

---

[2]Richard O. Davies, *Housing Reform During the Truman Administration.*

[3]Mary Hinchey, "The Frustration of the New Deal Revival, 1944–1946," unpublished doctoral dissertation, University of Missouri, 1965; Alonzo Hamby, "Harry S. Truman and American Liberalism, 1945–1948," unpublished doctoral dissertation, University of Missouri, 1965.

[4]The Eighty-first Congress has been the subject of considerable study in David B. Truman, *The Congressional Party.* This book will be discussed later in the essay.

[5]The most reliable biography published thus far is Jonathan Daniels,

It is readily apparent, however, that the research that needs to be done will have to be accomplished from within the larger framework of the populist-progressive-New Deal reform tradition. Only from within this perspective can we properly interpret the social welfare policies of Harry S Truman, whose "Fair Deal" was directly concerned with what he called "the experiment of achieving economic abundance and basic human rights in a society of free institutions and free men."[6] As President, the Man from Independence sought to provide each citizen, regardless of circumstances, the opportunity to enjoy economic and social security and opportunity. "We believe that our economic system should rest on a democratic foundation and that wealth should be created for the benefit of all," he told Congress in 1949. "We have pledged our common resources to help one another in the hazards and struggles of individual life."[7] The overpowering environment of modern society, Truman declared, required many government programs to protect and sustain the individual citizen. He lectured an unimpressed Republican Eightieth Congress to this effect in 1948: "We do not believe that men exist merely to strengthen the state or to be cogs in the economic machine. We do believe that governments are created to serve the people and that economic systems exist to minister to their wants." Emphasizing a viewpoint that remained consistent throughout his long political career, Truman said, "We have a profound devotion to the welfare and rights of the individual as a human being."[8] Just what this entailed, Truman frequently enumerated: "We are seeking to establish higher standards of living," he told a Jackson Day audience in 1946, "[requiring] a new health program, a new educational and social security program, an increased minimum wage, adequate housing, a further de-

---

The Man of Independence. The most recent biography, Alfred Steinberg, *The Man From Missouri: The Life and Times of Harry S. Truman,* is superficial and factually unreliable.

[6]Address at Jefferson-Jackson Day Dinner, Washington, D. C., February 24, 1949, in *Public Papers of the Presidents, Harry S. Truman, 1949,* 149.

[7]State of the Union Message to Congress, January 5, 1949, *Public Papers, 1949,* 2.

[8]State of the Union Message to Congress, January 7, 1948, *Public Papers, 1948,* 2.

velopment of our natural resources, and above all, a strong
and progressive America now and for all time."[9]

Ever since the United States began to react to its new environment in the late nineteenth century, the basic pattern of
reform has been inexorable: the increasing assumption of authority and responsibility for the protection and welfare of the
individual by the national government. The establishment of
the myriad government social service and regulatory functions
clearly amounts to a major "watershed" in American life;[10]
whether it occurred in the 1890's or the 1930's is of minor
importance here, because beyond question the rise of the social
service state had irrevocably reversed the traditional relationships between the individual and his government by the time
Truman took office. As scores of scholars have demonstrated,
both progressivism and the New Deal contributed significantly
to this reform movement, which emerged from the intellectual
and agrarian ferment of the latter quarter of the nineteenth
century. By the time the United States entered World War II,
the metamorphosis of American life had largely been accomplished.[11]

In order to understand fully the social welfare policies of
the Truman Administration, the preceding fifty years of reform
cannot be ignored, because what Eric Goldman terms the "Half
Century of Revolution" provided both the rationale and content
for the program the thirty-third President called his Fair Deal.
The reforms that Truman advocated were, for the most part,
New Deal retreads—programs that had originated in the
Roosevelt Administration. In many respects, there was not a
Fair Deal, as distinguished from the New Deal. Except for
the overriding problem of unemployment, the problems em-
phasized and the methods used to solve them were essentially

[9]*Public Papers, 1946,* 166.

[10]This important interpretative question is discussed in Richard S. Kirkendall, "The Great Depression: Another Watershed in American History?" in
John Braeman, Robert H. Bremner, and Everett Walters, eds., *Change and
Continuity in Twentieth Century America,* 145–89. This is the best bibliographic study of the New Deal, and it also serves as a logical point of departure for the student of the domestic policies of the Truman Administration.
[11]*Ibid.*

similar; both reform programs were firmly rooted in the assumption that the individual needed protection from his environment in the form of government social service programs. But here the similarity ends, because Truman's reform efforts did not benefit from the widespread public enthusiasm that characterized the first four years of the New Deal, and, unlike Roosevelt, Truman had to deal with a Congress blocked by political stalemate. Confronted by an entrenched and powerful antireform coalition of congressmen from rural America, Truman's appeals to the nation over the head of Congress were met by a national indifference that was conditioned by full employment, rising wages, overtime pay, and an apparent postwar reaction against major surgery upon the existing body politic.

The slender body of literature that deals with the social welfare activities of the Truman Administration somewhat surprisingly reflects no areas of serious disagreement. At the time of this writing, there is no evidence of the emergence of conflicting "schools" of interpretation. The Fair Deal was essentially "a modernization of Roosevelt's New Deal,"[12] and, as J. Joseph Huthmacher writes, it "anchored the nation securely within the mainstream of its domestic development during the postwar era."[13] The Truman Administration established no radically new programs, but it performed remarkably well in updating and expanding existing programs and, especially, in serving to assimilate the New Deal into American life.[14] One

---

[12]Louis W. Koenig, "Truman's Global Leadership," *Current History*, 38 (October, 1960), 227.

[13]J. Joseph Huthmacher, *Twentieth Century America; An Interpretation with Readings*, 344–45.

[14]Victor Albjerg, "Truman and Eisenhower; Their Administrations and Campaigns," *Current History*, 47 (October, 1964), 221–28; Mario Einaudi, *The Roosevelt Revolution*, 125, 334; Eric Goldman, *The Crucial Decade and After, America 1945–1960, passim*; Goldman, *Rendezvous with Destiny*, 314–35. At the time of this writing, Goldman's *Crucial Decade* stands as the only significant volume that attempts to survey the postwar era and to deal simultaneously with domestic and foreign policy. Goldman wrote the section dealing with the Truman Administration in 1956, and consequently his sources are primarily published materials and personal interviews. Although written in a lively style, *Crucial Decade* is uneven and superficial. Yet, ten years following its publication, it remains as the only useful survey of the Truman years.

major college text, however, seems rather overgenerous with its interpretation that the Truman domestic program constituted "a singularly constructive" period,[15] and Thomas Cochran must have ignored the sources when he labeled the Administration "businesslike and conservative."[16] Most interpretations agree generally, however, with Mario Einaudi that the Fair Deal was the logical extension of the New Deal[17] and with Arthur Link that Truman was the inheritor of the "progressive tradition" of William Jennings Bryan, Woodrow Wilson, and the two Roosevelts.[18]

The interpretations presented in college texts and other general works rely heavily upon Richard Neustadt's important essay, published in 1954.[19] Emphasizing the influence of the conservative coalition in Congress, Neustadt concludes that the Fair Deal scored an impressive number of legislative victories, perhaps far more than could be expected, in view of the structure of Congress. This political scientist, a former member of Truman's White House staff, points out that the Fair Deal secured the passage of the Employment Act of 1946, expanded considerably the Social Security program, and elevated the minimum wage from forty to seventy-five cents an hour. The Fair Deal also increased in size and scope the programs for soil conservation, land reclamation, flood control, rural electrification, and public power. The National Science Foundation was established, and the Housing Act of 1949, the signal legislative accomplishment of the Administration, dramatically expanded public housing and inaugurated the modern slum clearance and urban redevelopment programs. As Neustadt acknowledges, however, Truman was unable to overcome the opposition in Congress to the new programs of federal aid to education, a national health program, the Fair Employment Practices Commission, and the Brannan Plan for agriculture.

[15]Henry Bamford Parkes and Vincent P. Carosso, *Recent America, A History Since 1933,* 359–60.

[16]Thomas C. Cochran, *The American Business System, A Historical Perspective, 1900–1955,* 119.

[17]Einaudi, *The Roosevelt Revolution,* 125, 334.

[18]Arthur S. Link, *American Epoch, A History of the United States Since the Late 1890's,* 627.

[19]Richard E. Neustadt, "Congress and the Fair Deal; A Legislative Balance Sheet," *Public Policy,* 5 (1954), 351–81.

The general pattern of the Truman social reform program, therefore, lends considerable credibility to Eric Goldman's thesis that the Truman Administration fought a rear-guard action against the advancing postwar reaction that was spearheaded by the congressional coalition while simultaneously using executive powers and minor legislation to extend existing New Deal programs where feasible. Just as the Administration attempted to contain Russia's expansionist designs, so Truman's domestic policy sought to preserve the social service programs of the New Deal.[20]

While former New Dealers of an advanced liberal persuasion, such as Henry A. Wallace, condemned Truman's failure to expand drastically the government's role in social welfare, their frustrations might have been soothed somewhat by observing that Truman's efforts at least prevented an eradication or emasculation of the New Deal, as so ardently desired by such powerful persons as Joseph Martin and Harry Byrd. Truman obviously was no Harding or Coolidge in his attitude toward government action to solve social welfare problems, and he certainly did not preside over another postwar reversion to "normalcy." Thus, as Goldman wrote, "It was the Truman Administration that began codifying New Dealism in domestic affairs—slowing down its pace, pushing its attitude only in areas of outstanding need."[21] Even Mr. Truman agrees with this interpretation of the Fair Deal and sees it, as Goldman noted, as merely "an extension of the New Deal."[22] The relationship between the New and Fair Deals, however, needs further study. The wholesale disaffection of Roosevelt's advisers and leading "New Dealers" from the Truman Administration suggests that the concept of change as well as continuity must be used in analyzing the relationships between the two programs.

Assuming that the scholar is cognizant of the previous "Half Century of Revolution,"[23] the research on the social welfare

---

[20]Goldman, *Crucial Decade*, 65–66.

[21]Goldman, *Crucial Decade*, 293.

[22]Goldman, *Crucial Decade*, 92.

[23]This is the term Goldman uses to describe the previous fifty years of domestic reform.

policies of the Truman Administration should begin with the political structure of the United States during the Second World War. With the exception of Roland Young's narrow study of congressional politics,[24] we know little about the intricacies of domestic political activity during the war. I cannot accept Roosevelt's public announcement that "Dr. Win the War" had replaced "Dr. New Deal." The published sources indicate that this shift of program did not occur; to use David A. Shannon's phrase, "Politics continued almost as usual."[25] Especially important, the conservative coalition consolidated its gains of 1938 during the war years. The congressional elections of 1942 strengthened the coalition considerably, and even the venerable Nebraska insurgent, George W. Norris, was defeated by the arch-conservative Kenneth Wherry. Such

[24]Roland A. Young, *Congressional Politics in the Second World War;* this study provides the historian with some factual detail, but it fails to present the interpretative synthesis we need. Because he ignored the many relevant memoirs and manuscript collections, did not interview important participants, and relied almost exclusively upon the *Congressional Record* and published committee hearings and reports, Young failed to appreciate the political struggles occurring between the President and the Congress and between the forces of reform and conservatism. Young's narrow selection of topics (economic conversion, manpower utilization, price controls, taxes, military strategy, foreign policy, and reconversion) precludes a careful treatment of these conflicts, and the brevity of the volume forced the exclusion of the much-needed detail of the topics which are discussed. His use of a topical organizational framework necessarily prevented him from considering the interrelationships between rival committees and key congressional leaders, or between the state governments and the national government. Young's sparse treatment of the selected topics is clearly pointed up by the failure to discuss the National Resources Planning Board fight, the George Committee on Reconversion and Postwar Planning, or the origins of the Employment Act of 1946, other than a cursory mention of each. The important role of the Taft Subcommittee on Housing and Urban Redevelopment is not mentioned, and even the important G. I. Bill is treated merely on the basis of congressional debate and the obvious pressure tactics of the American Legion and other veterans' organizations. Never does this political scientist attempt to discuss the underlying assumptions of this legislation nor to pinpoint its relationship to congressional politics during the war. Young does, however, demonstrate that Congress played an important role in the war effort and that domestic politics was not shelved for the duration, although, curiously, the congressional elections of 1942 and 1944 are not related to the maneuvering within the Congress. Because he chose to write an institutional study of Congress and to limit his sources sharply, Young has provided the historian with little more than a proper starting place from which to develop his questions for a thorough study of the role of Congress during the Second World War.

[25]David A. Shannon, *Twentieth Century America,* 465.

conservatives as the Ohio Republicans, Robert A. Taft and John W. Bricker, became strong candidates for the Presidency, and the Democratic party also sported a representative collection of active critics of the New Deal. The entire scope of domestic political activity during the Second World War should provide many scholars with exciting and significant research topics, and not until we have sufficient monographic publication in this area can we fully understand the social welfare policies of the Truman Administration.

One important focal point of domestic politics during the war, which needs much study, was the anticipation of what would be accomplished during the postwar era.[26] The printed sources indicate that every interest group looked to the postwar period with high expectations: The conservatives hoped for a repeal of many New Deal experiments and a return to the True Way; veterans' organizations emphasized the serviceman's hopes for a good job, decent housing, and a college education; liberals dreamed of full employment and drastically increased government welfare programs. Scholars could profitably explore the great emphasis upon postwar planning. The many experiments of the New Deal had aroused considerable interest in the concept of social and economic planning. "Plan now for postwar America" became a recurring slogan, heard both within and outside the corridors of government. Many

---

[26]Mrs. Hinchey, "The Frustration of the New Deal Revival," provides an adequate study of this topic, although she ignores too many aspects of this very complex topic. Her primary concern is economic policy, and she ignores such closely related topics as agriculture or housing policy. She finds the movement for a full employment bill to be the touchstone of the New Deal revival. She ends the study with the 1946 congressional elections and concludes that the attempt largely failed, especially in the areas of labor and economic policy, although she observes, without discussion, that the New Deal was preserved in most areas. Her major theses are summarized in the introduction of the dissertation: "Harry S Truman attempted to fulfill the Roosevelt Administration's commitments in domestic policy. In his attempts to expand the New Deal after the war, however, Truman was plagued by a hostile conservative coalition in Congress and ultimately by dangerous inflationary pressures in the economy, both major problems during the war years. In addition, the failure of Truman's attempts to devise a strategy to unite the Democratic party and the frustration of the domestic program alienated the left wing and led to the disastrous defeat in the 1946 Congressional elections." (p. iv.) Mrs. Hinchey bases her study upon the Roosevelt and Truman Papers at Hyde Park and Independence.

conservatives, however, still clung tenaciously to *laissez faire* and sought to frustrate the new demands for social and economic engineering.

This concern with the quality of postwar life did not go unnoticed at 1600 Pennsylvania Avenue; President Roosevelt was already thinking about the postwar period as early as 1942. Following his directions, the National Resources Planning Board began drafting detailed plans for the postwar "reconversion" period—and beyond. The NRPB, led by such liberals as Alvin Hansen and Frederic Delano, envisaged another burst of reform that would compare favorably with the period 1933–1938. Above all, this presidential advisory group looked toward such areas as education, medical care, full employment, slum clearance, urban redevelopment, and veterans' housing. It hoped also to expand such existing programs as public housing, public power, social security, public works, and conservation of natural resources.[27]

Not everyone, however, concurred with this vision: a substantial segment of the population was convinced that the federal government had already intruded too far into the realm of social welfare. The surprising support received by John W. Bricker in his drive for the 1944 Republican presidential nomination reflected a growing discontent among many Americans with the trend toward increased federal welfare activity. This uneasiness was quite evident in Congress, especially when the House of Representatives killed the National Resources Planning Board. Conservatives in Congress had long been critical of this planning body, and, in February of 1943, ended its existence by refusing to appropriate further operational funds. The Senate promptly demonstrated its agreement with the House by creating its own postwar planning group under the chairmanship of Walter George, one of the Southerners Roosevelt had attempted to purge in 1938. To investigate the explosive housing issue the Senate established a special subcommittee, to be headed by Robert A. Taft, by no means an

---

[27]Charles E. Merriam, "The National Resources Planning Board: A Chapter in American Planning Experience," *American Political Science Review*, 38 (December, 1944), 1075–88.

ardent apostle of New Dealish planning.[28]

The conservative bloc in Congress, while adamant in its determination to prevent a postwar revival of the New Deal, had no qualms about advancing the social and economic welfare of the American veterans with expensive government programs. The Servicemen's Readjustment Act of 1944—the G.I. Bill of Rights—provided federal assistance to the veteran in such critical areas as housing, education, and vocational training. This legislation had a profound, although indirect, effect upon social mobility, the economic cycle, and the civil rights movement. The invasion of the veteran into the colleges and universities, alone, created a swift and dramatic change in American higher education; similarly, one can find in the housing provisions of this legislation a primary factor in the manner in which urban growth occurred in the postwar era, especially in the rapid proliferation of the "tract" housing developments that ring most American cities today.

The G.I. Bill, quite obviously, is a significant piece of social legislation, and it had a basic impact upon the domestic history of the United States during the Truman Administration. The impact of this law upon American society offers great opportunities for imaginative research; perhaps one fruitful approach would be to examine the manner in which specific programs, such as housing or education, affected individual communities or colleges. Equally significant would be a study of how social mobility was enhanced by such programs as the educational provisions of the bill or the manner in which the American Negro was spurred toward the fight for equal rights in his society. Just how the conservatives could rationalize their opposition to a New Deal revival with their support of this revolutionary legislation to aid veterans at high cost to the government also needs the consideration of the scholars researching this intriguing area of domestic reform.

Following the forceful demonstration of conservative opposition to a New Deal revival in the Resources Planning Board

---

[28]Davies, *Housing Reform During the Truman Administration,* discusses this development on pages 23–26. Mrs. Hinchey devotes several pages to this episode as well (2–9).

episode, Roosevelt counterattacked in his 1944 State of the Union message.[29] In this presidential election year, he boldly outlined a comprehensive reform program that included decent housing, educational opportunities, and medical care for all Americans. This "Economic Bill of Rights," Roosevelt wrote to his Vice-President, was his "blast" at the conservative bloc in Congress.[30]

Although Roosevelt talked eloquently, he did not go beyond the perfunctory outline of the general programs; he never translated his general goals into well-developed legislative proposals. At least in the cases of full employment and housing, he allowed Congress to assume the initiative;[31] the other programs apparently lay in limbo until the end of the war. Thus, when Roosevelt suddenly died on April 12, 1945, his successor was confronted not only with the formidable task of guiding the final military operations and planning for the postwar international settlement, but also of somehow formulating a complete domestic program as well. There is little wonder that the new President felt as if he had been buried by a celestial avalanche.[32]

Military and diplomatic decisions necessarily received Truman's first consideration, and he was not able to devote close attention to domestic problems until he boarded the U. S. S. *Augusta*, following the Potsdam Conference. As the *Augusta* plowed westward, Truman requested Samuel I. Rosenman to supervise the drafting of a detailed message that would outline his program in considerable detail. After Truman had presented his basic ideas to the former Roosevelt adviser, Rosenman reportedly erupted into enthusiastic praise for the reformist position Truman had sketched: "You know,

[29]Samuel I. Rosenman, ed., *The Public Papers and Addresses of Franklin D. Roosevelt, 1944–1945,* 41.

[30]Roosevelt to Henry A. Wallace, quoted in Hinchey, "The Frustration of the New Deal Revival," 9–10.

[31]Davies, *Housing Reform During the Truman Administration,* 23–28; Stephen K. Bailey, *Congress Makes a Law,* 1–60.

[32]Truman is quoted as telling the press, "Boys, if you ever pray, pray for me now. I don't know if you fellows ever had a load of hay fall on you, but when they told me yesterday what had happened, I felt like the moon, the stars and all the planets had fallen on me." (Goldman, *Crucial Decade,* 18.)

Mr. President, this is the most exciting and pleasant surprise I have had in a long time," Rosenman is reported to have told Truman.[33] Rosenman had undoubtedly been led by widely circulating rumors to believe that Truman would not seek to continue and expand the New Deal. The document went to Congress on September 6, 1945, just four days after General Douglas MacArthur accepted the formal Japanese surrender in Tokyo Bay.[34]

This message provided the cornerstone of Truman's social welfare program. It was definitely a Truman-inspired message, but it also had a resonant Roosevelt ring. Although Rosenman directed the preparation of this lengthy document, his papers show that he drew upon all relevant government agencies for ideas and even drafts of entire sections of the message.[35] Thus, the Message on Reconversion bore a definite New Deal imprint; the general authorship of Rosenman, in fact, symbolizes the close relationship between the Roosevelt and Truman programs.

The message was deeply rooted in the progressive tradition, but its immediate inspiration was the 1944 Economic Bill of Rights. In this message, Truman demonstrated beyond doubt his intention to make good on his predecessor's 1944 campaign promises. Most of the twenty-one points in the document were noncontroversial, such as increasing congressional salaries, selling excess ships, and stockpiling strategic materials, but his call for a comprehensive housing bill, a full employment bill, increases in unemployment benefits, a fair employment practices commission, and increase of the minimum wage gratified the uneasy liberal community and shocked—even angered—the conservatives. During Truman's first five months in office,

---

[33]Harry S. Truman, *Memoirs,* Vol. I, *The Year of Decisions,* 482–83. The memoirs are basic for the student of the Truman Administration. Although the two volumes are quite unbalanced in the distribution of time, they contain a wealth of factual material and, especially, provide ample demonstration of the Truman thought processes and the assumptions upon which his presidential decisions rested. The student of social welfare policy, however, will readily discover that the major concern of both volumes of the memoirs is foreign policy.

[34]The original document is in the Harry S. Truman Papers, PPF 200, Harry S. Truman Library.

[35]The Rosenman Papers are deposited in the Truman Library.

while he was preoccupied with foreign policy, the conservatives had apparently deluded themselves with the notion that the new President would begin to roll back the New Deal. The message, they contend, was a terrible blow, and Joseph Martin summarized this feeling in his memoirs: It was, he says, an obvious case of "out-New Dealing the New Deal," because Truman was endorsing "the same old dreary circuit of paternalism, controls, spending, high taxes, and vague objectives."[36]

The cry of betrayal from the aroused conservatives, however, seems to have expressed political viewpoint rather than actual surprise, because Truman's general position on social welfare had been clearly established. Although the exact circumstances of his nomination to the Vice-Presidency are unclear and probably will remain muddled forever, Truman definitely had been "cleared by Sidney," and this leader of organized labor would not have accepted anyone who was allied with the forces of reaction.[37] In fact, in his maiden presidential speech in April, Truman had briefly mentioned social welfare: "Here in America we have labored long and hard to achieve a social order worthy of our great heritage. In our time tremendous progress has been made toward a really democratic way of life. Let me assure the forward-looking people of America that there will be no relaxation in our efforts to improve the lot of the common people."[38] Even the barometer of liberalism, T. R. B. of the *New Republic*, had indicated a comfortable future to his apprehensive readers in June with the news that the new President was going to continue the New Deal: "His Administration is more homespun and less cosmopolitan than Roosevelt's, with a good deal more emphasis upon party regularity, but it is pretty evident in which direction it is going; it is going a little left of center."[39]

[36]Joseph W. Martin, *My First Fifty Years in Politics*, 177–78.

[37]Roosevelt reportedly approved Truman as the candidate for Vice-President after Sidney Hillman, the major spokesman for organized labor in political affairs, accepted the Missourian. Hillman, of course, refused to "clear" James F. Byrnes, the original leading challenger to the position held by Henry Wallace. Walter Johnson, *1600 Pennsylvania Avenue: Presidents and the People Since 1929*, 167.

[38]Quoted in Irving Brant, "Harry S. Truman," *New Republic*, 112 (May 7, 1945), 635–38.

[39]*New Republic*, 112 (June 18, 1945), 843.

Truman, of course, has always considered himself to be a strong "New Dealer," although his public career prior to 1934 fails to support this contention. Throughout his ten years in the Senate, however, as Eugene Schmidtlein demonstrates, Truman was solidly behind the Roosevelt program.[40] By September 6, 1945, however, Truman had decided that the growing public speculation on his domestic program had gone far enough, and he determined that the time had arrived to "let the Hearsts and McCormicks know that they were not going to take me into camp."[41]

The social welfare policies Truman pursued during his Presidency reflected not only his New Dealism as a senator but also his experiences as a farmer, unsuccessful businessman, and Jackson County politician of a Pendergast hue. All of these activities helped mold a deep sympathy for the average American. Truman's memoirs implicitly disclose the development of his liberalism. As a young man in Kansas City, he worked for a time with the Santa Fe Railroad as a paymaster. "I learned what it meant to work for ten hours for $1.50," he wrote.[42] As a member of the Pendergast political organization, Truman learned the political importance of good works—as a Presiding Judge of the Jackson County Court during the early days of the depression he saw how social welfare neatly fused with political expediency.[43] Hence, social welfare provided by government was an important dimension of Truman's political philosophy: "I was a New Dealer back in Jackson County, and there was no need for me to change," he recalls. "I be-

---

[40]Eugene F. Schmidtlein, "Truman the Senator," unpublished doctoral dissertation, University of Missouri, 1962. Schmidtlein provides the best study of Truman's often neglected senatorial career and his position within Missouri politics. The major significance of this study is that it does not overemphasize the Truman Committee's effects during the Second World War, and it discusses in detail Truman's support of New Deal programs and his concentrated work on the regulation of transportation.

[41]Daniels, *Man of Independence*, 297.

[42]Truman, *Year of Decisions*, 123.

[43]Lyle W. Dorsett, "A History of the Pendergast Machine," unpublished doctoral dissertation, University of Missouri, 1965, Chapter 8, demonstrates the close relationship of welfare and politics in Kansas City. This significant study discusses in part the relationship of Senator Truman with the Pendergast organization.

lieved in the program from the time it was first proposed."[44]
Thus, to Truman, his Message on Reconversion "symbolizes
for me my assumption of the office of President in my own
right. It was on that day and with this message that I first
spelled out the details of the program of liberalism and progressivism which was to be the foundation of my administration." It was, Truman affirms, "my opportunity as President
to advocate the political principles and economic philosophy
which I had expressed in the Senate and which I had followed
all my political life." And, he concludes, with a high degree
of accuracy, it "set the tone and direction for the rest of my
administration and the goals toward which I would try to
lead the nation."[45]

He never lost sight of the objectives he established on September 6, 1945. His published Presidential Papers document
beyond any doubt his commitment: "The basic objective," he
told Congress in his first State of the Union Message, "is to
improve the welfare of the American people."[46] On the first
anniversary of the death of Roosevelt, Truman observed, "The
domestic principles and policies which were laid down and
put into practice by President Roosevelt have come almost to
be accepted as commonplace today. Yet, they constitute a program of social reform and progress unequalled in the history
of the United States." Roosevelt, Truman said, accomplished
"a social revolution which swept out obsolete notions cluttering
our economy and substituted a bold program of decisive action
designed to improve the standard of living and the level of
security of the common man."[47]

Truman's social welfare policies, therefore, were based upon
the New Deal and, indirectly, upon the progressive tradition,
but unlike other reform Presidents, he faced new problems—

[44]Truman, *Year of Decisions*, 149; Truman writes elsewhere in his memoirs
that he always had been attracted by the New Deal: "I knew that the
program he was enunciating for the welfare and security of all classes of
Americans was a program that I could support wholeheartedly. In fact, it
was one I had already put into effect on the local level." (143)

[45]Truman, *Year of Decisions*, 481–82.

[46]January 21, 1946, *Public Papers, 1946*, 40.

[47]Truman, to Bruce Bliven, editor of *New Republic*, March 19, 1946, in
New Republic, 114 (April 15, 1946), 523.

conserving and improving what had already been accomplished. From the perspective of 1945, the specter of the repeal of the New Deal had become a vivid possibility; the fate of the progressive reforms following the First World War had not been forgotten. Truman was determined to prevent a repeat performance. At the same time, he sought to move on to new areas that he believed required attention.

The first order of business was to end the fear of widespread unemployment. The memory of depression hung over the nation as the war ended, and many fully expected another economic crisis. Stephen Bailey has demonstrated the slipshod manner in which the Employment Act of 1946 was enacted.[48] This significant legislation had been in the congressional mill since 1943, and Truman merely accepted it as part of his program. The affirmation of employment opportunities for all neatly meshed with his hope that the American workingman might be spared another severe depression.

Truman's aspirations for the achievement of new vistas of social legislation, however, never captured the public imagination; where Roosevelt's eloquence thrilled the depression-ridden nation, Truman's flat Missouri twang and modest physique produced only widespread indifference. Truman lacked a certain special something—charisma—that could evoke enthusiasm for his program. No matter how he tried—and try he did—Truman could not produce a ground swell of public support for his reforms.[49] "During his first two years in of-

[48]Bailey, *Congress Makes a Law.*

[49]Charles A. Madison, *Leaders and Liberals in 20th Century America,* is most critical of Truman's leadership. Although Madison acknowledges the near impossible situation Truman faced in Congress, he writes, "Unable to control members of his own party, lacking the imagination and the ingenuity to arouse the nation in favor of his reform measures, he made little impression on a Congress that chose to ignore some of his proposals, such as action on labor legislation and civil rights, and to enact others into law in so garbled or in so attenuated a form as to impair their original purpose." (455) Madison characterizes Truman as a man "with a mind governed by copybook maxims" who "on occasions, acted tactlessly or out of personal pique." (412) The emphasis of this long essay, however, is upon foreign policy, and social welfare policies receive little direct attention. Richard Neustadt, however, presents a more balanced and judicious discussion of Truman's leadership abilities in his *Presidential Power, The Politics of Leadership.* Although little attention is devoted to social welfare, Neustadt presents a useful study of

fice," Huthmacher cogently summarizes, "Truman appeared to be not only new at his job, but inept and indecisive. Liberals, with whom Truman sought to identify himself early in his administration, were dismayed by his seeming lack of forcefulness in pushing his program before Congress. On the other hand, conservatives took the President's professions of New Dealism at face value, and transferred to the new Administration all the venom that Roosevelt had engendered among them earlier."[50]

The crucial factor of leadership is perhaps best understood by examining Truman's relationship with American liberalism.[51] If one simply compares the written records of Truman and Roosevelt, the liberal community should have loved the Missourian; on almost all issues, Truman was far in advance of FDR. As James MacGregor Burns and William E. Leuchtenburg have demonstrated, throughout the New Deal years

the uses and limitations of presidential power as used by Truman. Johnson, in *1600 Pennsylvania Avenue,* is also concerned with this elusive term of presidential leadership, and entitles a section of his book, "Failures of Leadership: Truman." Johnson argues that Truman "could not furnish the inspired leadership which convinced the public he was leading a just cause." (223–24) Johnson acknowledges that, "Nevertheless, he grew in the presidency," and especially in his conduct of foreign policy. But in domestic policy, in meeting the challenges of inflation, labor, McCarthyism, and social welfare needs, Truman's record failed to meet the high standards Johnson sets for greatness.

[50]Huthmacher, *Twentieth Century America,* 343.

[51]Every student of Truman's domestic policies should consult Hamby, "Harry S. Truman and American Liberalism, 1945–1948." Hamby bases his dissertation upon the important manuscript sources and demonstrates how Truman's career paralleled the decline of liberalism in 1945 and 1946 and its rebirth in the election of 1948. Hamby carefully delineates Truman's problems with American liberalism and shows how their problems frequently were intertwined. "Having relied so long upon the magic personality of Roosevelt, liberals could not identify with an unobtrusive party regular who was unable to present an appearance of forceful, independent progressive leadership. Truman's lack of Roosevelt's great qualities of leadership combined with a liberal failure to achieve a sense of personal identification with the President, and these elements formed the most persistent and important facet of the progressive alienation from the President. But, the liberal movement was forced to accept the Truman leadership and with the surprising victory of 1948, liberalism recovered from its previous setbacks. Truman's victory in 1948 was a magnificent personal triumph—and it was also a victory for the liberal movement. Progressivism had been on the verge of another period of fragmentation and futility; instead, Truman's election unified it and infused it with a new sense of purpose and determination. Once again, liberalism was on the offensive." (From the Introduction.)

Roosevelt frequently dragged his feet on social reform, labor, public works, relief, and housing legislation.[52] Roosevelt never stormed any barricades for such reforms as a minimum wage or social security, and only the determined efforts of congressional liberals, such as Robert F. Wagner, carried the day for liberalism. Even at the time of his death, the "broker state" concept still pervaded Roosevelt's Administration, and FDR had yet to formulate a well-defined plan for postwar reform.[53]

Truman, however, never demonstrated Roosevelt's tepidity toward social reform, but he also never enjoyed the luxury of a friendly Congress—indeed, even of a united party receptive to his social welfare policies. Truman lacked Roosevelt's charm, sophistication, and facility with the language. Unlike Roosevelt, Truman never appreciated ideas and intellectuals for their own sake, and he replaced the Rooseveltian rhetorical liberalism with a brand of hardheaded political activism that somehow struck the liberals as too cold, too coarse, and too matter-of-fact. Truman's bluntness did not compare favorably with Roosevelt's eloquence, nor could he excite the American people as had Theodore Roosevelt or infuse in them the moral fervor and resolution as had Wilson. "Alas for Truman," T. R. B. complained, "there is no bugle note in his voice; little evidence that he has shown of being able to lift and inspire the masses."[54]

Whereas Roosevelt's suave style camouflaged his essential conservatism, Truman's pragmatic liberalism only re-emphasized his middle-class and middle-western origins. The replacement of ardent New Dealers by the "Missouri Gang" completed the alienation of the liberal community. As the mediocre likes of John W. Snyder, Harry Vaughan, John Steelman, Robert Hannegan, and George Allen entered the inner circles of the White House and such liberal favorites as Harold Ickes, Henry Wallace, and Wilson Wyatt departed, liberals felt unappreciated and unwanted. T. R. B. complained that the new group

---

[52] James MacGregor Burns, *Roosevelt: The Lion and the Fox;* William E. Leuchtenburg, *Franklin D. Roosevelt and the New Deal, 1932–1940.*
[53] Hinchey, "The Frustration of the New Deal Revival," *passim.*
[54] *New Republic,* 113 (December 10, 1945), 797.

of advisers was "too humdrum and prosaic" and lamented that the "gay, audacious, erratic New Deal days ended with the war."[55]

Truman's personal commitment to furthering social welfare is beyond question, but his selection of key advisers raises several important questions. None of his White House advisers had held important positions in the New Deal, and few can accurately be described as enthusiastic liberals. Truman's close relationship with John W. Snyder, who had considerable influence upon economic policy, cannot be explained except on the basis of personal friendship, because Snyder's conservatism was notorious among liberals. The entire Truman Cabinet reflected an inexplicable aversion to liberals, and the exodus of New Dealers in 1945 and 1946 quickly resulted in a lackluster Cabinet. Frequently, the administration of important social welfare programs fell to persons not recognized for reformist zeal. Because presidential decisions are made upon the advice and information received, Truman's Cabinet and White House staff needs considerable study before we can resolve the inner contradiction of a reformist President choosing a group of advisers and Cabinet officers that was, at best, lukewarm to the extension of the New Deal.

The suspicious liberals, however, were always ready to believe the worst of the man who had replaced Henry Wallace on the Democratic ticket in 1944. Within two weeks after Truman took office, the *New Republic* expressed its fears about Truman's devotion to reform; especially, it fretted about the new President's political skills: "Has Mr. Truman the imagination, the daring, the sensitiveness to new currents of popular need and pressure, to continue the advance as President Roosevelt would presumably have continued it?"[56] Following the imbroglio over price controls in the autumn of 1945, T. R. B. decided that Truman did not. "The trouble here is that the Administration has merely taken off the brakes, and the nation is coasting down the steep hill to 'normalcy' under its own huge dead weight," he lamented.[57] Truman was

---

[55]*New Republic*, 113 (July 14, 1945), 77.
[56]"President Truman's Task," *New Republic*, 112 (April 23, 1945), 540.
[57]*New Republic*, 113 (December 10, 1945), 797.

proving to be, at best, "a well meaning man who does as well as he knows how,"[58] and this certainly was not sufficient.

The liberals' dissatisfaction with Truman, despite his strong advocacy of social reform, suggests that liberalism itself was beginning to undergo a significant transformation. The so-called "bread and butter" reforms that had distinguished the New Deal evoked far less response from American liberals in the postwar era, because they were now turning toward the fight for civil rights for the American Negro and to the preservation of civil liberties. Perhaps even more important is the decline of the antibusiness theme in American liberalism as the "mixed economy" of the postwar era quickly ended the threat of massive unemployment.

In their criticism of Truman's domestic record, the liberals failed to recognize that the ability to secure new legislative welfare programs lay beyond any President's normal powers. Tremendous obstacles blocked Truman. The times simply were not propitious for new reform measures. The war years had numbed the catalytic effect of the depression, and the economic boom that began in 1940 continued throughout the Truman years with but a minor interruption in 1949; consequently, few individuals could be convinced of the need for starting new departures in social reform. A postwar reaction against reform precluded the enactment of most new programs. Truman's urgent appeals to the public met with an indifferent yawn because the American people were more concerned with the price of hamburger and the scarcity of houses and automobiles than with social welfare legislation. The New Deal had already effected tremendous changes in the individual's relationship with the government, and no new departures seemed necessary. Full employment, abetted by considerable overtime pay, proved to be a soothing tranquilizer. Later in the Administration, the influence of Senator Joseph R. McCarthy succeeded in associating many reforms with subversion; if this were not a sufficient brake, after June 25, 1950, military expenditures forced an abandonment of any serious intentions of establishing new and costly programs.

---

[58]*New Republic*, 115 (September 9, 1946), 280.

If the mood of the nation provided a depleted soil upon which to sow the seeds of the Fair Deal, the composition of Congress only compounded Truman's problems. Ever since the congressional elections of 1938, Congress had been firmly controlled by a coalition of Southern Democrats and conservative Republicans.[59] Although one cannot be too precise in analyzing the structure of this conservative coalition, since its composition fluctuated on any given issue, its hard core reflected the attitudes of rural America.[60] Although the agricultural regions benefited from the social welfare programs, the bulk of the programs were oriented toward urban America. Because the ethos of a rural society normally tends to oppose change, the natural result was concerted opposition to the Truman social welfare policies. Despite its minority status in a now predominantly urban nation, rural America effectively controlled the congressional committee system. This coalition was most powerful in the House of Representatives; here the legislative gates were rendered inaccessible by the labyrinth of committees that had fallen to the conservatives through the workings of the seniority system. Truman's comprehensive housing bill, for example, passed the Senate in 1946 and 1948 (and would have passed in 1947 had it been brought to a vote), but the lower house never had the opportunity of voting on it. The Banking committee killed it in 1946, the Rules committee in 1948. Had the bill ever reached the House floor, a speedy passage was assured.[61] Stuck on dead center, Congress did not respond to Truman's program, but conversely, it could not retreat to the days of Calvin Coolidge either. As Samuel Lubell points out,

---

[59]James MacGregor Burns, *The Deadlock of Democracy; Four Party Politics in America.*

[60]Allan P. Grimes, *Equality in America,* 89–126. Grimes demonstrates that the demand for reform legislation in modern America has risen primarily from urban areas; his book implicitly supports the hypothesis of "urban liberalism" recently advanced by J. Joseph Huthmacher in "Urban Liberalism and the Age of Reform," *Mississippi Valley Historical Review,* 49 (October, 1962), 231–41. The importance of the rural-urban split over most reforms is incisively discussed by James T. Patterson, "A Conservative Coalition Forms in Congress, 1933–1939," *Journal of American History,* 52 (March, 1966), 757–72.

[61]Davies, *Housing Reform During the Truman Administration.*

Truman was forced to mark time.[62] In a time of congressional deadlock, Truman's Administration made two significant contributions to the American reform tradition: (1) the prevention of repeal of New Deal reforms, and (2) the strengthening of existing programs via vigorous executive action.

Students of American politics could profitably devote considerable attention to the four Congresses with which Truman had to work. The new research tools of the political scientists should be utilized, as well as the traditional research methods of the historian. David Truman provides us with some useful quantitative information about the Eighty-first Congress, but he leaves too many questions unanswered, primarily because he does not ask the questions of the political historian.[63] We need not only the institutional studies of Congress but also biographies of such congressional leaders as Robert A. Taft, Alben Barkley, Sam Rayburn, and Joseph Martin. The composition of the so-called "conservative coalition" needs detailed study as does the ineffectual liberal bloc.

Directly related to Truman's relationship with Congress are the structural changes occurring within the Presidency itself. Truman was the first President who was forced to conduct a "dual presidency." Due to the development of Russian intransigence in the postwar period and the resulting Cold War, Truman had to conduct, simultaneously, fully developed domestic and foreign policies. While he worked to extract from Congress new departures in social welfare, he also had to rely

---

[62]Samuel Lubell, *The Future of American Politics,* 9–28. Lubell's stimulating interpretation of the politics of the Truman era must be consulted by all students of the Truman Administration. Lubell's interpretation of Truman as a President who purposely refused to move off center in domestic legislation seems overdrawn and contrived, although thorough research has not yet tested this hypothesis. Lubell provides a good starting point for the study of the politics of the Truman era.

[63]Truman, *The Congressional Party.* Truman (no relation to the President) has amassed considerable statistical data pertaining to the institutional roles of party regularity, presidential congressional leadership, and the "division and cohesion" of voting blocs within the Congress. Unfortunately, he does not synthesize his data into general theses, nor does he consider the importance of pressure groups and public opinion. Above all, he fails to place his study within a solid historical context. His conclusions are based primarily upon the *Congressional Record,* congressional hearings, and published reports.

upon it for financial support for his new concept of America's role in world politics. The impact of his absorption with foreign policy undoubtedly affected adversely his domestic reform program, but no research has been conducted to support this hypothesis. In this regard, one speculative question stands out: Did Truman compromise on domestic policy in order to get congressional support for his dramatic new departures in foreign policy?

There was, however, one area in which Truman definitely did not compromise. This was housing reform, which provided an outstanding exception to the dull pattern of legislative stalemate and executive caretaking.[64] This singular success of a highly controversial program demonstrates that the congressional blockade was vulnerable to a reform that attracted widespread public support. The Fair Deal enjoyed a fleeting moment of legislative triumph when the Housing Act of 1949 was signed by a jubilant President. This act created the present slum clearance and urban redevelopment program and markedly expanded the existing public housing program. Truman's activity in housing reform illustrates his deep commitment to improved social conditions for the nation's poor. Beyond any doubt he desired to provide every American family with an opportunity of enjoying "decent" housing. Truman was deeply disturbed by the appalling discrepancy between the nation's affluence and the condition of the millions forced to live in slum housing. "A decent standard of housing for all is one of the irreducible obligations of modern civilization," he told Congress in 1945. "The people of the United States, so far ahead in wealth and productive capacity, deserve to be the

---

[64]Davies, *Housing Reform During the Truman Administration*. This study is based primarily upon the Truman Papers and several related manuscript collections in the National Archives, the Library of Congress, and other agencies. Attempting to fuse social and political history into a meaningful synthesis of Truman's many activities in housing reform, Davies places the Truman housing program into the context of the progressive-New Deal tradition. He argues that Truman's interest in housing stemmed from three sources: (1) a personal desire to aid the low-income family to enjoy "decent" housing; (2) the political necessity of keeping the Roosevelt urban coalition intact for the purpose of winning elections; and (3) the great public demand for immediate action to deal with the widespread postwar housing shortage and to halt the growth of urban slums.

best housed in the world. We must begin to meet the challenge at once."[65]

Truman used every available presidential power to force Congress into facing this challenge; finally, after four years of intense political infighting, Congress passed the comprehensive housing bill, cosponsored by three unusual political bedfellows: Robert F. Wagner, Robert A. Taft, and Allen J. Ellender.[66] The Truman Papers show the President's strong position on housing reform; this is corroborated by the public record. "For some reason," David D. Lloyd, a White House staff member, recalled in 1961, "Mr. Truman was hot on housing."[67] This presidential interest and action, while important, alone would not have jarred the housing bill loose from the tenacious clutches of the House leadership. Ultimately, a public demand for housing legislation, prompted by the postwar housing shortage, proved decisive. On most issues, Truman could arouse little public interest, but middle-class America, thoroughly irritated by the shortage of apartments and houses, created such a demand for congressional action that the bill finally was passed. Ironically, however, the Housing Act of 1949 was concerned with the slum dweller and not with the middle-class family seeking a nice place in which to live. Truman and his associates neatly transferred the middle-class pressure created by the shortage into an effective tool with which to secure public housing and slum clearance from a reluctant Congress.

Truman apparently fought equally hard for other major domestic reforms, but he did not receive sufficient public support. Quite possibly, he might have compromised to get crucial appropriations for his foreign policy. He fervently desired, it is quite obvious, to create a national compulsory health program that would ensure every American of adequate medical care, but he could not convince the Congress—or the American Medical Association—of the need for such a program. "I have never been able to understand all the fuss some people make

---

[65]Message on Reconversion, September 6, 1945, Truman Papers, PPF–200.
[66]Davies, *Housing Reform During the Truman Administration*. See also Richard O. Davies, " 'Mr. Republican' Turns 'Socialist': Robert A. Taft and Public Housing," *Ohio History*, 73 (Summer, 1964), 136–43.
[67]Interview with author, July 20, 1961.

about government wanting to do something to improve and protect the health of the people," he comments in his memoirs. "I have had some bitter disappointments as President, but the one that has troubled me most, in a personal way, has been the failure to defeat the organized opposition to a national compulsory health insurance program."[68]

Although Truman never enjoyed the pleasure of public support for most of his social welfare policies, he nonetheless plodded doggedly ahead. Setback was compounded by failure. His record with the Democratic Seventy-ninth Congress was dismal; only the watered-down Employment Act and the Veterans' Emergency Housing Act (which became a bureaucratic nightmare and failed miserably) interrupted a succession of rebuffs from Congress. Many observers expected him to soften his reform requests when the first Republican-controlled Congress in seventeen years convened in 1947, but Truman merely intensified his efforts and bombarded the Congress with special messages urging enactment of a wide assortment of social welfare programs.

Inevitably, as the presidential election approached, altruism fused with political expediency. The important connection between Truman's social welfare policies and political strategy is basic to the proper understanding of his re-election. Many individuals consider Truman's victory over Thomas E. Dewey the greatest upset in American presidential elections. Certainly, the external appearances create such an impression; two secessions—Henry Wallace to the left, J. Strom Thurmond to the right—wracked the Democratic party and ultimately deprived Truman of at least eighty-six electroal votes. Even within the remnant of the Democracy, a "dump Truman" movement fizzled, at least partially because an attractive candidate, such as Justice William O. Douglas or General Dwight D. Eisenhower, could not be secured. In Washington, Democrats arranged to sell their houses or allowed leases to expire as they faced the inevitable. Most ominous, however, was the rejuvenated Republican party that had selected an impressive ticket of Dewey and Earl Warren. Even Walter Lippmann publicly wondered

---

[68]Harry S. Truman, *Years of Trial and Hope*, 23.

if the nation could survive until January 20; smug Republicans could find precious little Truman money, even at three to one.[69]

But, somehow, Harry S Truman won. For the popular radio newscaster, H. V. Kaltenborn, the shock was simply too much. His dumbfounded commentary on election night perhaps best expressed the astonishment of the American people, who had been convinced by the press and pollsters that a Dewey victory was certain. Then there was, of course, that priceless headline of Colonel McCormick's overanxious *Chicago Tribune*, which announced, a bit too soon, the restoration of legitimacy.

Samuel Lubell has demonstrated, however, that a Dewey victory would have been the real upset.[70] Throughout the campaign a fundamental factor had been concealed: There were more Democrats than Republicans. Probably better than any other American, Truman realized the significance of this simple demographic fact. "I want to say to you at this time that during the next four years there will be a Democrat in the White House," he told a group of Young Democrats in May. "And you are looking at him."[71]

The rising crest of Republican confidence concealed Truman's shrewdly prepared plan for victory. The grand strategy was ingenious in its simplicity: Truman merely sought to maintain intact the Roosevelt coalition that had worked so effectively in 1940 and 1944.[72] Beyond any doubt, Truman established himself in the voters' minds as the inheritor of the Roosevelt mantle, and he did so by shaping his entire campaign around social welfare policies. In fact, he presented the major

[69]Jules Abels, *Out of the Jaws of Victory*, presents the only book-length study of the 1948 campaign. Its journalistic style and evident indignation at Dewey's lackluster campaign detract from its value. Although Abels has written a useful book, the history of this election based upon the original materials is yet to be written.

[70]Lubell, *The Future of American Politics*, 241–43.

[71]May 14, 1948, copy of address in Charles S. Murphy Files, Truman Papers.

[72]Samuel J. Eldersveld discusses the crucial factor of urban voting in "The Influence of Metropolitan Party Pluralities in Presidential Elections Since 1920: A Study of Twelve Key Cities," *The American Political Science Review*, 43 (December, 1949), 1189–1206. Coupled with Lubell, this essay provides a provocative interpretation that should stimulate research into the area of urban voting patterns during the postwar period.

issue as a referendum on the New Deal. Because his opposition lolled in the languid atmosphere of overconfidence, he was never effectively challenged as he accused *all* Republicans of being completely opposed to the New Deal. "The Republicans don't like the New Deal," he told an audience in Akron. "They never liked the New Deal, and they would like to get rid of it." The Republicans, he said, were hiding behind Dewey's "soothing syrup" and were "waiting eagerly for the time when they can go ahead with a Republican Congress and a Republican President and do a real hatchet job on the New Deal without interference."[73]

Truman actually began his campaign on January 7, 1948, when he informed the Eightieth Congress of the state of the Union.[74] In this politically inspired message, he called for a wide assortment of social reforms, the scope of which prompted the *Philadelphia Inquirer* to observe, "Truman leaves out practically nothing but the beatitudes and the Ten Commandments."[75] From this time forward, Truman cleverly coupled social welfare with the practical consideration of getting himself re-elected. Scarcely a week passed that he did not dispatch a special message to Congress on some reform program. Special messages on civil rights, housing, rent controls, medical care, price controls, social security, and education descended upon the Republican Congress, and he made frequent reference to these reforms during his press conferences.[76]

Truman clearly perceived the political importance of these reforms. If the Republican Congress should have passed any of his programs, then he would have been able to tell the voters about his legislative triumphs; but if it turned down his suggestions, as seemed most likely, then he could blame the Republican leadership in the Congress. No matter what Congress did, therefore, Truman stood to reap the political harvest. When the Senate, under the whip of presidential aspirant Robert A. Taft, passed the comprehensive housing bill,

---

[73]*Public Papers, 1948* (October 11), 743.

[74]*Public Papers, 1948* (January 7), 1–10.

[75]January 8, 1948, in State of the Union File, Democratic National Committee Files, Truman Library.

[76]*Public Papers, 1948*, 1–457, *passim.*

Truman fired off a memorandum to the Administrator of the Housing and Home Finance Agency: "We must make every effort now to see that the House passes an equally good bill." Cogently pointing up the political implications of this legislation, he wrote, "I know that we face strong opposition; but if this legislation should fail, we must at least be sure that the responsibility for its failure is placed where it belongs."[77]

To dramatize the issues he had been creating since January, Truman embarked on a two-week train trip to the Far West in early June. Ostensibly, he undertook the journey to receive an honorary degree from the University of California at Berkeley, but the political motives of what he called "this nonpartisan, bipartisan trip"[78] soon became apparent. This was to be a stridently partisan campaign excursion. For the first time, he attacked the Eightieth Congress in a concerted manner, as he unveiled his new, folksy, off-the-cuff speaking technique. In Gary, Indiana, he flailed the Congress for refusing to admit war refugees; at Grand Island, Nebraska, he promised to use a pair of spurs, just received from a local welcoming committee, on the Republican congressional leaders.[79] And so it went. As the trip progressed, the "new" Truman emerged—a confident, articulate, and highly effective speaker.

As his audiences increased in size and enthusiasm, he undoubtedly realized that his strategy of focusing his campaign upon social welfare policies was sound. By the time he reached the Coast, he was now hearing his audiences respond to his criticism of Congress with "Pour it on, Harry!" and "Give 'em hell, Harry!" to which he grinned and replied, "I'm going to, I'm going to." He told his track-side listeners, "This Congress is interested in the welfare of the better classes. They are not interested in the welfare of the common everyday man."[80] Repeatedly, the phrases "special interest Congress" and "do-nothing Congress" were sprinkled in his short speeches. On

---

[77]Truman to Raymond M. Foley, April 23, 1948, Truman Papers, OF 63.

[78]*Public Papers, 1948,* Rear Platform Remarks, Crestline, Ohio (June 3), 284.

[79]*Public Papers, 1948,* 286, 297.

[80]*Public Papers, 1948,* Informal Remarks, Bremerton, Washington (June 10), 314.

his return trip, he significantly pointed out that the basic issue of the ensuing campaign would be "special privilege against the interests of the people as a whole."[81] By the time the trip ended on June 18 in Baltimore, Truman had succeeded in directing the nation's attention to the conservative congressional wing of the Republican party. Thus, when the Republican Convention adopted a platform that endorsed the basic social welfare policies he had been urging upon Congress, the GOP leadership had exposed itself at its weakest point—the liberal-conservative split over domestic issues.

The Democratic faithful, however, had failed to recognize Truman's strategy; dissension riddled the party. Wallace had already abandoned ship, and what would become the Dixiecrat party stomped out of the national convention in Philadelphia in protest over a strong civil rights plank in the platform.[82] The apathetic center that remained perfunctorily renominated Truman.

The President realized the precarious position of his party and attempted to instill new life into it with his acceptance speech. This exciting address proved to be one of the most significant and probably the most effective of his entire political career. Speaking before a benumbed convention at 2 A.M., he accepted the nomination few Democrats really wanted him to have and ridiculed the obvious disparity between the Republican platform and the record of "the worst" Eightieth Congress. On each of his social welfare policies, he pointed out, the Congress had refused to act, and yet, the GOP platform endorsed essentially the same program. "There is a long list of these promises in that Republican platform," he told a suddenly enthusiastic convention. "I have discussed a number of these failures of the Republican 80th Congress. Every one of them is important."[83] Because the Republican Convention had essentially endorsed the Truman social welfare pro-

---

81*Public Papers, 1948,* 314, 317, 356.

82See Karl M. Schmidt, *Henry A. Wallace: Quixotic Crusade,* for a discussion of the Progressive party of 1948. V. O. Key, Jr., *Southern Politics in State and Nation,* 329–44, contains the best discussion of the Dixiecrat movement.

83*Public Papers, 1948* (July 15), 409.

gram, he excited his audience with the announcement that he was going to give the Republican-controlled Congress the opportunity to enact its party's platform so that the voters could be certain that the Republican platform was a sincere pledge. "On the 26th day of July, which out in Missouri we call 'Turnip Day,' I am going to call Congress back and ask them to pass laws to halt rising prices, to meet the housing crisis— which they say they are for in their platform," Truman said. At the same time, he announced, Congress would have the opportunity of enacting his entire social reform program, which had been adopted by the Republican Convention.[84] Truman then hammered home his major point: "Now my friends, if there is any reality behind this Republican platform, we ought to get some action from a short session of the 80th Congress. They can do the job in fifteen days, if they want to. . . . Now what that worst 80th Congress does in the special session will be the test."[85]

The Turnip Day strategy proved more than successful; the Republicans stormed and sputtered, spent most of the two weeks bickering among themselves in the heat and humidity of a typical Washington summer, and adjourned without passing any significant legislation.[86] Truman's dramatic call for a special session had exposed a deep division within his opposition's ranks and, most important, had forcefully demonstrated that the Republican congressional delegation was not disposed to honor most of its party's campaign pledges.

The actual campaign was anticlimactic. By Labor Day Truman had shaped the issues to his own advantage, and Governor Dewey, aware of the embarrassing split within his own party and probably mesmerized by the predictions of his inevitable victory, failed to respond to Truman's charges, let alone take the offensive himself. Instead, Dewey contented himself by

---

[84]*Public Papers, 1948* (July 15), 410.

[85]*Public Papers, 1948* (July 15), 410.

[86]For a brief but workmanlike discussion of the special session of Congress, see R. Alton Lee, "The Turnip Session of the Do-Nothing Congress: Presidential Campaign Strategy," *The Southwestern Social Science Quarterly,* 44 (December, 1963), 256–67.

taking the "high road" and, consequently, never attacked Truman's vulnerable flanks.

Truman devoted almost every one of his 354 campaign speeches to social welfare policies; significantly, he concentrated his attention upon the Republican congressional leadership and not on his opponent. In making fallacious but politically useful connections between Dewey and the Republican right wing, Truman affirmed that the Eightieth Congress was "merely a symbol and instrument of Republican Party policy."[87] When he was not busy attacking the "Tafts and Tabers" and the "do-nothing Congress," he was reinforcing his own image as that of the inheritor of the New Deal tradition. Truman gave few speeches in which he failed to mention the magic name of Franklin D. Roosevelt. He repeatedly emphasized that the underlying issue of the election was "to preserve the gains made since 1933 when President Roosevelt took office." Time and again he returned to this central theme: "The Democratic Party gave the country a New Deal. And that New Deal paid off too. It was good for the country. It was good for labor. It was good for the farmer. It was good for every citizen in the United States." He warned, "These Republicans would like to turn back the clock" and restore the "boom and bust" policies of Harding, Coolidge, and Hoover. The Eighieth Congress, he charged, "repeatedly flouted the will of the people," and he warned that a Dewey victory would "deliver this country into the hands of the special interests and big business." In short, "The record of the Republican Party is a story of obstruction, objection, and reaction from the days of the Hoover depression to the end of the 80th Congress."[88] In contrast to this dismal situation, Truman pictured in Roosevelt and the New Deal the essential spirit of the American Way of Life: "The Democratic Party represents the people. It is pledged to work for agriculture. It is pledged to work for labor. It is pledged to work for the small businessman and the white collar worker." Getting to the crux of the matter, "The Democratic Party puts human rights and human welfare first."[89]

[87] *Public Papers, 1948* (October 8), 721.
[88] *Public Papers, 1948*, 695, 697, 731, 735, 851, 853.
[89] *Public Papers, 1948*, 505.

Truman's ten-month campaign, therefore, was exceedingly liberal in content, but equally conservative in purpose—liberal in the vast assortment of social welfare policies advocated, but conservative in that Truman sought primarily to hold intact the social service state erected by the New Deal and also to preserve for his own political advantage the support of the Roosevelt coalition.[90]

A scholarly assessment of the election of 1948, however, has not been written. While we know a great deal from the published sources and from Jules Abels' popular study, significant questions are yet to be answered. Why, for example, was the total vote in 1948 relatively small in relationship to eligible voters? Did the Wallace movement really serve as a "lightning rod" and prevent a "soft on communism" charge from being made against Truman? Similarly, did the Thurmond candidacy remove the stigma of racism from the Democratic party and thus help it in the northern states? What was the actual composition of the Dixiecrat party, and how did this dissident movement affect the final result of the election? Why did Dewey refuse to attack the Truman record? Finally, did the voters re-elect Truman because of a conservative motivation to preserve the New Deal from possible Republican repeal, or did foreign policy, which was scarcely mentioned throughout the campaign, play a hidden but crucial role in determining voter preference? One thing is quite evident, however. This was the last presidential election to be based primarily upon the rhetoric of domestic reform; by 1952 foreign policy clearly became the vital concern of most voters.

The election, however, did not diminish the power of the conservative coalition in the Congress. When the Democratic Eighty-first Congress met, Truman proved unable to transfer his popularity with the voters into success with his legislative program. Except for the Housing Act of 1949, Congress rejected outright his other controversial proposals. This same congressional bloc was to remain intact and later was to stifle

---

[90]For a discussion of one aspect of Truman's campaign, see Richard O. Davies, "Whistle-Stopping Through Ohio," *Ohio History,* 71 (July, 1962), 113–23.

the New Frontier. Not until the combination of *Baker v. Carr* (1962) and the 1964 Republican debacle would the congressional log jam be broken and a new flood of social welfare legislation stream off Capitol Hill.

This essay has focused primary attention upon the activities of the Truman Administration, but two significant developments in the realm of social welfare occurred during the Truman period that are only indirectly connected to the action of the Administration. They require, however, some consideration in an essay of this nature. The first of these is the general acceptance by the American people of the permanency of the social service state. Most liberals expected a concerted effort by conservatives in the immediate postwar period to eradicate the New Deal—but this movement never gained sufficient momentum. The near-complete acceptance of the social service state needs examination, especially on the local and state level. The factors contributing to this fundamental change in the American mind have never been studied in any systematic manner.

Another important development was the professionalization of social welfare. During the progressive era and the 1920's, social reforms originated primarily from within private reform organizations. Even during the New Deal, the impetus for many reforms came from outside of government. As the New Deal established new social welfare agencies, however, the reformers frequently assumed positions administering the various programs. Thus, by the time Truman took office, the demand for reform came, not from private reform groups, but increasingly from within various federal agencies. The growth of the professionalization of social welfare and the institutionalization of reform seemingly culminated with the establishment of the Department of Health, Education and Welfare in 1953 and the Department of Housing and Urban Development in 1965. These important changes in social service and social reform need careful research.

Harry S Truman left office, as he had entered, during a period of political deadlock. He had, however, preserved the social welfare programs of the New Deal and, through strong executive action and some enabling legislation, strengthened considerably many existing programs. His determined action would prove to be decisive in preserving the New Deal and in providing the critical bridge to the remarkably successful Great Society legislative program of Lyndon B. Johnson. Circumstances prevented Truman from establishing many new, exciting reform programs, but in a time of public indifference and political stalemate, he labored to provide the American people with his conception of a Fair Deal. The significance of these efforts should not be allowed to go unnoticed, or unappreciated, by the historians of the Truman Administration.

Bibliography
Books

Abels, Jules, *Out of the Jaws of Victory.* New York, Holt, Rinehart, and Winston, Inc., 1959.

Bailey, Stephen K., *Congress Makes a Law.* New York, Columbia University Press, 1950.

Burns, James MacGregor, *The Deadlock of Democracy: Four Party Politics in America.* Englewood Cliffs, Prentice-Hall, Inc., 1963.

————, *Roosevelt: The Lion and the Fox.* New York, Harcourt, Brace and World, Inc., 1956.

Cochran, Thomas C., *The American Business System: A Historical Perspective, 1900–1955.* Cambridge, Harvard University Press, 1957.

Commager, Henry Steele, *The American Mind.* New Haven, Yale University Press, 1950.

Daniels, Jonathan, *The Man of Independence.* Philadelphia, J. B. Lippincott Company, 1950.

Davies, Richard O., *Housing Reform During the Truman Administration.* Columbia, University of Missouri Press, 1966.

Einaudi, Mario, *The Roosevelt Revolution.* New York, Harcourt, Brace and World, Inc., 1959.

Goldman, Eric F., *The Crucial Decade and After, America 1945–1960.* New York, Vintage Books, 1960.

————, *Rendezvous with Destiny.* New York, Vintage Books, 1960.

Grimes, Alan P., *Equality in America.* New York, Oxford University Press, Inc., 1964.

Hays, Samuel P., *The Response to Industrialism, 1885–1914.* Chicago, University of Chicago Press, 1957.

Hofstadter, Richard, *The Age of Reform.* New York, Alfred A. Knopf, Inc., 1955.

Huthmacher, J. Joseph, *Twentieth Century America: An Interpretation with Readings.* Boston, Allyn and Bacon, Inc., 1966.

Johnson, Walter, *1600 Pennsylvania Avenue: Presidents and the People Since 1929.* Boston, Little, Brown and Co., 1960.

Key, V. O., Jr., *Southern Politics in State and Nation.* New York, Vintage Books, 1964.

Leuchtenburg, William E., *Franklin D. Roosevelt and the New Deal, 1932–1940.* New York, Harper and Row, Publishers, 1963.

Link, Arthur S., *American Epoch: A History of the United States Since the Late 1890's.* New York, Alfred A. Knopf, Inc., 1959.

Lubell, Samuel, *The Future of American Politics.* Garden City, N. Y., Doubleday & Company, Inc., 1955.

Madison, Charles A., *Leaders and Liberals in 20th Century America.* New York, Frederick Ungar Publishing Co., Inc., 1961.

Martin, Joseph W., *My First Fifty Years in Politics.* New York, McGraw-Hill, Inc., 1961.

Neustadt, Richard E., *Presidential Power: the Politics of Leadership.* New York, John Wiley & Sons, Inc., 1960.

Nye, Russell B., *Midwestern Progressive Politics.* East Lansing, The Michigan State University Press, 1950.

Parkes, Henry B., and Vincent P. Carosso, *Recent America, A History Since 1933.* New York, Thomas Y. Crowell Company, 1963.

Schmidt, Karl M., *Henry A. Wallace: Quixotic Crusade.* Syracuse, Syracuse University Press, 1960.

Shannon, David A., *Twentieth Century America.* Chicago, Rand McNally & Co., 1963.

Steinberg, Alfred, *The Man from Missouri: The Life and Times of Harry S. Truman.* New York, G. H. Putnam's Sons, 1962.

Truman, David B., *The Congressional Party: A Case Study.* New York, John Wiley & Sons, Inc., 1959.

Truman, Harry S., *Memoirs.* Garden City, N. Y., Doubleday & Company, Inc., 1955, 1956. 2 vols.

Young, Roland A., *Congressional Politics in the Second World War.* New York, Columbia University Press, 1956.

Public Documents

Rosenman, Samuel I., ed., *The Public Papers and Addresses of Franklin D. Roosevelt.* New York, Harper & Brothers, 1950. 4 vols.

Public Papers of the Presidents, Harry S. Truman, 1946, 1948, 1949. Washington, D. C., Government Printing Office, 1962, 1964.

Articles

Albjerg, Victor, "Truman and Eisenhower: Their Administrations and Campaigns." *Current History,* 47 (October, 1964), 221–28.

Davies, Richard O., " 'Mr. Republican' Turns 'Socialist': Robert A. Taft and Public Housing." *Ohio History,* 73 (Summer, 1964), 136–43.
———, "Whistle-Stopping Through Ohio." *Ohio History,* 71 (July, 1962), 113–23.
Eldersveld, Samuel J., "The Influence of Metropolitan Party Pluralities in Presidential Elections Since 1920: A Study of Twelve Key Cities." *The American Political Science Review,* 43 (December, 1949), 1189–1206.
Huthmacher, J. Joseph, "Urban Liberalism and the Age of Reform." *Mississippi Valley Historical Review,* 49 (October, 1962), 231–41.
Koenig, Louis W., "Truman's Global Leadership." *Current History,* 38 (October, 1960), 227.
Kirkendall, Richard S., "The Great Depression: Another Watershed in American History." In John Braeman, Robert H. Bremner, and Everett Walters, eds., *Change and Continuity in Twentieth Century America.* Columbus, Ohio State University Press, 1964.
Lee, R. Alton, "The Turnip Session of the Do-Nothing Congress: Presidential Campaign Strategy." *The Southwestern Social Science Quarterly,* 44 (December, 1963), 256–67.
Merriam, Charles E., "The National Resources Planning Board: A Chapter in American Planning Experience." *American Political Science Review,* 38 (December, 1944), 1075–88.
Neustadt, Richard E., "Congress and the Fair Deal: A Legislative Balance Sheet." *Public Policy,* 5 (1954), 351–81.
Patterson, James T., "A Conservative Coalition Forms in Congress, 1933–1939." *Journal of American History,* 52 (March, 1966), 757–72.

Unpublished Studies

Dorsett, Lyle W., "A History of the Pendergast Machine." Ph.D. dissertation, University of Missouri, 1965.
Hamby, Alonzo L., "Harry S. Truman and American Liberalism, 1945–1948." Ph.D. dissertation, University of Missouri, 1965.
Hinchey, Mary H., "The Frustration of the New Deal Revival, 1944–1946." Ph.D. dissertation, University of Missouri, 1965.
Schmidtlein, Eugene F., "Truman the Senator." Ph.D. dissertation, University of Missouri, 1962.

Newspapers and Periodicals

Chicago Tribune, November 3, 1948.
New Republic, 112 (April 23, 1945), 540; (May 7, 1945), 635–38; (June 18, 1945), 843.
———, 113 (July 14, 1945), 77; (December 10, 1945), 797.
———, 114 (April 15, 1946), 523.
———, 115 (September 9, 1946), 280.

Manuscript Collections

Democratic National Committee Records. Truman Library, Independence, Missouri.

Charles S. Murphy. Truman Library, Independence, Missouri.

Franklin D. Roosevelt. Roosevelt Library, Hyde Park, New York.

Samuel I. Rosenman. Truman Library, Independence, Missouri.

Harry S. Truman. Truman Library, Independence, Missouri.

Interview

David D. Lloyd. July 20, 1961.

Civil Rights and Civil Liberties

✦

WILLIAM C. BERMAN

THE PURPOSE OF THIS PAPER is to survey the Truman Administration's actions in the area of civil rights and civil liberties, to review the more significant works dealing with those actions, and to suggest possible research projects designed to expand our existing knowledge and to deepen our understanding of how the Truman Administration helped to shape the institutional patterns of postwar American society and politics.

At the outset I should say that I do not believe civil rights and civil liberties are identical or that they deal with or relate to the same set of problems or conditions. *Civil rights*, to put it simply, pertain to the quest for and the realization of equality of treatment and opportunity, whether in the field of housing, education, employment, or the ballot. Those rights are guaranteed by the Thirteenth, Fourteenth, Fifteenth, and Twenty-fourth amendments of the Constitution of the United States, plus various statutes passed by Congress and some state legislatures. *Civil liberties* cover, among other things, freedom of speech and the right of political dissent and protest. The First Amendment of the Constitution of the United States provides civil liberties with whatever legitimacy and historical respectability they have had as part of the American heritage and experience.

The death of Franklin Roosevelt and the onset of the Cold War ushered in a new era in the history of civil rights and civil liberties in America. It was the fate of the Truman Administration to have to cope with complex political and legal problems created by the surfacing of civil rights and civil liberties issues. The Administration moved on both fronts and in a direction and on a scale for which there were few precedents. From 1945 to 1953 the White House gave moral support and qualified political backing to spokesmen of equality in American life. But, especially after the *Amerasia* and Canadian spy cases, the Administration also yielded ground to domestic critics who demanded a broad governmental program to deal with possible subversion and disloyalty in federal ranks. Thus, the Truman Administration inadvertently let loose the Yahoos, and it was victimized by its own efforts to contain them.

Turning first to the matter of civil rights: My research leads me to conclude that the Truman Administration opened the doors of Freedom House for the American Negro.[1] That this was a remarkable development can best be illustrated by noting what progress was achieved in the Roosevelt years. In an unpublished doctoral dissertation, "The Negro and the New Deal," Allen Kifer has documented the thesis that little was accomplished in terms of a constructive break-through in civil rights from 1933 to 1941.[2] During this period Roosevelt was not interested in the Negro problem per se, and his Administration had no over-all commitment to civil rights. Frank Freidel observes in *F.D.R. and the South* that Roosevelt treated the issue with circumspection so as to prevent a rupture with Democrats from Dixie whose votes he needed in Congress.[3] After all, men like Theodore Bilbo and John Rankin of Mississippi were vociferous supporters of the New Deal.

President Roosevelt's first significant commitment to civil rights came in 1941. In response to mounting Negro pressure

[1]William C. Berman, "The Politics of Civil Rights in the Truman Administration."

[2]Allen Kifer, "The Negro and the New Deal."

[3]Frank Freidel, *F.D.R. and the South*, 71–102.

he issued Executive Order 8802 creating a Federal Fair Employment Practices Commission. Herbert Garfinkel's *When Negroes March* tells the dramatic story of how A. Philip Randolph threatened to bring 100,000 Negroes to Washington if the President resisted his request for prompt White House action to end discrimination in defense work.[4] The symbolic value of the order cannot be overestimated. Negro leaders, sensing for the first time the possibilities of power, were determined to press their fight against Jim Crow and discrimination in American life. Organization and the ballot could win them a place at the table where Madisonian realists played the game of interest politics in the traditional American way: Those who have are heard. Thus, during and after World War II there would be agitation for greater federal recognition of and support for Negro demands.

That those demands would be heard after 1945 by the occupant of the White House was due in part to changes taking place in American society. Negroes were becoming politically visible in the large urban communities of the North and of the Far West. A great internal migration, in progress for twenty years before 1945, was swelling the numbers of Negroes in the ghettos of Los Angeles, New York, Chicago, Cleveland, and Detroit. Translation of urban census statistics into political terms indicated that these potential voters could play a significant role in determining the outcome of future elections, especially on the national level. This thesis was advanced by Henry Lee Moon in *Balance of Power: The Negro Vote,* a book published on the eve of the 1948 presidential election.[5] Moon's work, which gave an accurate accounting of the Negroes' rise to national political prominence, was also a call to arms. The strategy was simple: The ballot could be used by Negroes to obtain reform and progress in race relations, and that party which proved most responsive would be the beneficiary of an important bloc vote.

Before discussing how President Truman sought and won that vote, it would be useful to examine first his relations with

---

[4]Herbert Garfinkel, *When Negroes March,* 27.
[5]Henry Lee Moon, *Balance of Power: The Negro Vote.*

the Democratic party. Such a study might explain how difficult it was for him to champion the cause of civil rights and why, eventually, he had no choice but to do so. Comfortable with the New Deal, yet at home with the South, Truman represented the centrist faction of the Democratic party, which included Sam Rayburn, Fred Vinson, Tom Clark, and Alben Barkley. This dual political presonality made him acceptable to Franklin Roosevelt and to the Democratic National Convention as the party's vice-presidential nominee in 1944 in lieu of Henry Wallace or James F. Byrnes. When Truman became President he was immediately pulled by the party's two ideological and political magnets, the liberal North and conservative Dixie. Inclined to go South, but needing the votes of the North, Truman stayed at dead center—using liberal rhetoric to compensate for lack of political motion. Samuel Lubell develops this theme in *The Future of American Politics.*[6] The need for a systematic analysis of the internal structure of the Democratic party of the 1940's continues, with attention directed to the formation and function of this centrist faction, which Truman represented.

President Truman's skill in political maneuvering was shown in 1945 and 1946 during debate in Congress over establishment of a permanent FEPC. As suggested by Louis Ruchames in *Race, Jobs, and Politics,* the President gave formal backing to the proponents of permanent FEPC legislation but did nothing to antagonize the bill's opponents. Rhetorical gestures would serve until such time as the Administration should be forced to support words with some kind of action.[7]

A series of racial murders that occurred in the South during the spring and summer of 1946 created political pressure that Truman could not ignore. As related by Walter White in *A Man Called White,* a group of nationally prominent liberals met with the President in September, 1946, to protest the murders.[8] To placate them Truman promised to establish a committee to investigate federal, state, and local law enforcement procedures and to recommend ways of strengthening "cur-

[6]Samuel Lubell, *The Future of American Politics,* 37–39.
[7]Louis Ruchames, *Race, Jobs, and Politics,* 126.
[8]Walter White, *A Man Called White,* 331–32.

rent law enforcement measures . . . to safeguard the civil rights of the people.'"[9] The Truman Civil Rights Committee, modeled after the famous Wickersham Commission of the Hoover Administration, was established by Executive Order 9808, December 5, 1946.

On October 29, 1947, after an exhaustive examination of all aspects of racial discrimination in America, the committee turned over to Truman its report, *To Secure These Rights*.[10] The report proved to be a political bomb, which had to be either defused or detonated. In calling for a massive federal attack on segregation, *To Secure These Rights* probably went far beyond what the President had wanted in 1946. It put him on the spot, because to ignore it would be politically dangerous but to endorse its recommendations without qualification would be equally foolhardy. How to retain the loyalty of the South and yet avoid alienating Negro voters of the North was the question Truman and his advisers had to resolve. A battle royal must have taken place in the upper echelons of the Administration between those who favored action and those who wanted to pigeonhole the report. Apparently, the views of Clark Clifford, Truman's leading adviser, prevailed: The report's recommendations (or some of them) were incorporated in a message the President sent to Congress on February 2, 1948.[11] In *Brothers Under the Skin*, Carey McWilliams suggests that Henry Wallace's announced intention of seeking the Presidency on a third-party ticket spurred the Administration into reaching its decision.[12] A careful study of how and by whom that decision was actually made is eagerly awaited.

Truman's recommendations for legislative action in the message of February, 1948, were promptly ignored. Sparks flew from the South, however, and soon Dixie was ablaze with rebellion. In due time a third-party movement was organized, and in November the Dixiecrats won a million votes for a lost

---

[9]The President's Committee on Civil Rights, *To Secure These Rights*, 7–9.

[10]The President's Committee on Civil Rights, *To Secure These Rights*, 7–9.

[11]U. S., *Congressional Record*, 80th Cong., 2d Sess., 1948, 94, Part 1, 928–29.

[12]Carey McWilliams, *Brothers Under the Skin*, 44.

cause. This aspect of the story has been handled by V. O. Key, Jr., in *Southern Politics in State and Nation.*[13]Perhaps there are other questions still to be asked about this episode: How did the Southern centrists, such as Governor Gregg S. Cherry of North Carolina, contain the rebellion? and What cooperation did they receive from the White House to dampen the flames? Seen from this perspective, there is possibly a need for a fresh review of Southern politics. Such a study might throw additional light on the role played by the centrist faction of the national party in keeping the organization intact despite losses on either flank.

The Democrats held their nominating convention in July of 1948, at which time the liberals, led by Hubert Humphrey, had their turn at rebellion. They were angry over the Administration's refusal to endorse a strong plank on civil rights, and they were determined to write one into the party platform even if it necessitated a fight on the floor.[14] The fight took place, and the liberals emerged victorious, causing a partial Southern bolt. Now, the Democratic party faced the prospect of battling three other political organizations for control of the White House and the Congress.

Once the campaign was on, it was essential for President Truman to give further evidence of his sincerity and good will on the civil rights question. He did so by issuing two executive orders, on July 26, 1948. The first, Executive Order 9980, called for the ending of discrimination in governmental hiring practices; the second, Executive Order 9981, prepared the way for eventual desegregation of the armed services. There was much opposition from Pentagon officials to the desegregation order, but in time it was executed and implemented. That this order marked a real departure from tradition was confirmed by Lee Nichols in *Breakthrough on the Color Front,* an account of events in the armed forces from 1948, when the executive order was issued, to 1954, when the book was published.[15] The caste system and patterns of racial discrimination had been effec-

---

[13]V. O. Key, Jr., *Southern Politics in State and Nation,* 335–45.
[14]Clifford Brock, *Americans for Democratic Action,* 97.
[15]Lee Nichols, *Breakthrough on the Color Front.*

tively challenged in one vital sector of American society. It is to Truman's credit that this challenge was posed. Politics and morality had merged—and, in this case, justice resulted.

From September to November of 1948 the President worked hard for votes. Running against the record of the Eightieth Congress, Truman set out to vanquish Governor Thomas Dewey of New York, whose civil rights record was respectable by the standards of the 1940's. On Election Day the incumbent fooled everyone but himself and Leslie Biffle. In retrospect, we can see that the Negro vote augmented Truman's chances, for it provided him with his margin of victory in such key states as Ohio, Illinois, and California. This election was clear demonstration that the politics of civil rights had become institutionalized on the national level. Negroes had at last crossed the threshold of influence.

An amusing account of the campaign from the point of view of a disgruntled Deweyite can be found in Jules Abels' *Out of the Jaws of Victory*.[16] An analysis of the reasons and forces behind Truman's success is to be found in Lubell's *The Future of American Politics*.[17] An explanation of how damaging the lack of Negro support had been to the Republican cause is contained in an article, "Does the Republican Party Want the Negro Vote?" written by Arnold Aronson and Samuel Spiegler for the December, 1949, issue of *The Crisis*, the monthly journal of the National Association for the Advancement of Colored People.[18] However useful these works are in assessing the great Democratic victory of 1948, they lack the specificity of historical scholarship. This situation will not be changed until the major papers of the leading participants of that Democratic campaign are made available to students and scholars of the period.

After the election, liberals expected that the White House and the new Democratic Eighty-first Congress, working together, would produce needed social change. They contem-

---

[16]Jules Abels, *Out of the Jaws of Victory*.
[17]Lubell, *The Future of American Politics*.
[18]Arnold Aronson and Samuel Spiegler, "Does the Republican Party Want the Negro Vote?" *The Crisis*, 56 (December, 1949), 364–68.

plated successful legislative action on civil rights now that the Fair Deal had endorsed a new deal for American Negroes. During 1949, for at least two reasons the White House deepened its commitment to the cause of civil rights: One, during the campaign President Truman had made promises to Negroes that he could not repudiate; two, the Cold War had become the dominant fact of international politics. For reasons of state it was necessary to combat the Soviet charge that America was a monolithic racist society.

Yet, notwithstanding the liberal upsurge of 1948, the main line of resistance to any political break-through was Congress. The informal conservative coalition of Southern Democrats and Northern Republicans remained powerful enough to hamstring and block all efforts to put new civil laws on the statute books. To emphasize the strength of the coalition, the Senate, confirmed in its prejudices and traditions, refused to liberalize its rule governing filibusters. Without a substantive change in Rule 22 all hopes of getting a meaningful civil rights program through the Eighty-first Congress would be permanently dashed. Faced with the prospect of inevitable defeat on civil rights, but unwilling to court the opposition of allied Negro and white liberal organizations, the President submitted a comprehensive civil rights program to Congress in 1949. Politicians on both sides of the question played their prescribed roles; for a year or so the debate waxed furious. Finally, with the advent of the Korean War, Congress simply shelved the Truman recommendations.[19]

President Truman's failure to get congressional action on civil rights was an extreme example of the legislative heave-ho Congress gave to many of his Fair Deal programs. Apparently the results of the 1948 election had been nullified by a Congress that was in no mood for serious work. James M. Burns has provided students of recent American history and politics with a useful matrix in which to place a discussion of why the executive-legislative impasse developed in the American political system. His book, *Deadlock of Democracy,* is a skillful diagnosis of what ailed the national government from the

---

[19]Berman, "The Politics of Civil Rights," 161.

1940's to the mid-1960's.[20] What is needed, however, is a detailed analysis of the organization and of the composition of the Democratic party in Congress, stressing the role played by Speaker of the House Sam Rayburn and other brokers of power, who may have blunted proposed liberal legislation to avoid a dangerous feud within the party. A close review of the civil rights fight in the Eighty-first Congress might reveal more than the distribution of the votes: why they took one configuration or another. To reiterate a point already made, such a study could conceivably illuminate the role of the centrist faction of the party in preserving the outlines of harmony and cooperation within the party organization itself. A starting point for any student of the problem would be Congressman Richard Bolling's *House Out of Order*.[21]

Obstructed for one reason or another in Congress, the Administration adopted other techniques to push ahead on the civil rights front. Utilizing administrative remedies, the White House inched along the relatively unexplored and unused highway of executive equity. This tactic has been succinctly discussed and analyzed by Richard Longaker in *The President and Individual Liberties*.[22] Longaker's thesis is that the powers inhering in the office of the Presidency were tapped to cope with a number of civil rights problems that otherwise might have been ignored. The awesome expansion of presidential power resulting from the depression of the 1930's and World War II made it possible for the Chief Executive to meet a current problem without always having to answer to Congress. For example, he could, if he had the will and the proper administrative assistants on whom he could depend for advice and the appropriate follow-through, initiate steps to mitigate or eliminate discrimination in the federal employment practices. Here was, in the administrative realm, an interstitial area where political and party considerations did not necessarily intrude.

The Truman Administration was blessed with a number of thoughtful, hard-working administrative assistants, such as

---

[20]James M. Burns, *Deadlock of Democracy*.
[21]Richard Bolling, *House Out of Order*.
[22]Richard Longaker, *The President and Individual Liberties*, 73–171.

Philleo Nash and Stephen Spingarn, who, operating apparently with the President's sanction, did what they could to enlarge the government's responsibilities in the area of civil rights. Complementing the work of the White House staff were the departments of Defense, Interior, and Justice. The Defense Department was in the process of abolishing a segregated military establishment; the Interior Department worked to integrate its facilities, especially in Washington, D. C.; but far the most significant and important, in terms of long-range effects, was the contribution of the Justice Department, specifically of the Solicitor General's Office and the Civil Rights Bureau. Between 1947 and 1953 the Justice Department assumed the role of *amicus curiae* in certain civil rights cases that had been accepted for adjudication by the Supreme Court. The mere fact that the federal government had acted in that capacity represented a radical departure from earlier policy, and this action occurred at a time when the Court's position on civil rights seemed to be more fluid and less doctrinaire than ever before.

As Robert Harris notes in *Quest for Equality,* the Supreme Court in the 1930's was already beginning to revitalize the equal-protection clause of the Fourteenth Amendment.[23] By the late 1940's it had broadened even more its opposition to legal discrimination, as was illustrated in the case of *Shelly v. Kramer.* This case raised the question of whether a restrictive housing covenant written into a property holder's title was legally binding.[24] In May, 1948, the Court declared that restrictive housing covenants were discriminatory in character and nonenforceable in federal courts. Earlier, in December, 1947, the Justice Department submitted an *amicus curiae* brief to the Court, requesting adjudication of the case and asking for legal condemnation of restrictive housing covenants.[25] The subsequent Court decision may have been influenced by this brief. In any event, the department's action was an important precedent in the legal battle against discrimination in Ameri-

---

[23]Robert Harris, *The Quest For Equality,* 109–67.
[24]Charles Abrams, *Forbidden Neighbors: A Study of Prejudice in Housing,* 220.
[25]Tom C. Clark and Philip B. Perlman, *Prejudice and Property.*

can life. The questions remain, Why was the Shelly brief filed with the Court? and What was the authorization for such action? A background examination of this brief could possibly illuminate the nexus between political necessity and the quest for legal equality.

That the *amicus curiae* brief was now included as a major weapon in the government's arsenal was made clear in 1950 when the Justice Department filed two additional briefs with the Supreme Court in the cases of *McLaurin v. Oklahoma* and *Sweatt v. Painter*. They contained a request that the Court repudiate the *Plessy–Ferguson* doctrine; in short, the government advocated a revolutionary break-through in race relations law. The Court, however, refused to resolve these cases within a broad constitutional context, but, in June, 1950, provided substantial relief to those citizens who had petitioned it. In *Desegregation and the Law*, Albert P. Blaustein and Clarence C. Ferguson, Jr., point out how these decisions established the appropriate legal climate for the Court's action in the case of *Brown v. Board of Education*.[26]

While members of his Administration grappled with the administrative complexities of the civil rights issue, President Truman confronted the realities of the political world, which was fraught with conflict and turmoil. Korea, McCarthyism, and charges of corruption had diminished the popular appeal of his Fair Deal program. As long as he remained in the White House, however, Truman used his power to shape party policy and to help select the party's presidential nominee for the 1952 campaign.

The Democratic party was in trouble in 1952. In addition to the external opposition, further internal division over the civil rights issue continued as a strong possibility. At the 1952 convention that issue, volatile as ever, reappeared in the guise of a controversy over the question of whether to force Southern delegates to accept a loyalty oath binding them to support the party's nominees. After a fierce floor fight, a compromise so-

---

26Albert P. Blaustein and Clarence C. Ferguson, Jr., *Desegregation and the Law*. Also see: Jack Greenberg, *Race Relations and American Law*, and C. Herman Pritchett, *Civil Liberties and the Vinson Court*.

lution was found. Sectional feelings had been ruffled, however, notwithstanding the settlement, which had been imposed on both sides. Alan Sindler has examined in depth the causes and resolution of the 1952 contretemps over the loyalty pledge in "The Unsolid South: A Challenge to the Democratic Party."[27]

Another feature of the 1952 convention was the conflict between the supporters of Senator Estes Kefauver and party regulars, including President Truman. Civil rights was a covert issue in this battle for the control of the Democratic party. Party stalwarts deemed Kefauver too outspokenly liberal and feared his nomination would offend moderates and reactionaries, whose votes the Democrats needed if they were to defeat General Eisenhower in November. Desire for party unity accounted for the nomination of Illinois Governor Adlai Stevenson for the Presidency and Alabama Senator John Sparkman for the Vice-Presidency. President Truman, of course, played a leading role in the selection of these centrist alternatives to Kefauver and Senator Richard Russell of Georgia. His action and intervention helped to preserve the delicate cohesiveness of the party. Once more the civil rights chasm had been bridged.

During the campaign of 1952 President Truman deliberately solicited the Negro vote for Adlai Stevenson, hoping that in the event of a close election the Negro vote would prove as decisive as it had been in 1948. But the Eisenhower landslide neutralized completely the votes Negroes cast for Stevenson, even though Stevenson received a greater percentage of Negro votes than Truman had received in 1948.

Following the election the Truman Administration capped its work in the area of civil rights by submitting a Justice Department brief to the Supreme Court in support of Negro petitioners in the case of *Brown v. Board of Education*. Once again the government requested that the Court repudiate *Plessy v. Ferguson* on the grounds of its patent unconstitutionality.[28] With this action the Administration could look forward to the arrival of Clio's servants.

---

[27]Alan Sindler, "The Unsolid South: A Challenge to the Democratic Party," in Alan F. Westin, ed., *The Uses of Power*, 229–85.

[28]Brief for the United States as *amicus curiae* in cases 8, 101, 191, 413, 448, Supreme Court of the United States, October Term, 1952.

Before concluding this survey of the themes, problems, and literature relating to the Truman Administration and civil rights, I should add that at the present time several works are in progress that, when completed, will (we hope) provide students with the kind of monographic studies the post-1945 period deserves and needs. According to archivists at the Truman Library, subjects now under investigation include the use of the presidential executive order as an instrument for policy making in the field of civil rights; the desegregation of the United States Armed Forces; the 1948 Democratic National Convention; the Southern-Democratic and Republican coalition during the Truman Administration from 1945 to 1953.[29]

Moving from civil rights to civil liberties, one must, once again, look first at the Roosevelt Administration's performance in this area. In reviewing the policy of the Roosevelt Administration, especially in the period of World War II, two points stand out: (1) The White House ordered the incarceration of thousands of Japanese-Americans because it feared they would engage in espionage and sabotage if they were left free; (2) aside from this inexcusable action, thanks to the decency of the President and the civil libertarian orientation of Attorney General Francis Biddle, the Administration eschewed the authoritarian excesses and assaults on the First Amendment that characterized the Wilson Administration after 1917. Biddle, in his autobiography *In Brief Authority,* spells out the Justice Department's respect for procedural due process and free speech in the years he served as Attorney General of the United States.[30] The death of Franklin Roosevelt in April, 1945, and the resignation of Biddle in June, 1945, brought to a close one chapter in the history of civil liberties in America. The succeed-

---

[29]Mrs. R. P. Morgan, candidate for the Ph.D. in Political Science at Louisiana State University, "The Use of the Presidential Executive Order as an Instrument for Policy Making in the Field of Civil Rights"; Richard M. Dalfiume, candidate for the Ph.D. in History at the University of Missouri, "The Desegregation of the United States Armed Forces"; Ann C. McDonald, candidate for the Ph.D. in History at St. Louis University, "The 1948 Democratic Convention"; Travis M. Adams, candidate for the Ph.D. in History at Vanderbilt University, "The Southern Democratic Republican Coalition During the Truman Administration."

[30]Francis B. Biddle, *In Brief Authority.*

ing one was to be shaped mainly by the Cold War and the Korean War.

Francis Biddle's replacement was the former Assistant Attorney General, Tom Clark of Texas, who lacked his predecessor's passionate concern for and interest in civil liberties. Clark was more concerned with the political fortunes of the Administration, which were tied to Truman's relations with Congress. Thus, he was well aware of the possible results from any congressional investigation into the hiring and firing procedures of the federal government. As early as 1946 the *Amerasia* case and the Canadian government's sensational exposé of a Soviet spy ring operating within the governmental bureaucracy of Canada brought the security issue to the fore. Alan Westin discusses this point in his essay, "Constitutional Liberty and Loyalty Programs."[31]

The *Amerasia* case dealt with the removal of classified government documents from the State Department and their subsequent publication in a magazine *Amerasia*, edited by an alleged Communist sympathizer. It was the subject of a House Judiciary Committee investigation, launched in April, 1946. Later in the same year a House Civil Service Subcommittee submitted a report calling for the establishment of uniform hiring practices throughout the federal government and asking that the White House create a committee to study the problem and make appropriate recommendations. Following the November, 1946, congressional election, the President complied with the Civil Service Committee's request. A temporary committee was created for the purpose of making the investigation. Its report, filed with the President on February 20, 1947, stressed the point that the employment of disloyal and subversive persons presented "more than a speculative threat to our system of government."[32] On March 21, 1947, Truman issued Executive Order 9835, creating the necessary machinery to cope with the problems raised by the report. Eleanor Bontecou has examined the genesis and evolution of that order in

[31]Alan F. Westin, "Constitutional Liberty and Loyalty Programs," in Alfred H. Kelly, ed., *Foundations of Freedom in the American Constitution*, 205.

[32]*Congress and the Nation: 1945–1964*, 113.

The Federal Loyalty-Security Program, a carefully researched study in administrative history.[33] A critical evaluation of the order and of the subsequent developments flowing from it, that is, the erosion of due process and a threat to the First Amendment, can be found in Alan Barth's work, *The Loyalty of Free Men.*[34]

The White House probably hoped that Executive Order 9835 would bolt the door on the closet in which a subversive skeleton or two sometimes rattled. But the Eightieth Congress, with a Republican majority, was determined to pry open that door. The Republicans were thinking about the 1948 election and were no doubt hoping to gain additional political leverage with the loyalty issue. Consequently, House Republicans offered a bill to replace the Truman Loyalty Board with one having a statutory basis; the bill passed the House but expired in the Senate.

In January, 1945, at the opening session of the Seventy-ninth Congress, the House of Representatives had revitalized the House Committee on Un-American Activities by giving it permanent standing. By 1947 this committee was ready to unleash its first thunderbolt in the direction of Hollywood. From this point on, the Communist issue would become its *raison d'être,* the Truman Administration its adversary. Robert K. Carr's *The House Committee on Un-American Activities: 1945–1950* is a sound history of the committee's expedition into the great American garden in search of real or imagined subversives.[35]

It was clear that the political sparring between Democrats and Republicans over the loyalty question in 1947 was only a prelude to a major fight that would capture the public's attention in 1948. In the spring of 1948 President Truman and the House Committee on Un-American Activities collided over the question of whether the White House would release to the committee the security file of the professionally respected director of the National Bureau of Standards, Dr. Edward Con-

---

[33]Eleanor Bontecou, *The Federal Loyalty-Security Program.*
[34]Alan Barth, *The Loyalty of Free Men.*
[35]Robert K. Carr, *The House Committee on Un-American Activities: 1945–1950.*

don. Truman refused to honor the committee's request and ignored a House resolution asking him to comply with it. For him, the retention of the Condon file was a matter of executive privilege that could not be compromised.[36]

Following this executive and legislative imbroglio, in May, 1948, the House of Representatives passed the Mundt–Nixon bill, which required the registration of the Communist party and its various front organizations with the Justice Department. The White House refused to discuss the bill, but the President did disclose that he opposed legislation outlawing a political party. The Mundt–Nixon bill, the forerunner of the McCarran Act of 1950, was pigeonholed in the Senate, as the Upper Chamber awaited the results of the 1948 election before considering such an extreme piece of legislation. Although the Republicans failed to enact the Mundt–Nixon bill into law, they succeeded in making something of a political issue out of the loyalty and security questions. The Truman Administration was placed on the defensive by the Republicans' charges that it was lax in protecting the country from possible subversion and had not administered its loyalty program with vigor. Given the climate that prevailed in the early summer of 1948, civil liberties were bound to suffer, caught as they were between an administration executing a careful retreat from a position that was politically exposed, and critics of that administration.

In his *Security and Liberty: The Problem of Native Communists, 1947–1955,* Harold W. Chase has argued that the Truman Administration sought to free itself in 1948 of the charge that it was soft on communism.[37] This is a reasonable hypothesis that might explain why the Justice Department suddenly initiated proceedings before a New York federal grand jury on July 20, 1948, to indict the leaders of the American Communist party for having violated the Smith Act. Did the Justice Department act as it did because the Administration had advance information about the imminent appearance of Elizabeth Bentley and Whittaker Chambers before the House

[36]For a review of the Condon affair, see: *Congress and the Nation,* 1693.
[37]Harold W. Chase, *Security and Liberty: The Problem of Native Communists, 1947–1955,* 27.

Committee on Un-American Activities? Could not the Smith Act indictment be construed as a face-saving gesture on the part of the Administration to offset the abuse that was soon going to descend from Capitol Hill in the direction of the White House? The politics of civil liberties, as it applies to the 1948 election, is a subject worth careful study and analysis. The state of the American Communist party at the time of the indictment and trial is discussed in David Shannon's *The Decline of American Communism* and in Lewis Coser and Irving Howe's *The American Communist Party*.[38]

The Bentley–Chambers testimony before the House committee produced shock waves throughout the country. Especially damaging was the testimony of Whittaker Chambers that linked Alger Hiss, a former State Department employee with well-placed friends inside and outside of government, with a Russian espionage ring that operated in Washington in the late 1930's. Apparently placed on the defensive by these revelations, President Truman, on August 5, 1948, called the House hearings "a red herring," a charge he reiterated in December, 1948, after the Hiss–Chambers confrontation had developed into a national *cause célèbre*.[39] The trials and ultimate conviction of Hiss on grounds of perjury quickly became a symbol for many of a *Generation on Trial,* to borrow the title of Alistair Cooke's study of the Hiss affair.[40] Truman's words were to return to haunt him many months before he left office.

Meanwhile, the Democrats scored their surprising victory in 1948, helped considerably by the presence of Henry Wallace on their left. The Wallace movement functioned as a lightning rod for the Democratic party, rendering harmless the accusations Republicans were wont to make about the malfeasance of the Administration. Notwithstanding the results of the 1948 election, the panic over alleged Communist subversion continued to mount. The Hiss affair kept the issue alive and kicking in 1949 and prepared the way for the emergence of post-World

---

[38]David Shannon, *The Decline of American Communism;* Cabell Phillips, *The Truman Presidency*, 365–72; Lewis A. Coser and Irving Howe, *The American Communist Party*, 469–78.

[39]*Congress and the Nation*, 1694.

[40]Alistair Cooke, *A Generation on Trial.*

War II's most successful political desperado, Wisconsin's Senator Joseph R. McCarthy.

The Democratic Eighty-first Congress was initially quiescent on matters pertaining to national security, its attention being riveted on the legislative proposals submitted by the White House in 1949. Thereafter, pressures for congressional action on security matters started to grow again, abetted no doubt by the victory of Mao Tse-tung's forces in the Chinese Civil War in 1949, the Hiss conviction in January, 1950, and the frustrations generated by the Korean War. Thus was a climate established for a new and more pernicious assault on the Administration and, incidentally, on the Bill of Rights. A ready-made thesis of conspiracy that involved the State Department, Alger Hiss, and Yalta with the loss of China was now packaged by the nativist entrepreneurs of both parties for national distribution. Here is a perverse example of Joseph Schumpeter's theory of creative innovation in the economic sphere transferred to the political arena.

Nineteen-fifty was the year the nativists came into their own: Senator McCarthy was now on the attack, his chief target the Truman Administration. Faced with such a dogged and wily opponent, the Administration was now in serious trouble as it confronted McCarthyism for the first time. Edward Shils, in his provocative essay *The Torment of Secrecy,* provides a sociological framework in which to place the phenomenon of McCarthyism.[41] He notes that its roots go deep into American history and that it was, in part, a product of continuing hostility to the New Deal dating back to the 1930's—a hostility that would be given a national outlet by McCarthy and his followers. Another interpretation of McCarthyism was advanced by Dennis Wrong in 1954 in his article "Theories of McCarthyism—A Survey."[42] Wrong pointed out that McCarthy did not operate in a historical vacuum. Although McCarthy's

---

[41]Edward A. Shils, *The Torment of Secrecy,* 77–105.

[42]Dennis Wrong, "Theories of McCarthyism—A Survey," *Dissent,* I:2 (1954); Daniel Bell, *The Radical Right;* Richard Hofstadter, *The Paranoid Style in American Politics and other Essays.* An important work, published after this essay was prepared, is Earl Latham, *The Communist Controversy in Washington: From the New Deal to McCarthy.*

career was self-made, the product of shrewd promotion via the mass media, one source of his strength was the incipient garrison-state ideology that the Truman Administration had helped to fashion earlier, by means of its loyalty program, Attorney General's list, and prosecutions under the Smith Act. This is a point which liberals sometimes overlook in their eagerness to vilify McCarthy and his works.

The Korean War not only helped to spawn McCarthyism, it also provided a seedbed for the rebirth of a modified Mundt–Nixon bill, which had been gathering dust in House and Senate committees since 1949. In August, 1950, the Senate Judiciary Committee, headed by Nevada's Senator Pat McCarran, and the House Committee on Un-American Activities, led by Georgia's John Wood, prepared legislation along the lines of the Mundt–Nixon bill for consideration on the floors of both houses. Sensing the possibility that such legislation could now pass Congress and fearing the damage to the First Amendment that would result from it, President Truman advised Congress on August 8, 1950, to consider an alternative, that is, ways and means of strengthening existing laws governing sabotage and espionage.[43] How the President reconciled his defense of the First Amendment and the right of political activity for Communists with the Administration's indictments under the Smith Act is not known. In any event, his advice went unheeded.

After the House had passed the Wood bill on August 29, 1950, the Senate moved quickly to consider the McCarran committee's draft for internal security legislation. At this time token opposition to the McCarran draft developed when a small bloc of liberal Democratic senators, led by West Virginia's Harley Kilgore, tried to substitute its own measure for that of the Judiciary Committee. The liberals proposed the creation of internment camps to house potentially dangerous individuals. They would be removed from society under orders of the Attorney General of the United States during a state of national emergency, which could be declared at the discretion of the President. Eventually, with the assistance of Scott Lucas

---

[43]David Horton, *Freedom and Equality: Addresses of Harry S Truman*, 35–43.

of Illinois, the Democratic party's majority leader in the Senate, the Kilgore measure was tacked on to the McCarran draft, which easily passed the Senate. On September 12, 1950, a House-Senate conference committee resolved the differences between the Wood and McCarran bills, replacing the former with the latter. On September 20, 1950, the McCarran bill passed both houses of Congress, only to be vetoed by President Truman on September 22, 1950.[44] This veto was overridden by a substantial margin on the same day by both houses, and thus the Internal Security Bill of 1950 became law. A legislative history of this act, perhaps modeled after Daniel Berman's history of the 1960 civil rights act, would be a worth-while study, as would a biography of Senator Pat McCarran, the architect of the bill in question.[45]

Despite the lack of a legislative history of the McCarran Act, there is a sizable literature regarding specific aspects of this controversial law. Among the more significant studies are: Zechariah Chafee's *The Blessings of Liberty*; Walter Gellhorn's *American Rights: The Constitution*; Harold Chase's *Security and Liberty: The Problem of Native Communists;* and Arthur E. Sutherland, Jr.'s article, "Freedom and Internal Security."[46]

Once he was obligated by law to administer the McCarran Act, President Truman nominated five individuals to serve as members of the Subversive Activity Control Board; the Senate later refused to confirm the nomination of one of the five, Charles LaFollette, whose liberalism Senator McCarran probably found unacceptable. Subsequent to the Truman nominations the Justice Department petitioned to SACB to force the registration of the Communist party as a Communist organization. The party refused to comply with the board's request and thereby precipitated a legal row in the federal courts on the

---

[44]Horton, *Freedom and Equality*, 46–57.
[45]Daniel M. Berman, *A Bill Becomes A Law: The Civil Rights Act of 1960.*
[46]Zechariah Chafee, Jr., *The Blessings of Liberty*; Walter Gellhorn, *American Rights: The Constitution;* Harold W. Chase, *Security and Liberty: The Problem of Native Communists, 1947–1955;* Arthur E. Sutherland, Jr., "Freedom and Internal Security," *Harvard Law Review*, 64 (1951), 383.

issue of whether it had the right to avoid self-incrimination.[47] The operation of the SACB in the Truman years, the difficulties the Administration encountered in its attempt to register the party, and the rejection of the LaFollette nomination have yet to be systematically examined and analyzed.

After activating the SACB the White House moved on another front, perhaps hoping to head off further congressional action in the area of internal security. On January 23, 1951, the President issued Executive Order 10207, creating the President's Commission on Internal Security and Individual Rights. This commission, headed by retired Fleet Admiral Chester W. Nimitz, was authorized to study existing laws relating to treason, espionage, and sabotage and to recommend ways to strengthen them. But before the Nimitz Commission could begin its work in earnest, it ran into that nemesis of the Truman Administration, Senator McCarran's Judiciary Committee. This committee refused to grant the Nimitz Commission an exemption already approved by the House that would allow members of the commission the right to continue their association with firms doing business with the government. On May 12, 1951, the commission resigned, claiming that the lack of an exemption would hamper its work. The White House had thus failed to seize the initiative in this field, much to the future detriment of both the Truman Administration and civil liberties. Professor Alan Harper's unpublished essay dealing with the origins and demise of the Nimitz Commission is deserving of a professional reading public.[48]

Nineteen fifty-one was not a good year for civil libertarians. The Supreme Court upheld the constitutionality of the Smith Act in the famous Dennis decision, the Senate created a new Internal Security Committee that spent its first year investigating charges brought against Owen Lattimore and the Institute of Pacific Relations, and the White House issued an executive order modifying and tightening rules pertaining to the loyalty program. Executive Order 10241, issued on April 28,

---

[47]Thomas I. Emerson and David Haber, *Political and Civil Rights in the United States*, 2d ed., 413–18.
[48]Alan D. Harper, "The Nimitz Commission."

1951, now authorized the Loyalty Review Board to dismiss federal employees "if there is a reasonable doubt as to the loyalty of the person involved."[49] In this manner certain borderline cases could be more easily handled than, say, under the 1947 order, which required at least proof of reasonable grounds for disloyalty. The 1951 order is discussed in Professor Ralph Brown's *Loyalty and Security*, the most balanced and comprehensive study of this enduring postwar political malaise.[50]

Nineteen fifty-two was the year of the great smear. Senator McCarthy was still on the rampage, slandering and vilifying the Democratic party at the merest mention of a newspaper headline. To the delight of such respected Republicans as Senator Robert A. Taft of Ohio, McCarthy's repeated charges had placed the Democrats on the defensive. The "Communists in government" issue, which had been slowly building since 1947, finally erupted with volcanic fury in the 1952 presidential election.

The presence of Richard Nixon on the 1952 Republican ticket indicated that the long-suffering Republican party was banking heavily upon this issue. The Democrats were not very successful in countering the rhetorical blasts of Nixon and McCarthy. The triangular relationship between McCarthyism, the Truman Administration, and civil liberties in the context of the 1952 election is also a subject that deserves serious study. Volume II of President Truman's memoirs, *Years of Trial and Hope*, and Richard Rovere's biography, *Senator Joe McCarthy*, are useful beginning points for such a project.[51]

Because of the difficulty in obtaining access to primary sources, students, until very recently, have been discouraged from investigating in depth the civil liberties policies and problems of the Truman Administration. Now it seems that enough material is available at the Truman Library to justify serious scholarly examination of some of the questions raised in this

[49]*Congress and the Nation*, 1665.

[50]Ralph S. Brown, Jr., *Loyalty and Security: Employment Tests in the United States*, 36.

[51]Harry S. Truman, *Years of Trial and Hope;* Richard Rovere, *Senator Joe McCarthy*.

paper.[52] In due time a comprehensive history of the politics of civil liberties in the Truman Administration will be written. And with that accomplishment, professional scholarship will take a giant stride forward into the little-known field of contemporary history.

To conclude: It seems clear from the foregoing analysis that the Truman Administration responded to political pressures generated by Negroes and nativists with a series of *ad hoc* policies that were designed to win or at least to prevent the loss of votes. In this respect the civil rights and civil liberties policies of the Truman Administration had a similar motivaton. On the other hand, the results were vastly different. In the area of civil rights the federal executive assumed limited responsibilities for the welfare of the American Negro. The Truman Administration's equivocal defense of civil liberties was hardly enough to counteract the poison injected into the body politic by the antagonists of the open society.

Before any thorough scholarly assessment of these differing policies can be made, however, available primary materials dealing with them will have to be considerably enlarged. Without access to the key policy-making papers of the major figures of the Administration, including the President, Clark Clifford, Charles Murphy, and Tom Clark, it will be difficult but not impossible to go beyond what is presently known, especially in the sensitive area of civil liberties and internal security. Perhaps in time the papers of Sam Rayburn, Alben Barkley, and Leslie Biffle will provide further information about the political aspects of these problems. The full story of this Administration's action in the fields of civil rights and civil liberties remains to be told.

---

[52]A well-documented and provocative essay on the subject of civil liberties and internal security has come to my attention: see Athan Theoharis, "The Rhetoric of Politics: Foreign Policy, Internal Security and Domestic Politics in the Truman Era, 1945–1950."

BIBLIOGRAPHY

Books

Abels, Jules, *Out of the Jaws of Victory.* New York, Henry Holt & Company, Inc., 1959.

Abrams, Charles, *Forbidden Neighbors: A Study of Prejudice in Housing*. New York, Harper and Brothers, 1955.

Barth, Alan, *The Loyalty of Free Men*. New York, The Viking Press, Inc., 1951.

Bell, Daniel, ed., *The Radical Right*. New York, Doubleday & Company, Inc., 1963.

Berman, Daniel M., *A Bill Becomes a Law: The Civil Rights Act of 1960*. New York, The Macmillan Company, 1962.

Biddle, Francis B., *In Brief Authority*. New York, Doubleday & Company, Inc., 1962.

Blaustein, Albert P., and Clarence C. Ferguson, Jr., *Desegregation and the Law*. New Brunswick, Rutgers University Press, 1957.

Bolling, Richard, *House Out of Order*. New York, E. P. Dutton & Company, Inc., 1965.

Bontecou, Eleanor, *The Federal Loyalty-Security Program*. Ithaca, Cornell University Press, 1953.

Brock, Clifton, *Americans for Democratic Action*. Washington, D. C., Public Affairs Press, 1962.

Brown, Ralph S., Jr., *Loyalty and Security: Employment Tests in the United States*. New Haven, Yale University Press, 1958.

Burns, James M., *Deadlock of Democracy*. Englewood Cliffs, Prentice-Hall, Inc., 1963.

Carr, Robert K., *The House Committee on Un-American Activities: 1945–1950*. Ithaca, Cornell University Press, 1952.

Chafee, Zechariah, Jr., *The Blessings of Liberty*. Philadelphia, J. B. Lippincott Company, 1956.

Chase, Harold W., *Security and Liberty: The Problem of Native Communists, 1947–1955*. New York, Doubleday & Company, Inc., 1955.

Clark, Tom C., and Philip B. Perlman, *Prejudice and Property*. Washington, D. C., Public Affairs Press, 1948.

Congressional Quarterly Service, *Congress and the Nation: 1945–1964*. Washington, D. C., Congressional Quarterly Service, 1965.

Cooke, Alistair, *A Generation on Trial*. New York, Alfred A. Knopf, Inc., 1950.

Coser, Lewis A., and Irving Howe, *The American Communist Party*. New York, Frederick A. Praeger, 1962.

Emerson, Thomas I., and Dennis Haber, *Political and Civil Rights in the United States*, 2d ed. Buffalo, Dennis & Company, 1958.

Freidel, Frank, *F.D.R. and the South*. Baton Rouge, Louisiana State University Press, 1965.

Garfinkel, Herbert, *When Negroes March*. Glencoe, The Free Press of Glencoe, Inc., 1959.

Gellhorn, Walter, *American Rights: The Constitution*. New York, The Macmillan Company, 1960.

Greenberg, Jack, *Race Relations and American Law*. New York, Columbia University Press, 1959.

Harris, Robert, *The Quest for Equality*. Baton Rouge, Louisiana State University Press, 1960.

Hofstadter, Richard, *The Paranoid Style in American Politics and Other Essays*. New York, Alfred A. Knopf, Inc., 1965.

Horton, David, ed., *Freedom and Equality: Addresses of Harry S Truman*. Columbia, University of Missouri Press, 1960.

Kelly, Alfred H., ed., *Foundations of Freedom in the American Constitution*. New York, Harper & Brothers, 1958.

Key, V. O., Jr., *Southern Politics in State and Nation*. New York, Alfred A. Knopf, Inc., 1949.

Latham, Earl, *The Communist Controversy in Washington: From the New Deal to McCarthy*. Cambridge, Harvard University Press, 1966.

Longaker, Richard P., *The President and Individual Liberties*. Ithaca, Cornell University Press, 1961.

Lubell, Samuel, *The Future of American Politics*. New York, Harper & Row, Publishers, 1966.

McWilliams, Carey, *Brothers Under the Skin*. Boston, Little, Brown and Company, 1951.

Moon, Henry Lee, *Balance of Power: The Negro Vote*. New York, Doubleday & Company, Inc., 1949.

Nichols, Lee, *Breakthrough on the Color Front*. New York, Random House, Inc., 1954.

Phillips, Cabell, *The Truman Presidency: The History of a Triumphant Succession*. New York, The Macmillan Company, 1966.

The President's Committee on Civil Rights, *To Secure These Rights*. New York, Simon and Schuster, Inc., 1947.

Pritchett, C. Herman, *Civil Liberties and the Vinson Court*. Chicago, University of Chicago Press, 1954.

Rovere, Richard, *Senator Joe McCarthy*. New York, Harcourt, Brace & World, Inc., 1959.

Ruchames, Louis, *Race, Jobs, and Politics*. New York, Columbia University Press, 1953.

Shannon, David A., *The Decline of American Communism*. New York, Harcourt, Brace and Company, Inc., 1959.

Shils, Edward A., *The Torment of Secrecy*. Glencoe, Free Press of Glencoe, Inc., 1956.

Truman, Harry S., *Memoirs*. Doubleday & Company, Inc., 1955, 1956. 2 vols.

Westin, Alan F., ed., *The Uses of Power*. New York, Harcourt, Brace and World, Inc., 1962.

White, Walter F., *A Man Called White*. New York, The Viking Press, Inc., 1948.

Public Documents

Brief for the United States as *amicus curiae* in Cases 8, 101, 191, 413, 448, Supreme Court of the United States, October Term, 1952. U. S., *Congressional Record,* 80th Congress, 2nd Session, 1948, XCIV (Part 1), 928–29.

Articles

Aronson, Arnold, and Samuel Spiegler, "Does the Republican Party Want the Negro Vote?" *The Crisis,* 56 (December, 1949), 364–68.

Sutherland, Arthur E., Jr., "Freedom and Internal Security." *Harvard Law Review,* 64 (1951), 383.

Wrong, Dennis, "Theories of McCarthyism—A Survey." *Dissent,* I:2 (1954).

Unpublished Studies

Berman, William C., "The Politics of Civil Rights in the Truman Administration." Ph.D. dissertation, Ohio State University, 1963.

Dalfiume, Richard M., "Desegregation in the United States Armed Forces, 1939–1953." Ph.D. dissertation, University of Missouri, 1966.

Harper, Alan D., "The Nimitz Commission." Manuscript in author's possession.

Kifer, Allen, "The Negro and the New Deal." Ph.D. dissertation, University of Wisconsin, 1961.

Theoharis, Athan G., "The Rhetoric of Politics: Foreign Policy, Internal Security and Domestic Politics in the Truman Era, 1945–1950." Manuscript in author's possession.

The Truman Presidency

✤

ELMER E. CORNWELL, JR.

T HE OTHER ESSAYS in this volume treat various of the areas of policy concern that faced the Administration of Harry Truman. The purpose of this essay is rather different. It is designed to deal with Mr. Truman's conduct of the Office of the Presidency, his impact on it, and the developments in the office that took place during his incumbency and to treat all of these—so far as possible—apart from patterns of policy per se.

As a problem in methodology, it is rather easier to analyze the things a given President did than it is to delineate the processes by which he did them. This is the case, in large measure, because of the nature of the Presidency. As Professor Neustadt has so well described presidential activity, it consists of a subtle array of techniques for the use of the prestige and persuasive "powers" attaching to the office, about which the Constitution and the law know nothing.[1] Besides leaving little formal record, much of this activity may actually leave *no* record more reliable than the memory of participants regarding oral discussions or agreements of which they had knowledge.

The point is well illustrated by a comparison of the Rich-

---

[1]Richard E. Neustadt, *Presidential Power: The Politics of Leadership.*

ardson edition of the *Messages and Papers of the Presidents*[2] with the present series of *Public Papers*[3] being issued by the National Archives and Records Service. Richardson took as his mandate the inclusion only of official messages to Congress, proclamations, and similar documents. The current effort, operating on a far more realistic theory of the nature of the Presidency and of presidential activity, includes transcripts of press conferences, transcripts of informal remarks made to visiting groups, texts of television speeches, correspondence, and a host of items that carry no official standing at all.

Admirable and infinitely valuable as this new series is to scholars working on the Presidency, it too, of necessity, falls far short of encompassing the full range and richness of the pattern of activity that represents the presidential role. Further, until some future Chief Executive decides (as none would be so foolish as to do) that all his telephone conversations, all his individual appointments, all informal conferences in his office, all his casual conversations with political associates are to be recorded verbatim, the record will remain incomplete.

These limitations on available information obviously hamper research on presidential policy, but they represent even more serious limitations for the political scientist or other scholar whose interest is in the Presidency as such, rather than what a particular President has done on a particular subject. The style or *modus operandi* of one White House occupant, almost by definition differs from that of all others before or since. We can describe in general, impressionistic ways what that difference in style is or was, but to reduce these necessarily glib generalizations to reasonably precise and documented propositions is extremely difficult.

Initially one must ask, of what major ingredients does a President's style consist, what are the crucial forces that shape it? Erwin C. Hargrove recently published a book entitled *Presi-*

---

[2]James D. Richardson, ed., *A Compilation of the Messages and Papers of the Presidents.*

[3]*Public Papers of the Presidents* is the full title. Annual volumes have been issued for all of the Truman, Eisenhower, and Kennedy years and for each year to date of the Johnson Administration.

dential Leadership: Personality and Political Style.[4] His emphasis is on the personality and on the psychological ingredients that shape the way a President approaches and conducts the office. Unfortunately for present purposes, he does not deal with Mr. Truman among his case studies.

This pioneering effort, together with an as yet very small number of roughly similar studies,[5] is based on the premise that, particularly in a one-man office like the American Presidency, the individual characteristics, drives, needs, skills, and so on of that man are inevitably going to be a major, if not *the* major, shaping influence. With this theory one could hardly disagree.

On the other hand, there are many situational factors that provide the framework within which a President works out his individual salvation—his style. The particular kinds of issues that are forced upon his attention for resolution during his incumbency and the mood of the nation set limits and shape practices. These latter are often described in relation to short-term, cyclical patterns. Cycles of reform and receptivity to strong innovating presidential leadership have recurred, followed by periods of quiescence, consolidation, and desire for rest.

Beyond these cycles there has also been a long-term secular trend of development, rapidly accelerated in recent decades, that has moved the Executive into the central energizing position in the whole national political system.[6] An increasingly positive and interventionist federal government and an increasingly receptive public have demanded this kind of leadership from the President. This trend in turn has represented a major imperative that has shaped the conduct of the Presidents since Hoover.

It is from this last area that one can draw the central theme for a discussion of the Truman Presidency. Harry Truman,

---

[4]Erwin C. Hargrove, *Presidential Leadership: Personality and Political Style.*

[5]See, for example, A. L. and J. L. George, *Woodrow Wilson and Colonel House: A Personality Study.*

[6]Effort is made to document this point in my "Presidential News: The Expanding Public Image," *Journalism Quarterly,* 36 (Summer, 1959), 275–83.

even more in some ways than Franklin Roosevelt, was the key transitional figure in the White House, bridging the shift from Coolidgean passivity to the hyperactivity, on a global scale, with which we today have become so familiar. Or, to restate this change in terms of the foregoing analysis, though one could center a discussion of the Truman Presidency on the man and the ways in which his personality and style permeated his conduct of the office, the object of this essay will be to show the impact of external, long-term developmental forces on the office and, ultimately, on the man.

One experienced observer of the Washington scene is reported to have recalled "an afternoon spent at the White House on a social call to President Coolidge in the latter's second term, when the only official business transacted was for the President to select from a group of recent photographs of his person those he wanted printed."[7] This may be unfair as a characterization of Mr. Coolidge's period in office, and to use the Vermonter as sole illustration of presidential passivity is also unfair. Yet, the contrast between today's Presidency and the office as it was in the 1920's is almost that sharp.

The federal government in those days did little by way of business regulation and next to nothing in the area of social welfare programs and engaged in as few and as simple relations with the rest of the world as was practical. Presidential responsibilities were correspondingly modest, hence, the President had but a tiny fraction of the present-day administrative establishment over which to preside, and, for the most part, he allowed the existing departments to go their own ways. Not until 1921, with the passage of the Budget and Accounting Act of that year, was there even a full theoretical recognition that the administrative branch of the government was in some sense a unity and that the President had a positive obligation to treat it as such.[8]

---

[7]John R. Steelman and H. Dewayne Kreager, "The Executive Office as Administrative Coordinator," *Law and Contemporary Problems*, 21 (Autumn, 1956), 696f.

[8]This obligation took the form of the establishment for the first time of the idea of an executive budget in the national government, with the President in ultimate charge of compiling such a coordinated financial plan.

Foreign affairs, for a disillusioned and isolationist nation, consisted in little more than occasional bouts with the reparations dilemma, half-hearted efforts to join the World Court, and expression of the simplistic idealism of the Kellogg–Briand Pact. The President, even in relation to these issues, stood aloof much of the time and left the initiative to his Secretary of State. Harding and Coolidge were little more involved in domestic policy than in foreign affairs—specifically, in providing leadership for Congress. Though Coolidge took a keen personal interest in pushing the Mellon tax reduction proposals (evoking but a mixed response from Congress), for the most part he kept hands off the issues before Congress. Indeed, there are many rather annoyed references in his press conferences to efforts *others* were making to get him to take a stand on their pet bills. Presidential prestige was looked upon as a passive ingredient in the legislative process, to be activated if, somehow, the man in the White House could be induced to lend his support to a measure.[9]

Only in the area of contact with the public via the communications media can one find significant activity and innovation during the 1920's. Calvin Coolidge's own rather striking—if surprising—abilities as a publicist, coupled with the advent of radio as a major channel of communication between President and public, reinforced one another. The Coolidge myth thrived, and he became virtually the personification of America's conscience and better self during the Roaring Twenties. He also demonstrated that the White House platform need not be used for promotion of policy, but could be as effectively used for what we today would describe as pure "image projection."[10]

Little need be said to recall the enormous change in the scale, the tempo, and the whole purpose of the presidential office that came about in less than a decade. We rightly think of the years Franklin Roosevelt was in the White House as

---

[9]See my *Presidential Leadership of Public Opinion*, 83f., on this point. An interesting collection of excerpts from Coolidge press conferences has been published, edited by Howard H. Quint and Robert H. Ferrell, entitled *The Talkative President*.

[10]See Cornwell, *Presidential Leadership of Public Opinion*, and "Coolidge and Presidential Leadership," *Public Opinion Quarterly*, 21 (Summer, 1957), 265–78.

the great watershed period in the modern evolution not only of the office but of our national governmental system itself. Virtually every descriptive generalization about the Presidency in the twenties must be amended or discarded for the thirties and since. The administrative establishment ballooned with the expansion of new federal responsibilities for providing social welfare and for policing and stabilizing the mixed economy. Hitler and the Second World War brought a new involvement with the world that will doubtless continue for the indefinite future. The Presidency was, inevitably, thrust into the forefront of all of these new areas of concern.

Multiple continuing roles as chief administrator, chief guardian of prosperity, chief of foreign affairs, and chief legislator replaced the presidential passivity that had so often been the rule earlier. Not only must he now actively coordinate and attempt to mesh the many cogs of the national government into some semblance of orderly operation, but the Chief Executive must also accept responsibility as primary initiator of policy. In a word, he must lead Congress. This latter task had never been easy for the Presidents who occasionally undertook it. However, in the era since the thirties, a new note of receptivity has crept into the congressional view of presidential leadership. The old suspicion and jealousy of prerogative is still there, but it is now paralleled by a feeling that the President *must* provide the agenda and even, at times, the spur to action.

Over much of this massive process of transition Roosevelt presided; actually, he did far more than merely preside. He himself supplied, or at least corralled and channeled, much of the dynamism. But this very creativity and restlessness—the virtuoso performance which was his administration—represent the problem as it was posed for his successor. As a problem it ran far deeper than the seemingly casual way in which Senator Truman was chosen to be Vice-President and then, when elected, was left in nearly total ignorance of both the President's mind and his mode of operation.

Roosevelt's supreme self-confidence, together with the highly personalized, informal, and almost secretive way in which he operated, were the chief hallmarks of his tenure.[11] In a way, these style characteristics of his were not inappropriate to the office he found waiting for him in March, 1933. It was simple and informal in both staffing and operation as well as in its rather tenuous relation to the rest of the national government and to the policy concerns of the American people.

Moreover, Roosevelt, consummate political craftsman that he was, sensed all the subtleties of the President's power position that Neustadt has so meticulously catalogued. His sure instinct told him that it was dangerous to sew oneself into a network of fixed relationships, staff or otherwise. Hence, he kept things fluid and played his role by ear, as much when setting up the administrative structure for wartime industrial mobilization as earlier when contriving the NRA or the WPA.

In short, under Franklin Roosevelt the Presidency truly became the vital center of national political life. His style of operation in the office was such, however, that it generated few of the mechanisms necessary to make possible the discharge of these responsibilities on a continuing basis. His encyclopaedic knowledge, his skill, and his virtuosity seemed to make a casual and outwardly chaotic White House enterprise work. But the formal institutional devices and channels that could provide continuity and could enable a less knowledgeable or gifted successor to carry on had yet to be devised in most cases.

That this lack of devices for continuity made the transfer of power on April 12, 1945, a frightfully difficult one for Harry Truman goes without saying;[12] more important, it left up to him much of the task of completing and implementing the Roosevelt Revolution in the Presidency—or what can more fairly and accurately be called, I think, the Roosevelt–Truman Revolution. The new President not only had to master the intricacies of the policies he must carry on and to discover such means as existed for doing so, but he faced the task of virtu-

[11]See Tugwell's characterization of Roosevelt's method of operation: Rexford G. Tugwell, *The Democratic Roosevelt*, 332f., 355.

[12]For comment on the transition and for a useful discussion of other aspects of the Truman Presidency, see Barton Bernstein, "The Presidency Under Truman," *Yale Political Review*, 4 (Fall, 1964), 8, 9, 24.

ally reconstructing the whole presidential enterprise to enable
it to carry its newly acquired burdens. One would not be justified in suggesting that Mr. Truman consciously addressed
himself to this problem save in piecemeal terms nor that he
was able to complete it. In any ultimate sense, the job of tool-
ing up the office to fill its growing role adequately will never
be completed. It is clear, however, in spite of these qualifications, that Harry Truman took the first and the longest steps.

The very fact that the new President had been thrust so
abruptly into the White House with no prior experience or
chance to acquaint himself with its inner workings had an
additional significance. All fledgling Chief Executives in some
degree come to the job unprepared, since the office is so completely unique and therefore unlike any prior experience an
occupant could possibly have had. Yet, the comprehensiveness
of Truman's lack of preparation would be hard to duplicate.
It probably meant, however, that he was even less inhibited
than a better prepared man would have been in developing
institutional innovations as he struggled with his new and
awesome tasks. Furthermore, anyone placed in such a position
who did not find ready-made mechanisms and channels through
which to operate would feel a strong impulse to contrive such
protective and supportive devices. That this must have been
the case with Harry Truman, one can safely surmise.

It is possible to be reasonably specific about the "agenda"
Truman faced along these lines. He was the first President to
come into office in the new era of American world leadership
and of continuing international crisis. In a sense, therefore,
his most pressing problems lay in contriving the institutional
means, military and otherwise, for making and carrying out
the kind of comprehensive foreign policy America had never
before needed or wanted.

On the domestic front, new dimensions had been added to
the age-old problem of presidential legislative and policy leadership. Both the public and the Congress had learned to expect
continuing initiative from the President. In the legislative reference service of the Budget Bureau Roosevelt had supplied
one useful tool, but more were needed; new strategies were

also needed for dealing on a continuing basis with this most intractable of national legislatures.

In the two supporting areas of White House staff and presidential public relations, the problems were considerable and the Roosevelt legacy again only partially useful. The new-model Presidency must, in the nature of things, find much of the thrust it can exert on policy in a citizenry it has aroused to demand action. Roosevelt demonstrated the need for this support graphically and unmistakably. No future President could afford to neglect the lesson. Yet nowhere was the Rooseveltan approach more personalized or less susceptible of transfer than here. It was hopeless for so different a personality as Harry Truman to attempt to emulate it; even if the Missourian had wanted to, changes in both technology and scale forbade it.

In the general area of staff arrangements, again, much of the Roosevelt method was *sui generis*: the brain trust, the corps of speech writers, the coterie of assistants and confidants who moved in and out of the charmed circle. On the other hand, it was FDR who, in 1939, established the Executive Office of the President and at a stroke launched the transformation of the Presidency from a somewhat helter-skelter one-man show into an institution.

Basic reorganization of the United States' machinery for making foreign and military policy was certainly a predictable outcome of the Second World War—though one wonders how much would have been done had Roosevelt lived to serve out his fourth term. It is perhaps significant that out of the experience of the First World War came the Budget and Accounting Act,[13] reflecting the fact that America's involvement then had, in a sense, been more financial than military. In any event, involvement required little attention on the part of the United States to the making of basic military policy, since this had been set by the Allies long before its entry as a belligerent. In the Second World War, the development of basic policy became largely an American responsibility and specifically President Roosevelt's. If weaknesses in the budget-making system

[13]Fritz Morstein Marx, "The Bureau of the Budget: Its Evolution and Present Role: I," *American Political Science Review*, 39 (August, 1945), 655.

had been highlighted during the first war, far more basic weaknesses in policy-making machinery emerged during the second. President Truman himself has written:

> One of the strongest convictions which I brought to the office of President was that the antiquated defense set-up of the United States had to be reorganized quickly as a step toward insuring our future safety and preserving world peace. From the beginning of my administration I began to push hard for unification of the military establishment into a single department of the armed forces.[14]

Here, as elsewhere, Truman's sense of orderly procedure, his very different personality traits, and the opportunity he had had to observe the weaknesses of the existing system in operation were involved. One can also assume that, confronted as he was with gigantic problems of dismantling our war machine, making peace, and planning for a but dimly discernible future, he sensed a compelling need for dependable mechanisms to which he could turn for assistance. This unprecedented array of new responsibilities could not be carried on the shoulders of one man with a few *ad hoc* assistants, however versatile he—and they—might be.

President Truman's crucial role in bringing this reorganization to fruition through the passage of the National Security Act of 1947 is a good illustration of the part the Chief Executive must often play in securing policy coordination or, as here, in forcing acceptance of the machinery for coordination. Paul Hammond portrays in some detail the lengthy discussions, looking toward some kind of reform, that had gone on before Truman took office.[15] Here was an almost classic example of the parochialisms endemic in a national bureaucracy and especially in the American. The forces that can be mobilized to block changes that threaten existing bureaucratic relationships are numerous and powerful.

The new President sent a message to Congress on December 19, 1945, in which he discussed at length his view of the unification problem and the principles that should guide its solu-

---

[14]Harry S. Truman, *Years of Trial and Hope: 1946–1953*, 49.

[15]Paul Y. Hammond, *Organizing for Defense: The American Military Establishment in the Twentieth Century*, Chapter 8.

tion. He advocated a single Department of National Defense with a single civilian head to sit in the Cabinet, a Navy, Army, and Air Force, mechanisms to coordinate these branches of the military establishment, and one Chief of Staff of the Department of National Defense plus commanders for each of the three military arms. These officers would constitute an advisory body to the Secretary and the President.[16]

The message seems to have had little direct impact on the negotiations that had been going on among the military service departments and the interested congressional committees. In fact, aside from providing ideas, many of which were later used in some form, these discussions served mainly to isolate and even, in time, to exacerbate the key differences of view (and of interest) that lay at the heart of the problems preventing unification. No less than eight bill drafts had been prepared in efforts to meet objections and yet fulfill the criteria the President had set forth. A ninth was introduced in April, 1946, only to be unanimously opposed by all spokesmen for the Navy.

In early May, President Truman writes, he called the Secretaries of the Navy and of War to the White House, urged the importance of unification, and asked them to bring a list of their disagreements to him. This was done on May 31, and indicated, to the President's disappointment, that the same key issues were still the stumbling blocks. Reluctantly he decided he had no choice but to resolve them himself, much as he would have preferred to have the services come to their own agreement. This he did, and by January, 1947, the last details had been worked out; the legislation finally passed in July, and James Forrestal was appointed as first Secretary of Defense in September.[17]

There has been so much discussion of the structure of the defense setup since, and so many changes, both legal and otherwise, that it is well to go back to the original provisions. The

---

[16]Truman summarizes this message in *Years of Trial and Hope,* 52 ff. See also, for the full text, "Special Message to the Congress Recommending the Establishment of a Department of National Defense," Item 218 in *Public Papers of the Presidents, Harry S. Truman, 1945.*

[17]See Hammond, *Organizing for Defense,* 221 f., and Truman, 53–55.

declaration of policy in Section 2 of the Act is, in part, as follows:

> ... [I]t is the intent of Congress to provide a comprehensive program for the future security of the United States; [and] to provide for the establishment of integrated policies and procedures for the departments, agencies, and functions of the Government relating to the national security; . . .[18]

Aside from the Department of Defense itself, the key piece of machinery provided for was the National Security Council, whose mission was "To advise the President with respect to the integration of domestic, foreign, and military policies relating to the national security. . . ."[19] Initially it was to consist of the President, the Secretary of State, the Secretary of Defense, the Secretaries of the Army, Navy, and Air Force, and the Chairman of the National Security Resources Board.

Placed directly under the NSC there was to be a Central Intelligence Agency. The NSRB was designed to advise the President concerning the coordination of military, industrial, and civilian mobilization—to rationalize, in other words, the functions that the WPB, its predecessors, and its rivals attempted to perform in World War II. The new Defense Department was to be a considerably looser structure than it has become since, with three more or less autonomous components. The Joint Chiefs of Staff, whose existence predated the Act, and who as a body were linked directly with the President in those days through Admiral Leahy as Chief of Staff to the President, now gained formal legal status, and they were placed directly under the Secretary of Defense. A Joint Staff was provided as the planning arm of the JCS, made up of equal numbers of officers drawn from the three services.

These were the primary elements in the new structure. This apparatus by no means solved all problems. The NSC, for example, could not, in the nature of things, become the kind of policy-making body some of its proponents envisioned. The history of the Cabinet makes it abundantly clear that no Presi-

---

[18]Quoted in Charles Fairman, "The President as Commander-in-Chief," *Journal of Politics*, 11 (February, 1949), 147. My summary of the Act relies on Fairman's account.

[19]Fairman, "The President as Commander-in-Chief."

dent is likely to allow his prerogatives to be thus "put in commission," as the British say. In fact, President Truman used to absent himself from meetings so his presence would not inhibit discussion; also, no doubt, he wished thus to emphasize that the council was to bring its thinking *to* him, not make decisions *with* him.[20]

One might almost say that the NSC machinery was as important for its symbolic role as for its actual impact on policy. It symbolized a recognition that foreign and military policy were indissolubly linked with each other and with the broad pattern of national policy as a whole. In a governmental system that fosters institutional parochialism and encourages piecemeal approaches as assiduously as the American, symbols of this kind are not without their importance. President Truman, in his memoirs, recalled finding, as an investigating Senator, "immense air installations located side by side at various points in this country and Panama where the Navy could not land on the Army's airfield, and vice versa."[21] Symbolic unification at the top could not end these absurdities at once, but it would help erode them in time.

President Truman's role in bringing about unification lay largely in the "authoritative mediation" that only he, as Chief Executive, was in a position to impose. He threw the weight of his office on the side of reform and forced the participants to take this compromise first step. The journey to unification was still a long one, from Forrestal to McNamara—and many

[20]President Truman discussed his conception of the NSC, *Years of Trial and Hope,* 62f. There is a fairly extensive literature on the operation of the NSC during the Truman Administration and after. See especially the hearings and documents issued by the Senate Subcommittee on National Policy Machinery of the Committee on Government Operations (86th Congress, 2d Session, 1961) and also H. P. Kirkpatrick, "Advisors or Policy-Makers: The National Security Council," *American Perspective,* 2 (February, 1949), 443ff.; Dillon Anderson, "The President and the National Security," *Atlantic Monthly,* 197 (January, 1956), 41–46; Robert Cutler, "The Development of the NSC," *Foreign Affairs,* 34 (April, 1946), 441–58; Paul Y. Hammond, "The NSC as a Device for Interdepartmental Coordination," *American Political Science Review,* 54 (December, 1960), 899–910; and Henry M. Jackson, "To Forge a Strategy for Survival," *Public Administration Review,* 19 (Summer, 1959), 157–63.

[21]Truman, *Years of Trial and Hope,* 50.

would say today that we have come too far. Yet, for good or ill, substantial unity and coordination have been established.

A more subtle, less frequently noted, yet perhaps equally important problem in regard to the making of foreign policy was (and is) the relationship between the President and his chief adviser, the Secretary of State. Here also President Truman laid down some important precedents. At the risk of making overly glib characterization, one may say that the usual pattern before 1945 was either for the President virtually to ignore his Secretary of State and allow that official to handle such foreign policy problems as might arise, or for the President to take the reins himself and become for practical purposes his own Secretary of State.

Using the 1920's, again for illustration, certainly Hughes and Kellogg were given very free rein by their respective superiors, Harding and Coolidge. The Washington Naval Conference was very much Secretary Hughes's show, and this freedom was hardly less true of Kellogg in relation to the Peace Pact that bears his and Briand's names. On the other hand, it was strikingly true both of Wilson and of Franklin Roosevelt that, especially when foreign policy forced itself insistently upon their attention, they became their own Foreign Ministers. Bryan left office in disagreement with his Chief, and Lansing chafed at his enforced isolation from the making of major decisions. Secretary Hull took the fact that Roosevelt bypassed him in favor of Sumner Welles or Harry Hopkins with rather better outward grace but with hardly more enthusiasm, presumably.

In an age when concerns of foreign policy were usually minor and peripheral to the main issues of American life and national policy and were only episodically important, this kind of ill-defined and oscillating relationship between the President and his chief adviser could be tolerated, if not recommended. In the vastly changed circumstances of the post-World War II world, it would not do. President Truman at first did not appear to sense the problem and its nuances. His naïveté is no better suggested than by his appointment of James F. Byrnes as his first Secretary of State. After listing his nominee's other qualifications, he notes that Byrnes rather than himself had been the logical choice for Vice-President in 1944, and that he, Truman, had worked for his selection. He goes on, "I thought that my calling on him at this time [to become Secretary] might help balance things up."[22]

That this was a serious error the President himself was soon to find out. He had made the wrong choice for the wrong reason. Because Byrnes apparently felt that he by rights should be sitting where Truman then sat and that he knew more about foreign policy than the President, he asserted far more independence than his boss was prepared in the long run to tolerate. Truman rightly came to sense that whatever had been true in the past, foreign policy had to be his paramount and continuing preoccupation.[23] He did not approve of Roosevelt's methods, but neither could he tolerate anything less than full and complete interchange and confidence between himself and his Secretary of State. "The Secretary of State should never at any time come to think that he is the man in the White House," he wrote, "and the President should not try to be the Secretary of State."[24]

Accordingly, in time, Byrnes resigned, was replaced on an interim basis by General Marshall,[25] and finally by Dean Acheson. In Acheson, Truman found a Secretary with whom he could develop the kind of working relationship that he felt was proper and one that, in general terms, represented a logical compromise with the oscillating pattern of the past. Acheson, in a revealing essay, describes this relationship. He emphasizes above all the constant two-way flow of communication as the key to this new pattern and especially the importance of face-to-face meetings with his Chief.[26]

[22]Harry S. Truman, *Year of Decisions: 1945*, 24.
[23]Truman, *Year of Decisions*, 486–93.
[24]Truman, *Year of Decisions*, 255.
[25]The great bond of affection and respect that existed between Truman and Marshall undoubtedly smoothed their relationship as President and Secretary of State immeasurably. See Robert H. Ferrell, *The American Secretaries of State and their Diplomacy: George C. Marshall*, 263–65.
[26]Dean Acheson, "The President and the Secretary of State," in *The Secretary of State*, edited for the American Assembly by Don K. Price, 45. McGeorge Bundy, in the Preface he wrote to his collection of Acheson speeches, *The Pattern of Responsibility*, wrote: "Mr. Acheson, more than any other Secretary of State in recent history, has accepted the responsibility of acting as a personal advocate for his chief." (ix).

The President refers in his memoirs to "weekly" conferences with Byrnes.[27] Acheson wrote that he saw the President rarely less than four times a week and, in crisis periods, every day. Regularly each Monday and Thursday they spent an hour and a half together, during which time they would first dispose of their respective agendas of specific items and then talk more generally, "talk in which I could learn from the President his thoughts of all sorts."[28] The Secretary could learn the President's mind and, on his part, alert him to future developments and discuss possible courses of action before a problem became a crisis.

Obviously, no such relationship can become a complete model for the future. As Dean Acheson himself wrote in the same essay, "everything depends on the temperament and character of the men involved."[29] Certainly, a Kennedy will play a central role himself, while an Eisenhower will defer to the presumed superior wisdom of a Dulles (though it is hard to imagine anyone but Eisenhower deliberately putting himself into that kind of secondary position). Yet, it seems clear that in the future no President will be able to delegate his responsibilities for foreign policy to the extent this could be done in the twenties, nor will any President be able to find the time and perhaps the talent to be his own Foreign Minister. Hence, the Truman–Acheson model is bound to be far more popular than either the Harding–Hughes or the Roosevelt–Hull patterns. Presidents may not consciously emulate Truman, but they will almost certainly arrive at a similar conclusion, impelled by similar forces.[30]

In the area of domestic policy and legislative leadership, though Harry Truman may have fewer successes to his credit, his experience was significant and instructive. Again, he had inherited a radically changed state of affairs from that which obtained before 1933. The Presidency, in the interim, had been such a commanding source of policy initiative that the results

[27]Truman, *Years of Trial and Hope*, 99.
[28]Acheson, "The President and the Secretary of State," 45.
[29]Acheson, "The President and the Secretary of State," 43.
[30]Douglas Southall Freeman, in his Introduction to the Bundy volume, wrote: ". . . future Secretaries can scarcely hope for a better situation than has existed between Acheson and President Truman."

amounted to the greatest legislative revolution in the history of the Republic. This precedent, coupled with the expectancy that followed the end of the war, doubtless persuaded Mr. Truman and his advisers that the wave of reform was not yet spent if indeed innovation had not become a permanent feature of the political landscape.[31]

At any rate, on September 6, 1945, a scant five months after coming into office and, by his own account, as soon as he could possibly find the time to prepare it, the President sent Congress a twenty-one-point message that, he said in his memoirs, constituted the platform of his Administration. It was the longest address by a President since T.R. had sent one of 20,000 words in 1901![32] This formidable gesture removed any doubt that he felt an obligation to provide Congress with a comprehensive agenda to match the New Deal and to extend it into what came soon to be called the Fair Deal.

This acceptance of the role of legislative leadership was impelled by neither foreign nor domestic crisis (as had usually been the case in the past) but rather by a quite new set of expectations, spawned in the preceding decade. No President who came to office after the New Deal era would be able to escape the responsibility of providing Congress with much of its agenda. This new responsibility carried no new power to win congressional support for presidential proposals, however, save possibly that represented by a greater willingness in the Congress to receive suggestions and guidance from the White House. The legislative branch sensed a need for leadership in the era of Big Government, while retaining its traditional quota of institutional jealousy of the Chief Executive.

From the President's side, to discharge these new responsibilities successfully, supporting innovations were called for in at least two directions. Formalized staff procedures would be

---

[31]See Richard E. Neustadt, "The Presidency and Legislation: Planning the President's Program," *American Political Science Review*, 49 (December, 1955), 1000.

[32]Truman, *Year of Decisions*, 416, 420. Text of message is in *Public Papers, 1945*, Item 128. For comment on the impact and significance of this message as well as a general evaluation of the Truman record with Congress, see Bernstein, "The Presidency Under Truman," 8ff. Note also Richard E. Neustadt, "Congress and the Fair Deal: A Legislative Balance Sheet," *Public Policy*, 5 (1954), 351–58.

essential to multiply the hands, eyes, and ears of a hard-pressed Chief Executive, and wary new approaches to the ever-suspicious congressional animal must be devised. Presidents faced with the year-in-and-year-out need to lead the legislative branch could not count on the drive of crisis or the euphoria of a "honeymoon" period to produce action. New strategies that would have general and continuing usefulness must be elaborated from the combined wisdom and experience of the past.

In the matter of staff, Mr. Truman inherited some useful developments from the Roosevelt era. The legislative reference service of the Bureau of the Budget, which had been established in the early twenties to study agency bills requiring expenditures, had been broadened to embrace all agency proposals in the thirties. Bills were now reviewed by this office before introduction in Congress, and enrolled bills were again processed by it for their accord with the program of the President on the way to the White House from Congress. This machinery gave the Chief Executive the means of maintaining continuing surveillance, not only on the activity of Congress, but of the flood of proposals spawned by the growing executive establishment.[33]

More directly related to legislative leadership, there had developed during the Roosevelt years an informal but quite effective set of procedures, centering on the role of speechwriter Samuel Rosenman, for soliciting departmental ideas that might be included in the State of the Union Message. This message had in turn become, quite naturally, the annual summary agenda the President provided for Congress. From the mass of material thus gathered, selection could be made, and drafts of the message prepared. These would be put in final shape by the speech writers working closely with Mr. Roosevelt.[34]

In 1945 President Truman still had Rosenman and another Roosevelt holdover who was a key cog in the process, Harold Smith, Director of the Budget. (The Bureau acted as clearing

[33]See detailed account of these developments in Richard E. Neustadt, "The Presidency and Legislation: The Growth of Central Clearance," *American Political Science Review*, 48 (September, 1954), 641–71.

[34]Neustadt, "Planning the President's Program," 1001.

house and "backfield" staff in this operation.) By 1946, however, both of these individuals had left the government. Furthermore, the newly created Council of Economic Advisers
was getting into operation, and the Office of War Mobilization and Reconversion under John Steelman was still in existence and filling a coordinating role.[35] The green Truman staff,
augmented by CEA and OWMR, duplicated each other's work
and got in each other's way in their overlapping efforts to
solicit the departments and frame the President's program (or
programs).[36]

Out of this experience, product of growing pains engendered
by new responsibilities and new contrivances to help fill them,
there had to develop more formalized procedures and more
regularized channels for doing what it had earlier been possible
to do on an almost casual basis. In other words, the new scale
of presidential activity plus a new set of White House occu-
pants who did not have the benefit of a decade of comradery,
inevitably called for a new level of routinization. From then
on, the program of the President would emerge as a carefully
meshed staff product each January. (The new Eisenhower
team, Neustadt tells us, scorned this machinery and produced
a brief and general State of the Union message in 1953. So
compelling were the expectations that had become rooted in
the preceding two decades, however, that for 1954 the new
team revived an even more elaborate version of the Truman
machinery and produced a full-blown presidential program that
second January.)[37]

On another staff front, President Truman's inaction left innovation largely up to his successors: the elaboration of White
House congressional liaison staff. Both he and Roosevelt made
use of staff people to supplement their own efforts at weekly
meetings with legislative leaders. Both were cool, however, to
an organized and continuing staff effort of this sort.[38] It was
left up to Eisenhower, as Neustadt rather skeptically suggests,

---

[35]For a study of OWM and OWMR, see Herman M. Somers, *Presidential Agency.*

[36]Neustadt, "Planning the President's Program," 1002.

[37]Neustadt, "Planning the President's Program," 982ff.

[38]Neustadt, "Planning the President's Program," 1016n56.

to establish "in his entourage an Army-type liaison operation, its several staff aides covering each corner of the Hill on regular patrols."[39] President Kennedy continued the same practice and further elaborated it; President Johnson retained Larry O'Brien to serve him as he had served his predecessor.[40]

Having a skillful Larry O'Brien around with staff and with a card-indexed file of preferences and foibles in Congress is of course no guarantee, as the modest Kennedy legislative record suggests. Nor is an institutionalized system for framing the presidential legislative program insurance of success. Both of these, however, fit logically into what seems to be emerging as the appropriate formula for handling Congress: maximum use of the party leadership machinery, coupled with an ideologically low-key, highly individualized approach through careful staff work; a full-blown program and agenda, with clear indication of priorities and delineation of objectives in detail through special messages accompanied with draft legislation; a general approach that plays down partisanship, takes into account the essentially consensual nature of the operation of Congress, and focuses accordingly on key individuals in the dispersed formal and informal power structures within Congress.

Only parts of this perhaps rashly ventured sketch for an optimum strategy squared with the Truman approach. He initiated the practice early of deluging Congress with massive legislative shopping lists but, paradoxically, coupled this at times with a former senator's reticence at "meddling in legislative tactics."[41] As time went on, an evolution occurred in this area. By January, 1947, the current practice of sending up three separate messages and thereby obtaining sharper focus on legislative needs—State of the Union, Budget Message, and Economic Report—had been inaugurated. Truman's earlier de-

39Neustadt, "Planning the President's Program," 1016.

40For developments down to and especially during the Kennedy Administration, see Edward P. Morgan, "O'Brien Presses on With the 'Four P's'," *New York Times Magazine* (March 25, 1962), 28–29, 116, 118; and also Stanley Kelley, Jr., "Presidential Legislative Leadership: The Use of Patronage," paper delivered at the 1962 Annual Meeting of the American Political Science Association.

41Neustadt, *Presidential Power,* 173.

mands for legislation, writes Neustadt, were emphatic if not especially specific. In 1948, tone and content shifted perceptibly in the direction of greater specificity and sharper delineation. After his re-election, these trends continued, with greater rationalization of sequential messages and bill drafts.[42]

As to general approach, the President seemed to oscillate between leaving up to Congress what they chose to do with his many proposals and rather vigorous intervention on key issues. When he became involved in an all-out effort, as with the price control issue in 1945–1946, he turned it into a slugging match. In this instance he doubtless damaged his prospects for future favorable action on other elements in his program by the way he bludgeoned Congress and alienated his own party's legislative leaders.[43] The calling of the special session of the Eightieth Congress in the summer just before the 1948 election, though brilliant election strategy as the November outcome suggests, probably had the same degree of impact in undercutting his long-term relations with the congressional establishment on both sides of the aisle.

Much of the recent research that has been done on Congress emphasizes its institutional aspects.[44] By contrast, much of the writing during the Roosevelt–Truman eras rested on the assumption that Congress is—or should be—an essentially partisan operation, more or less on the model of the House of Commons.[45] The recent literature is replete with references to the "inner club," "the establishment," and generally to the informal patterns of relationship and interaction that obtain.[46]

---

[42]Neustadt, "Planning the President's Program," 999f.

[43]Jay S. Goodman, "Harry S. Truman and Price Control: A Case Study," unpublished seminar paper, Brown University, 1963.

[44]See Donald R. Matthews, *United States Senators and Their World,* as an example of the current emphasis in the literature on Congress as institution. Others have done work based on the same insights and approaches, Richard F. Fenno, for example, in an article entitled: "The House Appropriations Committee as a Political System: The Problem of Integration," *American Political Science Review,* 56 (June, 1962), 310–24, applied them to a single committee and showed the same nonpartisan institutional forces at work.

[45]See, for instance, Roland Young, *This is Congress;* Thomas K. Finletter, *Can Representative Government Do the Job?* George B. Galloway, *Congress at the Crossroads;* and James MacGregor Burns, *Congress on Trial.*

[46]The phrase *inner club* seems to have been originated, at least in application to the Senate, by William S. White in his book, *Citadel: The Story of the United*

The tone is usually analytical, uncritical, and, in fact, by implication at least, defensive of the institutional *status quo.* The earlier writings were almost invariably reformist and highly critical. The most recent critical writing by insiders like Senator Clark, for instance, seeks to reform these *in*formal aspects, primarily.

These recent studies of Congress have provided a valuable corrective to the most stridently critical writings of the past and their invariable call for more vigorous partisanship and party discipline. The fact of the matter is that Congress functions only in part through partisan mechanisms. The crucial committee apparatus is only partially party-oriented, and the "inner club" is quite nonpartisan. Major legislative enactments more often than not are the result of the emergence of a bipartisan majority or even consensus, contrived through the mediation of the party leaders *and* via the nonparty elements in the congressional power structure.[47] Members' loyalty to the legislative institution seems often to be as strong as to their party. Donald Matthews points out that the Senate folkways frown on excessive partisanship.[48] William White, popularizer of this approach to Congress, has written: "[The Senate] is, oddly, not really a very partisan place, incredible though this statement may seem, as partisanship is normally understood— that is, as bitter and unending friction between two *parties.*"[49]

In light of this recent work it seems evident that no well-rounded appraisal of Truman's relations with Congress can be achieved without reading some of these more recent insights into his period in office. Is it not probable that, in using the Turnip Session in 1948 for what were regarded as purely partisan purposes, the President ran the grave risk of alienating Congress as an institution—the Democrats who would operate its party and committee machinery after the election as well as

---

States Senate; Senator Joseph S. Clark (D. Pa.) used another of these terms in the title of his little volume, *The Senate Establishment.*

[47]Ralph K. Huitt's depiction of the Johnson style as Senate Majority Leader shows these personal and nonpartisan aspects along with the partisan: "Democratic Party Leadership in the Senate," *American Political Science Review,* 55 (June, 1961), 333–44.

[48]Matthews, *United States Senators and Their World,* 98.

[49]White, *Citadel,* 24.

the Republicans who were the immediate campaign target? A quick survey of contemporary comment turns up no really satisfactory evidence to support this hunch, but does produce suggestive bits and pieces. Naturally, the Republicans were furious. New Hampshire Senator Styles Bridges is quoted in *Time* as having said that Mr. Truman would be answered by the "maddest Congress you ever saw."[50]

The Republican statement issued in answer to the President's message to the special session ran, in its opening paragraph, in part:

This session was called . . . solely as a political maneuver in the campaign for his own reelection, . . . *It was called without consultation with the leaders of Congress,* after Congress had adjourned with the full acquiescence and approval of the minority leaders.[51]

Many Southern Democrats expressed themselves angrily but, admittedly, as much because of the civil rights fight the President promised to force upon them as for any other reason. Doubtless many reactions, though couched in outwardly partisan and regional interest terms, were mixed with feelings that the Congress itself had been affronted as an institution. Cabell Phillips has written that the special session opened July 26 "with much . . . offended congressional dignity. . . . Some members, to emphasize their resentment, did not even rise from their seats as the President entered and left the chamber."[52] In any event, moves of this kind by the President and the general stridency of his dealings with the legislative branch poisoned relations between them and helped to ensure that little of the Fair Deal would end up on the statute books.[53]

By contrast, Presidents Kennedy and Johnson risked censure from their more militant fellow partisans by treating Congress

---

[50]*Time* (July 26, 1948), 15.

[51]*New York Times* (July 28, 1948), 4 (emphasis added).

[52]Cabell Phillips, *The Truman Presidency: The History of a Triumphant Succession,* 266.

[53]A case can be made that the times were no longer ripe for innovation, and that this explains his failures. This implies a theory of congressional action that completely leaves out the role of the President as an important variable, however. Furthermore, President Truman did get very important foreign policy innovation through using, in this area, more skillful, conciliatory, nonpartisan—and more successful, tactics.

in largely institutional terms, carefully cultivating committee chairmen and key opposition figures like Senator Dirksen, Republican minority leader. Recall Kennedy's long delay in signing the executive order ending discrimination in federally aided housing lest he annoy the Southern patriarchs in Congress and jeopardize his program generally.[54] One suspects, given the conditions that prevail, that this institutional emphasis will pay more consistent dividends in an era in which the President is expected to lead on a continual basis.

This formula is no easy prescription for a White House encumbent, however. It brings into focus again the conflict, inherent in the office, between the President's role as "President of all the people" and builder of consensus (in and out of Congress) and his role as party leader (also, in and out of Congress). If he seeks to fill the first of these and eschews the second, he may get along well with Congress and preserve his public image, but he also denies himself use of some important leadership weapons. Eisenhower's leadership suffered from too great a nonpartisan emphasis, much as Truman's did from excessive partisanship. Where to strike the balance is a nice question. In no area of presidential operation are final answers or pat formulae less likely to emerge than here.

The problem of presidential leadership of opinion in the post-Roosevelt period has been a difficult one—and not merely because FDR's act was so hard to follow, though his inimitableness was part of the difficulty. Chief Executives committed to leadership in both foreign and domestic affairs—whether committed by conviction or only by the forces of circumstance we have been examining—must do so in part by massing the public for support of their programs. An aroused and sympathetic citizenry is the last best hope of moving Congress to action, but foreign policy, too, rests on shifting sand until it is grounded in firm public acceptance.

Harry Truman came into office facing these imperatives.

[54]Kennedy's effort to force congressional acceptance of an Urban Affairs Department—with Robert Weaver as first Secretary—backfired in large measure because he became too partisan in that case. See Arthur M. Schlesinger, Jr., *A Thousand Days*, 711; and Theodore C. Sorensen, *Kennedy*, 481–82.

He followed a President who had rescued the press conference and turned it into a vital channel of communication and who made magnificent use of radio—both, through personal magnetism and virtuosity. Hence, the precedents available after 1945 were clear in theory but extremely hard to implement in practice. Take the press conference. FDR is said to have thoroughly enjoyed the dazzling performances of which he was often capable. Truman, in a preconference aside to a stenographer, is recorded as saying once in 1949: "I am getting so I dread these press conferences."[55]

The Missourian had no real choice save to work out his own approach to the press, and he had to do so in a period of rapid growth in the press corps and of changing demands born of technological innovation. The result was a process of formalization, even institutionalization, which no one fully and consciously intended. A first step was the move from the oval office locale to the Indian Treaty Room across the street, dictated by the numbers of reporters entitled to attend. The size and acoustics of the new room required microphones; microphones suggested recording of the exchanges. The radio broadcasting corporations, which felt inhibited in the conferences by the nonquotation rule, won the right, increasingly, to reproduce on the air short portions of these recordings. Thus, by the time General Eisenhower came into office, all that remained to be done was the allowing of full quotation and either direct broadcast or recording and filming for later use on the air and the television screen. The press conference had become an institution.

Mr. Truman's problem in dealing with the press, then, was more complex than that posed by his lack of Roosevelt's ability to use the President-reporter relationship to advantage or by his lack of a sense of pattern in either the product of a single news conference or of the news flowing from the Administration as a whole. The "institutionalization" of the news conference cut him off from certain opportunities for briefing and educating the press that had been inherent in the less formal,

---

[55]Cornwell, *Presidential Leadership of Public Opinion,* 170. The discussion of opinion leadership draws heavily on this source.

more private Roosevelt sessions. That Truman sensed this need is evidenced in the use he made of the special off-record meetings with groups of editors and news analysts.[56] In any larger sense, however, he never solved it. Neither did Eisenhower. President Kennedy solved the problem by making himself generally accessible to all comers among the press corps on an individual basis, thereby carefully reopening private channels that had been largely closed since Wilson's day.

These changes by Truman in the press conference came without deliberate planning in the White House. The same seems also to have been true of the use made by the new President both of radio and of the new medium, television. Mr. Truman went on the air no less frequently than his predecessor, but so closely identified had presidential broadcasting become with the Roosevelt fireside chats that many people wrote the White House, pleading that the new President follow suit. The broadcasts he had been making all along simply did not register as presidential broadcasts, apparently.[57] Beyond developing a more distinctive style of his own to rival his predecessor's, there was little Truman could have done about this baffling problem.

More, presumably, could have been done both in the substantive use of radio for leadership and in the use of television, for which no hampering Roosevelt tradition existed. Through the end of 1951 (the last year for which the *Public Papers* volume had appeared), the President broadcast seventeen radio or radio-and-television "messages to the American People" (as they are carried in the indexes). These messages fall, essentially, into the "fireside chat" category. All the other broadcasts so listed were brief comments on the opening of a Red Cross or Community Chest campaign, lighting the Christmas tree, and so forth. Nor does this group of seventeen include State of the Union messages or other speeches to live audiences, which were also broadcast. In other words, these were Truman's direct uses of the electronic media for leadership of national opinion.

---

[56]Cornwell, *Presidential Leadership of Public Opinion,* 166f.
[57]Cornwell, *Presidential Leadership of Public Opinion,* 268f.

Seven of these seventeen related to foreign affairs, most of them to the Korean War crisis.[58] Of the remaining ten, another seven dealt with price controls and closely related matters or, in any event, did not deal with Fair Deal programs like health insurance or the Brannan Plan.[59] The other three were addresses on: the status of the reconversion program, January 3, 1946; on the railroad strike, May 24 of the same year; and on the President's veto of Taft-Hartley, June 20, 1947. Interesting is the almost complete lack of radio-television speeches discussing with the public the elements of the Fair Deal with which Congress was making so little progress.

Actually, the 1946 speech on reconversion was a lengthy, point-by-point commentary on Congress' handling of the various proposals the President had laid before it in his agenda of the previous September. *Indictment* might be a more appropriate term than *commentary*. The speech is filled with phrases like: Progress has been distressingly slow; it [Congress] has done neither [follow his recommendations or enact its own]; Congress has done little—very little; and so forth. The tone of this speech, coming as it does less than nine months after Mr. Truman took office, is instructive. It is a far less subtle, far more heavy-handed approach to the legislative branch via the public than Mr. Roosevelt used. It suggests quite vividly, both in its tone and its early date in the Truman incumbency, that the President never made much effort to court the Congress as institution but, rather, treated it with hostility from the start. It is useful to note that this speech came well before the election of the Eightieth Congress and preceded the sharply partisan turn that President-Congress relations then took.

Significantly, the only other instance in this listing in which the President dealt with a major pending legislative item besides economic controls was his plug for the Marshall Plan in October, 1947, in the last part of a speech that called again upon a forthcoming special session to deal with price controls. It is interesting to note that this speech was delivered

---

[58]Delivered on August 9, 1945; September 1, 1945; July 19, 1950; September 1, 1950; December 15, 1950; April 11, 1951; and November 7, 1951.
[59]Delivered on October 30, 1945; June 29, 1946; October 14, 1946; October 24, 1947; July 13, 1949; September 9, 1950; and June 14, 1951.

during the period when he was using special off-the-record press conferences with editorial writers and commentators to very good effect in preparing the ground for this same major innovation in foreign policy.

The effective use of television represents a difficult challenge to the Presidency, at least as difficult as that which radio posed earlier. One is not sure that THE video formula which corresponds in success with the Roosevelt chat technique has been discovered even yet, if indeed there is one. On the other hand, it seems fair to say that the Truman people took too little notice of the fact that television is not the same as radio, nor merely an adjunct to radio.[60] Clearly, it makes its own very special demands on the public figure who would use it with maximum effect. Not until the rather far-fetched efforts of Robert Montgomery and the Eisenhower staff were attempts made to harness it explicitly to the White House enterprise.

Unquestionably, some of the most significant Truman innovations in the presidential establishment came in the area of staff and its use. Roosevelt had been responsible for the formation of the Executive Office, but much remained to be done toward the full institutionalization of the Presidency, especially in the inner circle: the White House Office itself. Aside from the addition of the six anonymous assistants in 1939, the office functioned on the same basis that had obtained at least since Jackson's day. Presidents traditionally had had very few assistants paid out of funds allocated for that purpose to the White House. Rather, they borrowed individuals from departments and agencies, who remained for all practical purposes presidential employees but were still carried on the rolls of the agency and were paid by it. Accordingly, the listing of White House Office personnel amounted to sixty at most until after Truman had taken over. Then, at his in-

---

[60]Interviews with members of the Truman staff turned up no evidence that special thought had been given to the question of how television should be used.

sistence, the system was regularized, and all those working for the President were transferred to a central presidential payroll. Immediately, the number so listed jumped to just under three hundred—reflecting no doubt the true state of affairs for some time past.[61]

This move alone, though only symbolic in its operational importance, nonetheless did give further concrete form to the White House staff operation. In dealing with staff members, Roosevelt had always deliberately kept lines and relationships very loose and flexible—even chaotic, one might plausibly suggest. This informality did not fit the emerging Truman style, and he soon instituted daily morning staff meetings over which he presided and which comprised (at least on one occasion when John Hersey was a guest) some dozen people: the Appointments, Press and Correspondence secretaries, The Assistant to the President (Steelman), the Special Counsel, three administrative assistants, two of his three military aides, and the Executive Clerk.[62]

Accounts suggest that the President handled these sessions very informally, going around the room to ask each person about his day's concerns, and raising matters himself that he wanted handled or that were in process. Some specialization was evident, but a good deal of fluidity of assignment remained. Though John Steelman carefully cherished his title as The (capital T) Assistant to the President, neither he nor anyone else played a Sherman Adams role under Harry Truman. Steelman himself notes that his position grew out of the Directorship of OWM/OWMR, which had been created by Roosevelt to mesh aspects of the war effort and had been held by Jimmy Byrnes, Fred Vinson, John Snyder, and then Steelman.[63] By all accounts, The Assistant was not much more than *primus inter pares* in the corps of assistants.

The Council of Economic Advisers provides a particularly interesting case study in the onward march of presidential staff-

---

[61]Cornwell, *Presidential Leadership of Public Opinion*, 208f.

[62]John Hersey, "Ten O'Clock Meeting," *New Yorker* (April 14, 1951), 38–55.

[63]Steelman and Kreager, "The Executive Office as Administrative Coordinator," 693.

ing. At least two developments of the Roosevelt era underlie this notion of providing institutional staff advice to the President in conjunction with the formal acceptance of governmental responsibility for the stability and health of the economy (in the Full Employment Act of 1946). On the one hand, there had been the brain trust that FDR put together before he became President, which included Moley, Tugwell, and others and which supplied him with much of his economic advice, once he got into office. On the other, there was the position of economic adviser to the Executive Council and later to the National Emergency Council, which was held during the short lives of these two bodies by Winfield Riefler. This latter position was set up to supply these coordinating bodies with such basic information about economic trends as could be gleaned from the rather primitive sources then available. There is much interesting discussion in the NEC transcripts of this problem: the recovery effort was functioning largely in the dark with little reliable data on either the target problems or the progress being made.[64]

Judging by a rather poignant utterance of President Harding's, even that passive Chief Executive felt on occasion the need for this kind of staff information and advice:

I don't know what to do or where to turn in this taxation matter. Somewhere there must be a book that tells all about it, where I could go to straighten it out in my mind. But I don't know where the book is, and maybe I couldn't read it if I found it! And there must be a man in the country somewhere who could weigh both sides and know the truth. Probably he is in some college or other. But I don't know where to find him.[65]

How much more would Presidents after the Great Depression, and especially after the legislation on full employment, need information and advice! They must have accurate data on the condition of the economic terrain and also counsel of the brain-trust sort on strategy for coping with emerging disequilibria.

Machinery for supplying these wants—and whether *formal* machinery was really called for—became matters of much dis-

[64]Lester G. Seligman and Elmer E. Cornwell, Jr., *New Deal Mosaic: Roosevelt Confers with His National Emergency Council*, 13, 17, 21.
[65]William Allen White, *Autobiography*.

cussion during passage of the Full Employment Act.[66] One of the recurrent themes in this discussion was desire to regularize what had remained, in the eyes of many, dangerously unsystematic and elusive under Roosevelt. That is, those who saw the Roosevelt brain-trusters as dangerous radicals with ill-defined behind-the-scenes influence wanted to institutionalize the President's sources of advice in such a way as to make them more responsible and visible.[67] This impulse apparently lay in the background not only of the establishment of CEA but perhaps of NSC and other agencies as well. Professor Neustadt writes that "It is no more than mild exaggeration to call NSC 'Forrestal's Revenge,'. . ."[68]

Whatever the motives, it is clear again in this instance that new assumptions of responsibility by the White House were bound to spawn increasingly formalized means for their discharge. Here—and elsewhere—the record does not always show direct and deliberate presidential action to bring new staff aids into being.[69] But as noted at the outset, individual presidential styles are not the only shaping forces at work in molding the institution. In this instance Truman's major contribution seems to have been a willingness to utilize the new council, once it was established, a willingness born both of acceptance of the theory behind its establishment and of a liking for formalized staff procedures. The initial impulse to create the group came from outside the Truman White House and, ultimately, from the generally felt need that produced the Full Employment Bill. Interwoven with this impulse was the reactionary anti-Roosevelt strand that shaped much postwar thinking about the office.

It would appear that the intentions of this latter group were in large part frustrated in the years following 1952. Even dur-

[66]See Stephen K. Bailey, *Congress Makes a Law, passim;* also Edwin G. Nourse, *Economics in the Public Service;* Corinne Silverman, *The President's Economic Advisers;* and Edward S. Flash, Jr., *Economic Advice and Presidential Leadership.*

[67]Lester G. Seligman, "Presidential Leadership: The Inner Circle and Institutionalization," *Journal of Politics,* 18 (August, 1956), 416 and *passim.*

[68]Richard E. Neustadt, "Approaches to Staffing the Presidency: Notes on F.D.R. and J.F.K.," *American Political Science Review,* 57 (December, 1963), 860.

[69]Bailey, *Congress Makes a Law,* 222.

ing the Truman years, the transition from Nourse's to Keyserling's leadership added flexibility to CEA as a presidential staff arm that was beyond the narrow focus on making available impartial economic expertise. Leon Keyserling represented a necessary transition to a blending of this expertise with advocacy of White House policies.[70] Only thus could this institutionalized brain trust have secured for itself a trusted role in the inner circle. The President must have *his* men around him; he would have little use for neutral technicians thrust upon him from outside.

In describing the transition from the Democratic Truman Administration to the Republican Administration of Eisenhower as it affected CEA, Corinne Silverman outlines the changes that Arthur F. Burns, Eisenhower's new chairman, demanded and received in the form and operation of the council.[71] These alterations, coupled with the fact that most of the forty-member economic and clerical staff changed, suggests recognition of the special relationship that had to be developed between each new White House incumbent and CEA. Whatever Congress intended, it succeeded only in providing a flexible set of forms into which new content could be injected by each new President. Or, as Edward Flash has written: "It [CEA] has not developed as a permanent entity with bureaucratic formality, specified procedures, and self-sustaining operations. Instead, it has emerged more as a variable group of individuals directly identified with and dependent upon the President."[72]

As time has gone on there seems to have been a clear and significant trend in the development of a public advocacy role for the council. With increasing frequency mentions have appeared of speeches given outside of Washington by the chairman, explaining and defending presidential policies in his area of concern, such as "guidelines" for price and wage increases. Here perhaps is a further subtle form of institutionalization of the presidential enterprise. The President now has a staff member who can combine the roles of providing expert advice and

---

[70]See Silverman, *The President's Economic Advisers, passim.*
[71]Silverman, *The President's Economic Advisers,* 15.
[72]Flash, *Economic Advice and Presidential Leadership,* 293.

supplementing the Chief Executive's own efforts in explaining the resulting policy decisions.

The relationship of innovations and changes in the Truman era to those in succeeding incumbencies is suggested by this last point. Each new President from Eisenhower on has filled the office in his own inimitable way. Each has brought variations, subtle or otherwise, to the use he has made of the staff contrivances he found waiting for him. But note: Each HAS begun where his predecessor left off. None of these developments of the Truman period has been discarded. The idea of meshing foreign and military policy through explicit processes of consultation, if not through the NSC in the precise manner intended by Congress or followed by Truman, has certainly survived. In fact, John Kennedy retreated to the refuge of the NSC after the Bay of Pigs nightmare. Personality, as Acheson foretold, has certainly dictated the relations between Presidents and their Secretaries of State, but in no case, even that of Dulles, has practice strayed very far from the Truman model.

On the domestic side, the Truman-elaborated methods for providing Congress with its annual agenda have become firmly institutionalized. The only significant innovation here has been perhaps a continued development of the practice of following up brief mention in the State of the Union Message of legislative goals with special messages elaborating each subject. It is true, of course, that the strategy of, and staffing for, White House dealings with Congress owe less to the Missourian than to his successors.

Presidents after 1952 experimented a great deal with uses of the communications media to reach the public, addressing themselves to the problem with more deliberate attention than Mr. Truman expended. The results of these efforts, though representing significant extensions of the developments made in the Truman era, have not always reflected in success the concern that has gone into them. No one, at any rate, has tried seriously to turn the clock back to pre-Truman practices, save possibly Lyndon Johnson.[73] Within the White House itself,

---

[73]Johnson succeeded in making a partial return to the less formal Roosevelt press conference practices, though over continuing demands from the press corps for the mass Kennedy-era conferences.

in sheer statistical terms, the trends of the forties have been projected on a rising curve into the fifties and sixties. The average number in the White House office force for the Truman years (after consolidation in the White House payroll) was about 250, for the Eisenhower period 350, and for the short Kennedy tenure about 420.[74] On the subtler matter of the use and organization of staff, following the hyper-rationalization of the General's system, something much closer to the less formal Truman practice—with a dash of Roosevelt —seems to have been the Kennedy–Johnson style. No administration has made less than full use of the Council of Economic Advisers, each content to adapt it by staffing it to taste from the range of views available in the economic profession.

In short, to a surprising degree the institutional innovations in the Presidency we associate with the Truman incumbency have stood the test of time and have provided precedents for the future. Each new President, within broad limits, is free to restructure the office to suit his own style. That adaptations following 1952 have been so relatively modest is testimony to the impact of the inescapable demands that now are made on the Presidency, but also to the soundness of the institutional foundation Harry Truman laid.

If this essay is to serve its primary purpose, it must not only provide some insight into the Truman Presidency based on work already done, but it must also embody suggestions for future investigation. We know all too little about the Truman Presidency—or about most presidential incumbencies, for that matter. Considerable work has been done on the policies of the Truman and other administrations (though this too is far from sufficient), but about the office itself, its evolution, and the styles of those who have filled it, there is very little indeed. It is hoped that the interpretation of the Truman Administration as a transitional period of key importance and of perhaps unique impact, offered in the foregoing pages, will itself be suggestive to other students. Undoubtedly, there are other de-

---

[74]These figures are from various issues of the *Statistical Abstract of the United States.*

velopments in staffing and operation besides those mentioned that could be studied from this point of view.

There is no pretense here of providing more than a partial insight into the office of the President between 1945 and 1953, but even a partial interpretation may prompt insights into other parts of the total pattern. For example, efforts to evaluate Harry Truman's leadership as President probably must be judged with reference to this special transitional quality of his Administration—from the personalized to the institutionalized Presidency.

Truman came to the White House under conditions that raised—far more insistently than it had ever been raised before —the broad question of the relationship of the *President* as an individual to the *Presidency* as an institution. Prior to the 1930's any such distinction would rightly have been brushed aside as a semantic quibble. The office then was a one-man show, always had been, and remained so at least until the 1939 order establishing the Executive Office of the President. But, given the accelerating process of institutionalization sketched here and over which Mr. Truman presided, willy-nilly, and the accompanying intra-White House delegation of presidential functions; given the general vast growth of the scale on which the whole presidential enterprise had to be conducted during the 1940's and 1950's; and given the intense and continuing preoccupation with foreign policy that was forced upon Harry Truman and his successors, this distinction became a very real one, posing urgent problems.

Truman faced, whether he fully sensed it or not, considerably more acute questions than even FDR had faced, of how he should allocate his limited time among the impossible demands upon it. He needed to decide even more carefully than Roosevelt which functions of the Presidency most insistently demanded the direct attention of the President and what kinds and amounts of attention should be devoted to them. Or, to put all of this in terms of presidential leadership: What were the optimum ways of exercising that leadership, in light of the fact that it was bound to be much more of an institutional product than ever before? It might well be that many of the uncertainties of Harry Truman's leadership stemmed from his perceptions or misperceptions of this problem and from his efforts (conscious or otherwise) to solve it. The question, in other words, was not solely one of his adroitness as a leader qua leader, but also of how to lead, in these new and complex institutional circumstances.

One wonders, for example, how many of his actions and decisions that seemed to fly in the face of either the facts or the theoretical logic of a situation were the results of faulty staff work, or of the faulty transmission to the President of the results of adequate staff work, or of the failure of the President to realize that he should have demanded more detailed staff effort and more detailed briefing in a given instance? How many of his difficulties with Congress reflected a failure to realize that a vast amount of the President's time —*personal* time—was needed for building support for White House proposals? Or, more to the point, how many of these difficulties resulted from a failure to realize that he did not have, personally, all of the necessary time and that carefully contrived staff aids were essential that could not only run interference for him but could also draw upon his personal efforts when they were essential, while leaving him alone when they were not?

The Truman leadership and its relation to White House staff is placed in an interesting light by a lengthy passage Cabell Phillips quotes from an interview with Clark Clifford. Phillips has just made the point that the President's policy instincts were liberal but quite vague. Clifford begins by noting that he and others, following the 1946 defeat, had become acutely aware of the Administration's lack of sense of direction, and a group decided to meet informally from time to time.

The idea was that the six or eight of us would try to come to an understanding among ourselves on what direction we would like the President to take on any given issue. And then, quietly and unobtrusively, each in his own way, we would try to steer the President in that direction. . . . Most of the Cabinet and the congressional leaders were urging Mr. Truman to go slow, to veer a little closer to the conservative line . . . it was two forces fighting for the mind of the President, . . . and I don't think Mr. Truman ever realized it was going on.[75]

If Clifford is right, then one of the problems of the Truman leadership clearly was the President's lack of personal sense of policy direction. All Presidents have, of course, been influenced in policy choices by those around them. Truman, however, needed advice on a far wider range of policy questions than any predecessor had ever faced, and yet seems to have brought to his evaluation of advice less clearly developed personal preferences. In an era demanding presidential policy leadership, staff and advisers were bound to try to fill any such vacuum.

Careful case studies of individual decisional situations and individual efforts at legislative leadership by the White House could throw much light on the Truman presidential leadership as a whole. Such studies would have to do more than delineate the substantive policy lines worked out or pursued with Congress. They must focus on processes and modes of operation. Data to study these latter are far from easy to come by, but reconstruction of sequences of events should be possible, at least to a limited extent, in many instances.

Shifting to the area of presidential public relations for further illustration, note, for example, the presidential press conference, which had become a weekly event under Truman. (It had been semiweekly under Roosevelt.) It is easy enough to say that Truman's ineptitude here was no more nor less than a comparison of his skill with that of the Old Master. But this is probably too simple an explanation. Some, at least, of the problem was that of coping with growing scale and a concomitant progressive formalization.

Presidential and staff effort was not always allocated in optimum ways. Quite evidently the failure to develop more formalized methods of preparation and briefing for the press conference was such a misallocation until nearly the end of Truman's tenure.[76] Probably more time thus spent would have

---

[75]Phillips, *The Truman Presidency*, 164.
[76]Cornwell, *Presidential Leadership of Public Opinion*, 172.

paid dividends. Along the same lines, the processes of framing the opening conference statements—which had come more and more into use, suggesting again the formalization of the whole business—and the writing of speeches, seem to have been poorly conceived. Admittedly, we have only glimpses of these processes, but apparently they were elaborate collegial efforts into which the President entered only rather late in the game.[77]

This raises not only the question of allocating the President's time, but also the more subtle question of when and how the man who is President must inject himself into an increasingly institutionalized leadership process to ensure that the essential elements of personal style and personality will make their impact. Unless this is done skillfully, the whole pattern of White House utterances may take on a dull, impersonal, dessicated, "committee-product" quality, in which there will remain no touch of the President as a human being with whom the public can identify. Again, it is the question of the President as a person in the Presidency as institution. The latter should not be allowed to obscure and smother the former.

Among the other lessons suggested by Eisenhower's long periods of illness was the fact that an institutionalized Presidency can operate virtually without a President at its center. The *Public Papers* volumes for 1955 and 1956 (the heart attack occurred in September, 1955) show a diminished but nonetheless steady outflow of press releases from the White House, suggesting the extent to which the Presidency functions autonomously when the Chief Executive is present and active as well as when he is inactive. The questions are, What is the essential difference when the President *is* actively involved? What must he do personally that his staff cannot do for him? What can he do better than staff could do for him? One of the keys to the success of presidential leadership in the era of the institutionalized Presidency must be the ability to answer these questions correctly.

---

[77]For an example of press statement drafting see: John Hersey, "The Wayward Press," *New Yorker*, December 16, 1950, p. 78f; and for a description of speech drafting under Truman, see Hersey, "Profiles: Mr. President," Part 5, "A Weighing of Words," *New Yorker* (May 5, 1951), 36–53.

Bureaucracy is a two-edged sword. When critical scale and size limits are reached, bureaucratization is essential to the functioning of organizations, the Presidency no less than any other. But it can envelop and smother the vital and creative forces of an institution in the process of enabling it to operate. That this has not yet happened to the Presidency nearly as much as it seems to have happened to the Papacy, for example, is a tribute to the skill and insight both of Presidents and those around them. As a potential problem, however, it is very real and important, perhaps not for a man with the enormous ego of Lyndon Johnson, but clearly it is for men constructed on the more modest lines of a Truman or an Eisenhower.

In summary, the foregoing discussion illustrates the ways in which insights gleaned from a study of the Presidency's institutional development can be turned to account by the student interested in the more personalized and personal aspects of the style of a particular President. Another way in which both presidential style and the operation of the office might be illuminated is through content analyses of the Presidents' utterances. Patterns of leadership regarding major policies could thus be identified, and generalizations about leadership techniques and perceptions result. Also, studies of content that focus on the tone of utterances rather than the substantive content might well be revealing. A comparative study of the tone and thrust of references to the Congress, made in speeches, messages, and press conferences, might provide the basis for comparing approaches to legislative leadership and for correlating these in at least rough ways with levels of success. One is struck, for example, as noted earlier, with the pointedly critical tone of the repeated references to Congress in President Truman's radio address on reconversion, made in January, 1946. Since so much of the pattern of relationship between President and legislative branch is made up of, or affected by, the cumulative impact of the rhetoric used on both sides, a study of these subtle but real factors would unquestionably be profitable.

It goes without saying that more work needs to be done on Harry Truman as a person. What were his key values and personality characteristics that in turn shaped his understanding of the Presidency, of power, of social change, and all the other perceptual and behavioral ingredients that blended into his way of functioning as President—in a word, again, his style? Careful accumulation of biographical data on important White House figures around the President that would highlight their backgrounds, relations to the President, their perceptions of their roles, the President's role, the problems he faced, the values that should guide his handling of them, and so on, is vital.

What relationships did staff people have outside the White House? What pattern of contacts did they have with the agencies of the executive branch and with other elements in the institutional environment within which the Presidency operates? Obviously, though the President has many such contacts himself, formal and informal, most of these relationships must be mediated through his staff aides. In the same manner, what kinds of access did organized interests and groups have to the White House, through whom, in relation to what policy areas, and with what measurable results? Again, what about the role of an agency like the Bureau of the Budget as a highly formalized staff arm of the President? Its relations with him, with his more immediate staff aides, with the agencies of the executive branch, with outside interest groups, and with the Congress are certainly of great interest, or should be, to any student of the Presidency as institution.

In short, the unanswered questions about Harry S Truman's Presidency are legion. Anything more complete than this illustrative listing would consume many pages. By the same token, no such listing should do more than excite the curiosity and energize the efforts of other investigators. Almost any resulting focus a student might select for his own work will, in so untilled a field, inevitably turn up new information and insights to add to our pitifully inadequate present stock.

BIBLIOGRAPHY

Books

Bailey, Stephen K., *Congress Makes a Law*. New York, Columbia University Press, 1950.

Bundy, McGeorge, *The Pattern of Responsibility.* Boston, Houghton Mifflin Company, 1952.

Burns, James MacGregor, *Congress on Trial.* New York, Harper & Row, Publishers, 1949.

Clark, Joseph S., *The Senate Establishment.* New York, Hill & Wang, Inc., 1963.

Cornwell, Elmer E., Jr., *Presidental Leadership of Public Opinion.* Bloomington, Indiana University Press, 1965.

Ferrell, Robert H., *The American Secretaries of State and Their Diplomacy: George C. Marshall.* New York, Cooper Square Publishers, Inc., 1966.

Finletter, Thomas K., *Can Representative Government Do the Job?* New York, Reynal and Hitchcock, 1945.

Flash, Edward S., Jr., *Economic Advice and Presidential Leadership.* New York, Columbia University Press, 1965.

Galloway, George B., *Congress at the Crossroads.* New York, Thomas Y. Crowell Company, 1946.

George, A. L., and J. L. George, *Woodrow Wilson and Colonel House: A Personality Study.* New York, The John Day Company, Inc., 1956.

Hammond, Paul Y., *Organizing for Defense: The American Military Establishment in the Twentieth Century.* Princeton, Princeton University Press, 1961.

Hargrove, Erwin C., *Presidential Leadership: Personality and Political Style.* New York, The Macmillan Company, 1966.

Matthews, Donald R., *United States Senators and Their World.* Chapel Hill, The University of North Carolina Press, 1960.

Neustadt, Richard E., *Presidential Power: The Politics of Leadership.* John Wiley & Sons, Inc., 1960.

Nourse, Edwin G., *Economics in the Public Service.* Harcourt, Brace & World, Inc., 1953.

Phillips, Cabell, *The Truman Presidency: The History of a Triumphant Succession.* New York, The Macmillan Company, 1966.

Price, Don K., ed., *The Secretary of State.* Englewood Cliffs, N. J., Prentice-Hall, Inc., 1960.

Quint, Howard H., and Robert H. Ferrell, *The Talkative President.* Amherst, The University of Massachusetts Press, 1964.

Schlesinger, Arthur M., Jr., *A Thousand Days.* Boston, Houghton Mifflin Company, 1965.

Seligman, Lester G., and Elmer E. Cornwell, Jr., *New Deal Mosaic: Roosevelt Confers with His National Emergency Council.* Eugene, University of Oregon Books, 1965.

Silverman, Corinne, *The President's Economic Advisers.* University, University of Alabama Press, 1959.

Somers, Herman M., *Presidential Agency*. Cambridge, Harvard University Press, 1950.
Sorensen, Theodore C., *Kennedy*. New York, Harper & Row, Publishers, 1965.
Truman, Harry S., *Memoirs*. Garden City, N. Y., Doubleday & Company, Inc., 1955, 1956.
Tugwell, Rexford G., *The Democratic Roosevelt*. Garden City, N. Y., Doubleday & Company, Inc., 1957.
White, William Allen, *Autobiography*. New York, The Macmillan Company, 1946.
White, William S., *Citadel: The Story of the United States Senate*. New York, Harper & Row, Publishers, 1957.
Young, Roland, *This Is Congress*. New York, Alfred A. Knopf, Inc., 1943.

Public Documents

Richardson, James D., ed., *A Compilation of the Messages and Papers of the Presidents*. Supplements. New York, Bureau of National Literature, Inc., 1897. 21 vols.
Public Papers of the Presidents: Harry S. Truman. Washington, D. C., Government Printing Office, 1961–1966. 8 vols.

Articles

Anderson, Dillon, "The President and the National Security." *Atlantic Monthly,* 197 (January, 1956), 41–46.
Bernstein, Barton J., "The Presidency Under Truman." *Yale Political Review,* 4 (Fall, 1964), 8ff.
Cornwell, Elmer E., Jr., "Coolidge and Presidential Leadership." *Public Opinion Quarterly,* 21 (Summer, 1957), 265–78.
———, "Presidential News: The Expanding Public Image." *Journalism Quarterly,* 36 (Summer, 1959), 275–83.
Cutler, Robert, "The Development of the N.S.C." *Foreign Affairs,* 34 (April, 1946), 441–58.
Fairman, Charles, "The President as Commander-in-Chief." *Journal of Politics,* 11 (February, 1949).
Fenno, Richard F., "The House Appropriations Committee as a Political System: The Problem of Integration." *American Political Science Review,* 56 (June, 1962), 310–24.
Hammond, Paul Y., "The NSC as a Device for Interdepartmental Coordination." *American Political Science Review,* 54 (December, 1960), 899–910.
Hersey, John, "The Wayward Press." *New Yorker* (December 16, 1950), 78ff.

————, "Ten O'Clock Meeting." *New Yorker* (April 14, 1951), 38–55.

————, "Profiles: Mr. President." Part 5, "A Weighing of Words." *New Yorker* (May 5, 1951), 36–53.

Huitt, Ralph K., "Democratic Party Leadership in the Senate." *American Political Science Review,* 55 (June, 1961), 333–44.

Jackson, Henry M., "To Forge a Strategy for Survival." *Public Administration Review,* 19 (Summer, 1959), 157–63.

Kirkpatrick, H. P., "Advisors or Policy-Makers: The National Security Council." *American Perspective,* 2 (February, 1949), 443ff.

Marx, Fritz Morstein, "The Bureau of the Budget: Its Evolution and Present Role." *American Political Science Review,* 39 (August, 1945), 653–84; (October, 1945), 869–98.

Morgan, Edward P., "O'Brien Presses on With the 'Four P's'." *New York Times Magazine* (March 25, 1962), 28–29, 116, 118.

Neustadt, Richard E., "Approaches to Staffing the Presidency: Notes on F.D.R. and J.F.K." *American Political Science Review,* 57 (December, 1963), 855–64.

————, "Congress and the Fair Deal: A Legislative Balance Sheet." *Public Policy,* 5 (1954), 351–58.

————, "The Presidency and Legislation: The Growth of Central Clearance." *American Political Science Review,* 48 (September, 1954), 641–71.

————, "The Presidency and Legislation: Planning the President's Program." *American Political Science Review,* 49 (December, 1955), 980–1021.

Seligman, Lester G., "Presidential Leadership: The Inner Circle and Institutionalization." *Journal of Politics,* 18 (August, 1956), 416ff.

Steelman, John R., and H. Dewayne Kreager, "The Executive Office as Administrative Coordinator." *Law and Contemporary Problems,* 21 (Autumn, 1956), 696ff.

"The Turnip Session." *Time,* 52 (July 26, 1948), 14–15.

Unpublished Studies

Goodman, Jay S., "Harry S. Truman and Price Control: A Case Study." Seminar paper, Brown University, 1963.

Kelley, Stanley, Jr., "Presidential Legislative Leadership: The Use of Patronage." Paper delivered at the Annual Meeting of the American Political Science Association, 1962.

Newspapers

New York Times, July 28, 1948.

Appendix A

HOLDINGS OF THE TRUMAN LIBRARY*

THE GROUPS OF PAPERS listed below have come to the Harry S. Truman Library primarily from former President Truman and from other persons who were active in the Truman Administration or were otherwise associated with Mr. Truman. The Library is now urging an even larger number of such persons to deposit their personal papers in the collections for research use. A considerable number of them have already agreed to do so. These include former Cabinet officers, other officials of the Truman Administration, and individuals who were significantly associated with Mr. Truman during some part of his career. In most cases the private papers of former government officials complement the official records of their agencies in the National Archives.

Papers opened to research by the Library are available on an equal basis to all persons engaged in serious study. A small portion of the collection is closed, in accordance with the stipulations of the donors. While it is the purpose of the Library to open as much of its holdings as possible for research use, donors have the legal right to stipulate conditions of access, which usually consist of lists of categories of papers that are to be closed. Examples of categories closed for the present are those that may be prejudicial to the conduct of the United States' foreign relations or that contain information that could be used to injure or embarrass living persons. This latter provision is designed only to protect legitimate personal privacy.

In addition to the papers, the Library has collections of books, transcripts of oral history interviews, microfilm, and audiovisual materials for the use of scholars.

Persons wishing to use papers and other materials should make advance application to the Director of the Library, informing him of the nature and purposes of their projects.

This list has been prepared by the staff of the Truman Library.

PHILIP C. BROOKS
Director
Harry S. Truman Library

---

*This is a list of the holdings in January, 1967. For information on additions, see the Research Newsletters of the Truman Library Institute.

GROUPS OF HISTORICAL MATERIALS

Group   *Cubic Feet*

1. Papers of Harry S. Truman as Senator and Vice-President,
   1934–45   85
2. Papers of Harry S. Truman as President, from the
   Central Files of the White House, 1945–53   2171
3. Files of Assistants, Aides, and Counsels to the
   President, 1945–53   112
4. Files of the White House Social Office, 1945–53   26
5. Files of the White House Office of Social
   Correspondence, 1945–53   76
6. Files of the White House Telegraph Office, 1945–53   5
7. Files of the White House Telephone Office, 1945–53   8
8. Files of the White House Official Reporter, 1945–53   15
9. File of Budget Bureau Reports to the President on
   Pending Legislation, 1945–53   37
10. Motion Picture Collection
11. Sound Recording Collection
12. Still Picture Collection
13. Museum Collection
14. Correspondence of President Harry S. Truman not part
    of the White House Central Files, 1945–53   less than 1
15. Post-Presidential Papers of Harry S. Truman, 1953—   29
16. Records Received from the Department of State
    Pertaining to the Truman Administration, 1945–48   3
17. General Historical Documents Collection, 1750—   1
18. Miscellaneous Historical Documents Relating to
    Harry S. Truman, 1884—   less than 1
19. Records of the President's Air Policy Commission,
    1947–48   13
20. Records of the President's Airport Commission, 1952   5
21. Records of the President's Committee on Civil Rights,
    1946–47   13
22. Records of the President's Commission on the Health
    Needs of the Nation, 1951–52   22
23. Records of the President's Commission on Immigration
    and Naturalization, 1952–53   6
24. Records of the President's Commission on Internal
    Security and Individual Rights, 1951   3
25. Records of the President's Advisory Committee on the
    Merchant Marine, 1947   6
26. Records of the President's Commission on Migratory
    Labor, 1950–51   5

27. Records of the President's Committee on Religion and
    Welfare in the Armed Forces, 1948–51   14
28. Records of the Missouri Basin Survey Commission,
    1952–53   11
29. Records of the Harry S. Truman Library, Inc., 1950–63   24
30. Papers of Jesse M. Donaldson, 1947–52 (Postmaster
    General, 1947–53)   1
31. Papers of John D. Clark, 1946–52 (Member of the
    Council of Economic Advisers, 1946–50; Vice Chair-
    man of the Council of Economic Advisers, 1950–53)   1
32. Records of the President's Scientific Research Board,
    1946–47   7
33. Records of the President's Water Resources Policy
    Commission, 1950–51   20
34. Papers of Samuel I. Rosenman, 1945–49 (Special
    Counsel to the President, 1945–46)   2
35. Records from the Democratic National Committee,
    1943–52   9
36. Papers of Frank McNaughton, 1938–52 (Washington
    Correspondent for *Time* magazine, 1941–49)   8
37. Papers of Charles G. Ross, 1945–50 (Press Secretary
    to the President, 1945–50)   2
38. Papers of Stephen J. Spingarn, 1933–64 (Administrative
    Assistant to the President, 1950; Member of the
    Federal Trade Commission, 1950–53)   18
39. Records of the Washington Office of the Cooperative
    League of the United States, 1936–49   59
40. Papers of Wallace J. Campbell, 1939–64 (Director,
    Washington Office of the Cooperative League of
    the USA, 1948–59)   26
41. Papers of Oscar L. Chapman, 1931–53 (Secretary
    of the Interior, 1949–53)   42
42. Papers of Myron G. Taylor, 1938–52 (Personal
    Representative of President Harry S Truman
    to the Vatican, 1945–50) (closed)   1
43. Papers of Charter Heslep, 1945–50 (Radio Broadcaster)   1
44. Papers of Henry A. Bundschu, 1939–56 (Independence,
    Missouri, lifelong friend of Harry S. Truman)   less than 1
45. Papers of Lina D. Adams, 1940–62 (Receptionist,
    Democratic National Committee, 1946–60)   less than 1
46. Papers of J. Howard McGrath, 1934–52 (U. S. Senator
    from Rhode Island, 1947–49; Chairman of the
    Democratic National Committee, 1947–49; Attorney
    General, 1949–52)   75

47. Papers of Alfred Schindler, 1934–55 (Under Secretary of Commerce, 1945–46) 11

48. Papers of Edwin A. Locke, Jr., 1941–53 (Special Assistant to the President, 1945–46; Coordinator of U. S. technical and economic aid to the Near East with the personal rank of Ambassador, 1951–52) 2

49. Papers of Nathaniel P. Davis, 1916–57 (Minister-Counsellor at the U. S. Embassy in Manila, 1946–47; Ambassador to Costa Rica, 1947–49; Minister to Hungary, 1949–51) less than 1

50. Records of the Harry S. Truman Library Institute for National and International Affairs, 1955–64 5

51. Papers of Frieda Hennock, 1948–55 (Member of the Federal Communications Commission, 1948–55) 9

52. Papers of John M. Redding, 1943–58 (Publicity Director, Democratic National Committee, 1947–50; Assistant Postmaster General, 1950–53) 9

53. Papers of James E. Webb, 1928–62 (Director of the Bureau of the Budget, 1946–49; Under Secretary of State, 1949–52) 33

54. Papers of Stanley Andrews, 1950–64 (Administrator, Technical Cooperation Administration, 1952–53) 1

55. Papers of James Boyd, 1927–64 (Director, U. S. Bureau of Mines, 1947–51) 5

56. Papers of Edward D. McKim, 1940–63 (Chief Administrative Assistant to the President, 1945; long-time friend of Harry S Truman) less than 1

57. Papers of Dillon S. Myer, 1943–53 (Commissioner of the Federal Public Housing Authority, 1946–47; Commissioner of the Public Housing Administration, 1947; Commissioner of Indian Affairs, 1950–53) less than 1

58. Papers of Joseph M. Jones, 1947–48 (Special Assistant to the Assistant Secretary of State for Public Affairs, 1946–48) 1

59. File of White House Press Releases, 1945–53 3

60. Papers of N. T. Veatch, 1926–33 (consulting engineer to the Jackson County Missouri Highway Department, 1926–33) less than 1

61. Records of the National Aircraft War Production Council, 1942–45 10

62. Transcript of Taped Interviews with Alben Barkley by Sidney Shalett, 1953 (biographer of Alben Barkley) less than 1

63. Papers of John W. Snyder, 1945–53 (Secretary of the
    Treasury, 1946–53)   26
64. Papers of Charles S. Murphy, 1951–61 (Special
    Counsel to the President, 1950–53)   5
65. Records of the President's Committee on Equality
    of Treatment and Opportunity in the Armed
    Services, 1949–50   4
66. Papers of Monrad C. Wallgren, 1929–59 (Chairman of
    the Federal Power Commission, 1950–51)   2
67. Papers of Frederick J. Lawton, 1943–63 (Director
    of the Bureau of the Budget, 1950–53; Member of
    the Civil Service Commission, 1953–63)   4
68. Papers of John C. Houston, 1945–54 (Special Assistant
    in the White House Office, 1950–51)   less than 1
69. Papers of Frank A. Waring, 1946–51 (Chairman of the
    Philippine War Damage Commission, 1946–51)   1
70. Selected Documents (duplicates) from the Records of the
    Commission on the Renovation of the Executive
    Mansion   less than 1
71. Papers of John W. Gibson, 1941–53 (Assistant
    Secretary of Labor, 1946–50; Chairman of the
    Displaced Persons Commission, 1950–52)   16
72. Papers of Warner W. Gardner, 1937–47 (Assistant
    Secretary of the Interior, 1946–47)   2
73. Papers of Raymond M. Foley, 1946–53 (Commissioner
    of the Federal Housing Administration, 1945–47;
    Administrator of the Housing and Home Finance
    Agency, 1947–53)   2
74. Papers of Herschel V. Johnson, 1929–53 (Ambassador
    to Brazil, 1948–53)   5
75. Papers of Philip M. Kaiser, 1948–54 (Assistant
    Secretary of Labor in Charge of International
    Affairs, 1949–52)   1
76. Papers of Paul M. Herzog, 1937–60 (Chairman of the
    National Labor Relations Board, 1945–53)   4
77. Papers of Frank Pace, Jr., 1946–53 (Director of the
    Bureau of the Budget, 1949–50; Secretary of the
    Army, 1950–53)   7
78. Papers of Sumner T. Pike, 1920–61 (Member of the
    Atomic Energy Commission, 1946–51)   5
79. Papers of James H. Foskett, 1919–54 (Naval Aide to
    the President, 1946–48)   1
80. Papers of Theodore Tannenwald, Jr., 1947–57 (Assistant
    Director and Chief of Staff to the Director for
    Mutual Security, 1951–53)   3

81. Papers of J. Weldon Jones, 1929–54 (Financial Adviser
to the United States High Commissioner to the
Philippines, 1935–40; Assistant Director of the
Bureau of the Budget, 1941–55)   8
82. Papers of Bryce B. Smith, 1924–62 (Mayor of
Kansas City, Missouri, 1930–39)   1
83. Papers of Joseph J. O'Connell, Jr., 1944–47 (General
Counsel of the Department of the Treasury, 1944–47)   1
84. Papers of Stephen A. Mitchell, 1903–60 (Chairman
of the Democratic National Committee, 1952–55)   28
85. Records of the National Committee Against Limiting
the Presidency, 1940–51   less than 1
86. Papers of Clinton P. Anderson, 1945–48 (Secretary
of Agriculture, 1945–48)   5
87. Papers of Sidney R. Yates, 1949–62 (Member of the
U. S. House of Representatives for the 9th District
of Illinois, 1949–62)   40
88. Records of the President's Materials Policy Commission,
1951–52   47
89. Newspaper clipping file of the Library of the
Democratic National Committee, 1946–63   74
90. World War I U. S. Army Maps showing actions in
which the 35th Division participated, 1917–19   less than 1
91. Papers of Lou E. Holland, 1918–60 (Kansas City,
Missouri, businessman and civic leader; Chairman
of the Smaller War Plants Corporation, 1942–43)   95
92. Records of the Committee for the Marshall Plan, 1947–51   1
93. Papers of Harry J. Anslinger, 1946–63 (U. S.
Commissioner of Narcotics, 1946–63)   less than 1
94. Records of the National Security Committee, 1947–50   1
95. Papers of Robert E. Freer, 1933–62 (Member of the
Federal Trade Commission, 1935–48)   18
96. Records of the United States Secret Service pertaining to
the protection of President Harry S Truman, 1945–53
(closed)   14
97. Papers of Major General Ralph E. Truman, 1944–53
(cousin of Harry S. Truman and Commanding General
of the 35th Division, 1938–42) (closed)   less than 1
98. Papers of David H. Stowe, 1947–52 (Administrative
Assistant to the President, 1949–53)   2
99. Papers of Joel D. Wolfsohn, 1937–52 (Assistant
Secretary of the Interior, 1952–53)   4
100. Papers of William M. Rigdon, 1945–52 (Assistant
Naval Aide to the President, 1945–53)   1

101. Papers of David D. Lloyd, 1949–63 (Administrative
     Assistant to the President, 1951–53)   22
102. Papers of Michael J. Galvin, 1933–63 (Under Secretary
     of Labor, 1949–53)   8
103. Papers of W. John Kenney, 1946–49 (Under Secretary
     of the Navy, 1947–49)   1
104. Papers of Harry H. Vaughan, 1945–53 (Military
     Aide to the President, 1945–53)   1
105. Papers of Gordon R. Clapp, 1933–63 (Chairman of
     the Board of Directors of the Tennessee Valley
     Authority, 1946–54; Chairman of the United Nations
     Economic Survey Mission for the Middle East, 1949)   1
106. Papers of James K. Knudson, 1930–63 (Member of
     the Interstate Commerce Commission, 1950–54)   1
107. Papers of John T. Koehler, 1949–51 (Assistant
     Secretary of the Navy, 1949–51)   less than 1
108. Papers of William L. Clayton, 1939–64 (Under
     Secretary of State for Economic Affairs, 1946–47)   14
109. Papers of Ellen Clayton Garwood, 1958–60 (daughter
     and biographer of William L. Clayton)   less than 1
110. Papers of Stanley Woodward, 1950–64
     (Ambassador to Canada, 1950–53)   less than 1
111. Papers of Tom L. Evans, 1920–65 (Kansas City,
     Missouri, businessman and civic leader and long-time
     friend of Harry S Truman)   4
112. Papers of Thomas C. Blaisdell, Jr., 1933–51 (Assistant
     Secretary of Commerce, 1949–51)   4
113. Papers of Sherman Minton, 1949–56 (Associate Justice
     of the United States Supreme Court, 1949–56)   3
114. Papers of Harold L. Enarson, 1941–53 (Special Assistant
     in the White House Office, 1950–52)   3
115. Papers of Gerhard Colm, 1944–46 (Assistant Chief,
     Fiscal Division, Bureau of the Budget,
     1940–46)   less than 1
116. Records of the President's Committee on Foreign Aid,
     1947   11
117. Papers of Francis P. Matthews, 1943–52 (Secretary
     of the Navy, 1949–51; Ambassador to Ireland,
     1951–52)   23
118. Papers of William A. Brophy, 1941–62 (Commissioner
     of Indian Affairs, 1945–48)   5

MICROFILM COLLECTION

M-1   Papers of George Washington, 1745–1799
M-2   Public Papers of Earl J. McGrath, January 1949–June 1953

M-3   Papers of the Adams Family, 1639–1889
M-4   Press Conferences of President Franklin D. Roosevelt, 1933–1945
M-5   Papers of Zachary Taylor, 1814–1931
M-6   Papers of William Henry Harrison, 1734–1939
M-7   Papers of Abraham Lincoln, 1833–1916
M-8   Papers of Chester A. Arthur, 1843–1938
M-9   Papers of Franklin Pierce, 1820–1869
M-10   Papers of John Tyler, 1691–1918
M-11   Papers of Grover Cleveland, 1828–1945
M-12   Papers of James Monroe, 1758–1839
M-13   Papers of Martin Van Buren, 1787–1860
M-14   Papers of Andrew Johnson, 1814–1932
M-15   Papers pertaining to Harry S. Truman, from the Franklin D. Roosevelt Library
M-16   Index to White House Press Releases, April 1945–January 1953
M-17   Correspondence between Arthur W. Wilson and Harry S. Truman and others, from the Cornell University Library, 1919–61
M-18   Papers of Dr. Michael M. Davis, 1939–55, including the records of the Committee for the Nation's Health, Inc.
M-19   Correspondence between Harry S. Truman and Alben Barkley, 1944–55, from the University of Kentucky Library
M-20   Letters regarding Presidential primaries, received by Richard H. Hansen from Governors of States and other prominent individuals, 1955–60
M-21   Papers of Mrs. Joseph M. Short as Secretary to the President, 1952–53
M-22   National Archives Case File 054-115 Truman Library, 1949–58
M-23   Selected documents from records of the Office of Public Buildings and Grounds relating to the White House, 1869–1930
M-24   Papers of Edward Jacobson and miscellaneous documents in the American Jewish Archives relating to Harry S. Truman, 1945–62
M-25   Papers of William McKinley, 1847–1902
M-26   Papers of Benjamin Harrison, 1787–1938
M-27   Papers pertaining to Monrad C. Wallgren, from the University of Washington Library
M-28   Papers of James Madison, 1723–1836
M-29   Scrapbooks of Edward R. Stettinius, Jr., in the University of Virginia Library
M-30   Correspondence and other materials relating to the question of Presidential disability, from the papers of Richard H. Hansen, 1950–60

ORAL HISTORY INTERVIEWS

OH-1   Nathan Thomas Veatch
OH-2   Edgar G. Hinde
OH-3   Mrs. W. L. C. Palmer
OH-4   Henry P. Chiles
OH-5   Ted Marks
OH-6   Walter Matscheck
OH-7   John R. Steelman (closed)
OH-8   Donald Hansen
OH-9   Irving Perlmeter
OH-10 Frederick J. Lawton
OH-11 Harry H. Vaughan
OH-12 Mildred L. Dryden (Mrs. William J. Dryden)
OH-13 James L. Sundquist
OH-14 Edward D. McKim (closed)
OH-15 Jonathan Daniels
OH-16 Mize Peters
OH-17 George Meader
OH-18 Mr. and Mrs. Randall Jessee
OH-19 Ethel Noland
OH-20 William D. Hassett
OH-21 William J. Bray
OH-22 A. J. Stephens
OH-23 Charles F. Curry
OH-24 William L. Batt, Jr.

EUROPEAN RECOVERY PROGRAM INTERVIEW PROJECT

Belgium: Baron Hervé de Gruben

Denmark: Per Haekkerup
                Thorkil Kristensen
                Povl Westphall

England: Sir Roger Makins
                Lord Plowden

France: Robert Marjolin

Germany: Konrad Adenauer
                Baron von Susskind
                Gustav A. Sonnenhol

Greece: Constantinos A. Doxiadis
                John S. Pesmazoglu
                Constantine Tsaldaris

Norway: Knut Getz Wold
              Halvard M. Lange
              Konrad Nordahl
              Erling Wikborg

U. S. A.:   Paul Hoffman

Appendix B

BIBLIOGRAPHY OF WORKS DRAWING UPON
THE TRUMAN LIBRARY

Books

Appleton, Sheldon, *The Eternal Triangle? Communist China, the United States and the United Nations.* East Lansing, The Michigan State University Press, 1961.

Bernstein, Barton J., and Allen J. Matusow, eds., *The Truman Administration: A Documentary History.* New York, Harper & Row, Publishers, 1966.

Cornwell, Elmer E., Jr., *Presidential Leadership of Public Opinion.* Bloomington, Indiana University Press, 1965.

Curti, Merle, *American Philanthropy Abroad: A History.* New Brunswick, Rutgers University Press, 1962.

Davies, Richard O., *Housing Reform During the Truman Administration.* Columbia, University of Missouri Press, 1966.

Druks, Herbert M., *Harry S Truman and the Russians, 1945–1953.* New York, Robert Speller & Sons, Publishers, Inc., 1966.

Ferrell, Robert, *George C. Marshall.* American Secretaries of State and Their Diplomacy, New Series 1925–1961, Vol. 15. New York, Cooper Square Publishers, Inc., 1966.

Flash, Edward S., Jr., *Economic Advice and Presidential Leadership: The Council of Economic Advisers.* New York, Columbia University Press, 1965.

Gerson, Louis L., *The Hyphenate in Recent American Politics and Diplomacy.* Lawrence, University of Kansas Press, 1964.

Henry, Laurin, *Presidential Transitions.* Washington, The Brookings Institution, 1960.

Hewlett, Richard G., and Oscar E. Anderson, Jr., *The New World: A History of the United States Atomic Energy Commission.* Vol. I. University Park, The Pennsylvania State University Press, 1962.

Jados, Stanley J., ed., *Documents on Russian–American Relations.* Washington, The Catholic University of America Press, 1965.

Kirkendall, Richard S., *Social Scientists and Farm Politics in the Age of Roosevelt.* Columbia, University of Missouri Press, 1966.

Lee, R. Alton, *Truman and Taft–Hartley: A Question of Mandate.* Lexington, University of Kentucky Press, 1966.

Longaker, Richard P., *The Presidency and Individual Liberties.* Ithaca, Cornell University Press, 1961.

Mabee, Carleton, *The Seaway Story.* New York, The Macmillan Company, 1961.

Matusow, Allen J., *Farm Policies and Politics in the Truman Years.* Cambridge, Harvard University Press, 1967.

Phillips, Cabell, *The Truman Presidency: The History of a Triumphant Succession.* New York, The Macmillan Company, 1966.

Robinson, Edgar E., and others, *Powers of the President in Foreign Affairs, 1945–1965.* San Francisco, The Commonwealth Club of California, 1966.

Robinson, James A., *Congress and Foreign Policy-Making: A Study in Legislative Influence and Initiative.* Homewood, Ill., The Dorsey Press, 1962.

Smith, A. Robert, *Tiger in the Senate: The Biography of Wayne Morse.* Garden City, N. Y., Doubleday & Company, Inc., 1962.

Steinberg, Alfred, *The Man from Missouri: The Life and Times of Harry S. Truman,* New York, G. P. Putnam's Sons, 1962.

Stromberg, Roland N., *Collective Security and American Foreign Policy: From the League of Nations to NATO.* New York, Frederick A. Praeger, Inc., 1962.

U. S., Commission on Civil Rights, *Report . . . 1959.* Washington, D. C., Government Printing Office, 1959.

Venkataramani, M. S., *Undercurrents in American Foreign Relations: Four Studies.* New Delhi, Asia Publishing House, 1965.

Warren, Sidney, *The President as World Leader.* Philadelphia, J. B. Lippincott Company, 1964.

Whitah, Donald R., *Safer Skyways; Federal Control of Aviation, 1962–66.* Ames, Iowa State University, 1966.

Articles

Bernstein, Barton J., "Charting a Course between Inflation and Depression: Secretary of the Treasury Fred Vinson and the Truman Administration's Tax Bill." To be published in *The Register of the Kentucky Historical Society.*

———, "Clash of Interests: The Postwar Battle Between O.P.A. and Agriculture." *Agricultural History,* 41 (January, 1967).

———, "Reluctance and Resistance: Wilson Wyatt and Veterans' Housing in the Truman Administration." *The Register of the Kentucky Historical Society,* 65 (January, 1967), 47–66.

———, "The Postwar Famine and Price Control, 1946." *Agricultural History,* 38 (October, 1964), 1–6.

———, "The Removal of War Production Board Controls on Business, 1944–1946." *The Business History Review,* 39 (Summer, 1965), 243–60.

————, "The Truman Administration and Its Reconversion Wage Policy." *Labor History,* 6 (Fall, 1965), 214–31.

————, "The Truman Administration and the Steel Strike of 1946." *The Journal of American History,* 52 (March, 1966), 791–803.

————, "Walter Reuther and the UAW–GM Strike of 1945–1946." *Michigan History,* 49 (September, 1965), 260–77.

Billington, Monroe, "Freedom to Serve: The President's Committee on Equality of Treatment and Opportunity in the Armed Forces, 1949–1950." *Journal of Negro History,* 51 (October, 1966), 262–74.

Bose, Tarun, "The Point Four Programme: A Critical Study." *International Studies,* 7 (July, 1965), 66–97.

Cornwell, Elmer E., Jr., "The Presidential Press Conference: A Study in Institutionalization." *Midwest Journal of Political Science,* 4 (November, 1960), 370–89.

Davies, Richard O., "Whistle-Stopping Through Ohio." *Ohio History,* 71 (July, 1962), 113–23.

————, "'Mr. Republican' Turns 'Socialist': Robert A. Taft and Public Housing." *Ohio History,* 73 (Summer, 1964), 135–43.

Dorsett, Lyle W., "Kansas City Politics: A Study of Boss Pendergast's Machine." *Arizona and the West,* 8 (Summer, 1966), 107–18.

Gustafson, Merlin, "Church, State and the Cold War, 1945–1952." *Journal of Church and State* (Winter, 1965), 49–63.

————, "Religion and Politics in the Truman Administration." *The Rocky Mountain Social Science Journal,* 3 (October, 1966), 125–34.

————, "The Church, the State, and the Military in the Truman Administration." *The Rocky Mountain Social Science Journal,* 2 (October, 1965), 2–10.

Hawley, Ellis W., "The Politics of the Mexican Labor Issue, 1950–1955." *Agricultural History,* 11 (July, 1966), 157–76.

Kirkendall, Richard S., "A Second Look at Presidential Libraries." *The American Archivist,* 29 (July, 1966), 371–86.

Lee, R. Alton, "Federal Assistance to Depressed Areas in the Post-war Recessions." *The Western Economic Journal,* 2 (Fall, 1963), 1–23.

————, "The Army 'Mutiny' of 1946." *The Journal of American History,* 53 (December, 1966), 555–71.

————, "The Turnip Session of the Do-Nothing Congress: Presidential Campaign Strategy." *The Southwestern Social Science Quarterly,* 43 (December, 1963), 256–67.

Lorenz, A. L., "Truman and the Press Conference." *Journalism Quarterly,* 43 (Winter, 1966), 671–79, 708.

Venkataramani, M. S., "The Soviet Union and the Indian Food Crisis of 1946." *International Studies,* 4 (April, 1963), 395–412.

Doctoral Dissertations

Berman, William C., "The Politics of Civil Rights in the Truman Administration." Ohio State University, 1963.

Bernstein, Barton J., "The Truman Administration and the Politics of Inflation." Harvard University, 1963.

Branyan, Robert L., "Anti-Monopoly Activities During the Truman Administration." University of Oklahoma, 1961.

Cornwell, Clifton, Jr., "A Rhetorical Study of the Spokesmanship of Scientists in the Decade after Hiroshima." University of Missouri, 1965.

Dalfiume, Richard M., "Desegregation of the United States Armed Forces, 1939–1953." University of Missouri, 1966.

Davies, Richard O., "The Truman Housing Program." University of Missouri, 1963.

Dorsett, Lyle W., "A History of the Pendergast Machine." University of Missouri, 1965.

Druks, Herbert M., "Harry S Truman and the Russians, 1945–1953." New York University, 1964.

Farrar, Ronald T., "Charles G. Ross: His Life and Times." University of Missouri, 1965.

Flash, Edward S., Jr., "The Council of Economic Advisers." Cornell University, 1961.

Freidell, Theodore D., "Truman's Point Four: Legislative Enactment and Development in Latin America." University of Missouri at Kansas City, 1965.

Gustafson, Milton O., "Congress and Foreign Aid: UNRRA, the First Phase, 1943–1947." University of Nebraska, 1966.

Hamby, Alonzo L., "Harry S. Truman and American Liberalism, 1945–1948." University of Missouri, 1965.

Harris, Merne, "The MacArthur Dismissal—A Study in Political Mail." The State University of Iowa, 1966.

Hartmann, Susan M., "President Truman and the 80th Congress." University of Missouri, 1966.

Hedley, John H., "The Truman Administration and the 'Loss' of China: A Study of Public Attitudes and the President's Policies from the Marshall Mission to the Attack on Korea." University of Missouri, 1964.

Hinchey, Mary H., "The Frustration of the New Deal Revival, 1944–1946." University of Missouri, 1965.

Iselin, John Jay, "The Truman Doctrine; A Study in the Relationship between Crisis and Foreign Policy-Making." Harvard University, 1965.

Lee, R. Alton, "Harry S. Truman and the Taft-Hartley Act." University of Oklahoma, 1962.

Lorimer, Sister M. Madeline, "America's Response to Europe's Displaced Persons, 1948–1952: A Preliminary Report." St. Louis University, 1964.

Maher, Sister Patrick Ellen, "The Role of the Chairman of a Congressional Committee: A Case Study of the Special Committee of the Senate to Investigate the National Defense Program, 1941–1948." St. Louis University, 1962.

Mathews, Naiven F., "The Public View of Military Policy, 1945–1950." University of Missouri, 1964.

Matusow, Allen J., "Food and Farm Policies of the First Truman Administration, 1945–1948." Harvard University, 1963.

McClure, Arthur F., II, "The Truman Administration and Labor Relations, 1945–1948." University of Kansas, 1965.

Morgan, Ruth L., "The Presidential Executive Order as an Instrument in Policy-Making." Louisiana State University, 1966.

Poen, Monte M., "The Truman Administration and National Health Insurance." University of Missouri, 1967.

Ross, Davis R. B., "The Return of Ulysses: The Veteran and American Society, 1944–1949." Columbia University, 1967.

Schmidtlein, Eugene F., "Truman the Senator." University of Missouri, 1962.

Smith, Cordell A., "The Marshall Mission: Its Impact upon American Foreign Policy toward China, 1945–1949." University of Oklahoma, 1963.

Stinnett, Ronald F., "A Pentadic Study of Democratic National Committee Dinner Speaking, 1936–1958." University of Minnesota, 1961.

Street, Kenneth W., "Harry S. Truman: His Role as Legislative Leader, 1945–1948." University of Texas, 1963.

Tarr, Curtis W., "Unification of America's Armed Forces: A Century and a Half of Conflict, 1789–1947." Stanford University, 1962.

Theoharis, Athan, "The Yalta Myths: An Issue in American Politics, 1945–1955." University of Chicago, 1965.

Waltrip, John R., "Public Power during the Truman Administration." University of Missouri, 1965.

Willson, Roger E., "The Truman Committee." Harvard University, 1966.

Wilson, Wesley C., "1946; General George C. Marshall and the United States Army Mediate China's Civil War." University of Colorado, 1965.

Masters' Theses

Bickerton, Ian J., "President Truman's Recognition of Israel." Kansas State University, 1966.

Bradford, Nancy Dixon, "The 1952 Steel Seizure Case." University of Southern California, 1967.

Carneal, Thomas W., "President Truman's Leadership in the Field of Civil Rights Legislation." University of Missouri at Kansas City, 1965.

Christensen, Lawrence O., "The Brannan Plan in Congress." Northeast Missouri State Teachers College, 1964.

Curtis, Dan, "A Rhetorical Analysis of Harry S Truman's Use of Proofs from Selected Speeches in the 1948 Presidential Campaign." Central Missouri State College, 1966.

Davis, Reynold J., "A Study of the Federal Civil Rights Programs during the Presidency of Harry S. Truman." University of Kansas, 1959.

George, James H., "The Background of the Truman Doctrine, April, 1945 to March, 1947." University of Wisconsin, 1966.

Gustafson, Milton O., "The Vandenberg Resolution: A Study in Bipartisanship." University of Nebraska, 1963.

Hanna, Michael S., "An Examination of the Audience Adaptation of Harry S Truman during the June, 1948, Whistle-Stop Tour." Central Missouri State College, 1964.

Jones, David L., "Senator Harry S Truman: The First Term." University of Kansas, 1964.

Kennedy, Dorothy M., "Democratic Party Splits in the Campaign of 1948." Central Missouri State College, 1964.

Lorenz, Alfred L., Jr., "Harry S. Truman and the Presidential Press Conference." Southern Illinois University, 1965.

Moll, Kenneth L., "Nuclear Strategy, 1945–1949: America's First Four Years." University of Omaha, 1965.

Olmstead, John, "Truman Speaking: Common Man Image," Central Missouri State College, 1964.

Radosh, Ronald, "The Economic and Political Thought of Henry A. Wallace." University of Iowa, 1960.

Tripp, Eleanor B., "Displaced Persons: The Legislative Controversy in the U. S., 1945–1950." Columbia University, 1966.

Urban, Harold V., "Harry S. Truman: Apprenticeship, April to September, 1945." University of San Francisco, 1966.

Index